The Tellicherry

Michael Dwyer

THE
Tellicherry
FIVE

The Transportation of Michael Dwyer
& the Wicklow Rebels

KIERAN SHEEDY

The Woodfield Press

Published in association with
Radio Telefís Éireann
and
Wicklow County Council

RTÉ

This book was typeset in Ireland by
Gough Tyypesetting Services for
THE WOODFIELD PRESS
17 Jamestown Square, Dublin 8.

A catalogue record for this title
is available from the British Library.

ISBN 0-9528453-4-5

Printed in Ireland by
Genprint Ltd.

Contents

The restored cottage at Derrynamuck, Co. Wicklow, from where Michael Dwyer escaped in 1799

Acknowledgments

This is a companion volume to my previous work *Upon The Mercy Of Government* based on the RTE Radio Documentary series of the same name. In the intervening decade further material has come to light, particularly with the indexing of the Colonial Secretary's Papers in Australia up to the year 1825, while descendants of the Dwyer, Devlin, Mernagh and Byrne families have also been engaged in valuable genealogical work which gives greater insights into the lives of the five Wicklow rebels.

This present volume has been published as part of the 1798 Rebellion Bi-Centennial commemorations and I am grateful to Blaise Treacy, Wicklow County Manager and Joan Kavanagh, Wicklow Heritage Centre for initiating the project. I received valuable assistance in Australia from Maureen Tucker (descendant of Hugh Byrne) and Ann Cunningham, Fred and Peter Mayberry (descendants of John Mernagh), Brigadier Stan Devlin – a descendant of Arthur Devlin – who was in the process of writing a history of the family), Noel Dwyer (descendant of Michael Dwyer), Alan Brown (descendant of Eliza Dwyer); and also Dr Ann Maree Whitaker (author of *Unfinished Revolution*), James J. Macken (author of *Martin Burke – The Father of Pittwater*); Jim Barrett (author of *Life In The Burragorang*), Michelle Vale (author of *Warby: My Excelllent Guide)*; Fr. Brian Maher, Canberra, genealogist Perry McIntyre, Sydney; Stephen Barlow, New South Wales Land Titles Office; Angela Young, Mossvale; Jim Munro, Campbelltown; Lloyd and Patricia Oakman, Glenalvon, Campbelltown, Joe Morley, Sydney; the staffs of the National Library of Ireland, National Archive of Ireland; State Library of New South Wales (Mitchell Library and General Reference Library); Archive Office of New South Wales; Land Titles Office, Sydney; Campbelltown Public Library, King's Cross Public Library, Sydney; Public Record Office, Hampshire; Public Records Office, London.

Kieran Sheedy

August 1997

Sarah Byrne, wife of Hugh Vesty Byrne (photograph *c.*1860)

PART ONE

"This daring chief, whose outrages were qualified with much generosity of temper, defied danger and frequently ran to the bayonet's point."

(*Freeman's Journal*, 14 September 1799)

"His Excellency is not inclined to extend mercy to such of those rebels as shall surrender within a period to be mentioned, upon any other terms than those of transportation for life."

(Letter of Lord Lieutenant, The Earl of Hardwicke, 21 December 1801)

"I have reason to believe that the assurance given to Dwyer that his life shall be spared have been somewhat stronger than there has been warrant."

(Letter of Brigadier-General Beresford, 15 December 1803)

"Your terms! Your terms! I know what your terms are better than yourself. You have no terms at all!"

(Dr Edward Trevor, Superintendent, Kilmainham Jail to Michael Dwyer 1805)

The original type of house built by the early settlers. Drawing by Fred Mayberry, Sydney – a descendant of John Mernagh

Dwyer/Byrne Memorial Stone, Glenmalure, Co. Wicklow

CHAPTER ONE

1798-1803

Garrett Byrne of Ballymanus had got the tactics exactly right when he instructed his Wicklowmen to avoid a general battle, but to attack instead the
enemy forces with small parties, in surprise attacks, before retreating to the
shelter and safety of Glenmalure valley and the Seven Churches. It was July
1798, and following the defeat of the United Irishmen at Vinegar Hill in
Wexford, numbers of fleeing rebels were harrassed relentlessly by units of the
regular army, militia and yeomanry as they retreated northwards towards the
cover of the Wicklow mountains. It was here that the native Wicklow rebels,
many of whom had fought in the Wexford campaigns, came into prominence
– men of the calibre of Miles Byrne, Garrett Byrne, Michael Dwyer and the
latter-day general, Joseph Holt.

They were born into the final quarter of the nineteenth century when the
stultifying and repressive Penal Law legislation which had discriminated against
both the majority Catholic population and Protestant Dissenters was being
slowly dismantled. Likewise, the economic sanctions, imposed on the country
by an unsympathetic British parliament were being relaxed while hopes for an
improvement in the overall quality of life had permeated even into the fastnesses
of the Wicklow mountains where a multiplicity of small farmers struggled to
eke out a subsistence. The writings of the expatriate Englishman, Thomas
Paine, incorporated into the American Constitution, had led indirectly, to
limited demands being made, initially among members of the Protestant business classes, for greater economic freedom; the Irish Volunteer movement
briefly threatened to flex its muscles and Grattan's parliament held out the
prospect, at least, of modest reform. But as the final decade of the century
progressed, the sense of euphoria, which briefly seemed to unite all factions
in the country evaporated just as swiftly. The issue of Catholic Emancipation
revealed the impotence of Grattan's parliament, and as the awesome power of
the masses, let loose in the excesses of the French Revolution manifested
itself, and as copies of Thomas Paine's pamphlet "The Rights of Man" began
to flood the country, the frightened ruling classes hastened to batten down
the hatches. The Society of United Irishmen, increasingly identified with the
notion of republicanism, came under suspicion; help was sought from France,
but the French fleet was unable to land at Bantry and in 1798 the local
populace in Wexford, goaded into spontaneous rebellion by a savage and
undisciplined military operation – underwritten by the passing of a Coercion

Act – were finally crushed at Vinegar Hill.

Prior to the 1798 Rebellion, Michael Dwyer had been given the rank of Captain in a local unit of the United Irishmen and is reputed to have set off on his own for Wexford to take part in several engagements, including the defeat at Vinegar Hill. On his return to his native Wicklow he quickly established himself as a resourceful leader and in the month of July was stationed in Glenmalure where he came to the notice of Miles Byrne:

> He [Dwyer] had already acquired a great reputation in those mountainous districts, for every time the cavalry appeared to reconnoitre near the entrance to the glen he was sure to be on their flank, or in an ambuscade before daylight . . . and as both he and the men who generally accompanied him were of his country and good marksmen, they took delight in terrifying the cavalry who instantly wheeled about and fled the moment a shot was fired at them. So, by Dwyer's bravery and exertions, we were in perfect safety during the night to repose and recover from our fatigues of the Wexford campaign.[1]

During the autumn while the rebels attempted to break out of the county Dwyer was content to remain within the confines of the mountains and following the surrender of Holt in December he became the undisputed leader of the remainder. Recognising the difficulty of dislodging them, General Moore had offered a form of amnesty or "protection" if the rebels agreed to lay down their arms. Dwyer considered the option carefully, but the bloodthirsty disposition of some corps of local yeomanry[2] highlighted the dangers which faced rebels who accepted the amnesty and decided to return home. Rowley Valentine was quoted as saying that "it matters little whether Dwyer took a protection or not, that the first sight of him he would get, he would shoot him."[3]

Such hardline attitudes were all the more unfortunate for Dwyer as he had fallen in love with a local girl Mary Doyle from the townland of Knockandarragh, and they married in the house of John Cullen in November 1798. But they would face long periods of separation as Dwyer continued to evade capture in the mountains. His first cousin, Hugh Byrne, was faced with a similar dilemma as he had married a Dublin girl, Sarah Dwyer (no relation) earlier in the year. Hugh Byrne had also taken a prominent role in the Wicklow campaign, being noted by Miles Byrne as having led a group of 20 men at Spinian's Hill and, likewise, there was no possibility of him returning safely to his job in a Rathdrum brewery. Martin Burke, a member of one of the best known families in Imaal, had fought in Wexford and remained active in the

---

1. *Memoir of Miles Byrne*, p. 219.
2. "A Forgotten Army" by Alan Blackstock. (*History Ireland*, Winter 1996).
3. *Memoir of Miles Byrne*, p. 52.

Wicklow campaign while John Mernagh, the young giant from Glenamalure, and whose family had suffered eviction,[4] did not consider the possibility of surrender. As for Arthur Devlin, a first cousin of both Michael Dwyer and Hugh Byrne,[5] he opted to join an army regiment in England, but found that it did not fit easily into his particular way of life.

During the early part of 1799, as an uneasy peace prevailed throughout the country, there was no let-up for the military forces in Wicklow as the rebels continued to engage in guerilla warfare and, in the process, became the acknowledged protectors of the locals against the excesses of the yeomanry, matching reprisal houseburnings, robbing the homes of loyalists for firearms and engaging in occasional robberies. On the night of 15 February 1799, during a heavy snowstorm, Michael Dwyer, accompanied by 11 of his comrades, took shelter in the townland of Derrynamuck which consisted of three houses belonging to the families of Hoxeys, Tooles and Miley Connell. But the military received intelligence of their whereabouts and a contingent of men, led by Capt. Roderick McDonald, surrounded them. The rebels in the first two houses surrendered, having negotiated terms, but when the members of the Connell family had been released from the third house, Dwyer and three others decided to resist. Following an exchange of fire Patrick Costello and Sam McAllister, a deserter from the Antrim Militia, were fatally wounded, and in a heroic gesture to save Dwyer, Sam McAllister proceeded to open the door of the cottage in order to draw the fire of the soldiers which action enabled Dwyer to rush out in the darkness and make his escape while they paused to reload. The eight captured prisoners were taken to Baltinglass and despite having made terms prior to their surrender were court-martialled a week later and were subsequently hanged.[6]

Despite this setback, and rumours to the effect that Dwyer had been fatally injured at Derrynamuck, the tactics of the rebels in Wicklow continued and the situation in which the military forces found themselves was summed up in the course of a leading article, headed OUTRAGES which was published in the 14 September 1799 edition of the *Freeman's Journal*:

> Our accounts also state, that in the neighbourhood of Baltinglass, on the Ballymore Eustace side, outrages re-appear, and do some straggling mischief. The mountainous situation of that part of the county Wicklow is favourable to such ruffians, affording them abundance of fastnesses,

---

4. The ruins of the cottage where the Mernagh family were housed by the Byrne family of Bolenaskea following their eviction were pointed out to the author by the late Billy Byrne in 1988.
5. Michael Dwyer's paternal grandfather was Charles Byrne of Cullentragh. His father, John Dwyer married Mary Byrne; his uncle Sylvester was the father of Hugh Vesty Byrne and his aunt Winifred who married Bryan Devlin was the mother of Arthur Devlin.
6. *Michael Dwyer – Battle of Doire na Muc*, a booklet by Elaine Hoxley and Caoimhin de Lion.

where it known and pursued they hide by day, and come out at night to some appointed rendezvous, to proceed in most cases strong enough against any private dwelling, however at present fortified by the precautions which late disturbances rendered necessary. . . . It is to be lamented that a few honest, loyal persons must suffer in consequence, though at the moment a military post might not be a mile distant. The guard cannot so spread itself out as to cover all the vicinage, and the offenders, often lying about the place, and well acquainted with the bye-roads, disguising and equipping themselves for the assault, return home, and hid their robbing habiliments. The military may on the summons come too late; and should they even follow suspected persons to their cottages; they may find them all innocent a-bed. Thus some for a considerable time elude the vigilance of the soldiers and even cavalrymen (yeomen). But at last and long run Paddy the Grinder, Na bach libh, is found out, identified and hanged for his crimes, or sent to act Patrick in Prussia.

Frequently last year, when after the decamping of General Moore from the Glen of Imaal, it was the purlieu ground of Holt's flying light horse, whose floating quarters were behind the hills back towards the Seven Churches, the Boys, as the natives call them, used to burn down a dwelling in the glen, while the military were near in pursuit. Dwyer actually lived for some months on the banks of the Slaney, between the surrounding fire of the Baltinglass, Stratford and Donard military, and in the sight of the constant co-operation of the Humewood and Saunders Grove Yeomanry. This daring chief, whose outrages were qualified with much generosity of temper, defied danger, and frequently ran to the bayonet's point. He once with a few of "the boys" wounded two of Captain Hume's men, whom he overtook by themselves, pursued to the Slaney, where it is fordable at the little town of Stratford, and paused some minutes, still firing at them as they crossed the river, though the drum was beating to arms, and an officer with a detachment of the Clare militia turned out to seize him. On the approach of the military, he made to the mountains and escaped in safety. By night, 'twas a matter of notoriety. He kept his quarters at a farmhouse belonging to a widow, whom he had some time lived with as a servant, and who in the troubles was obliged to retire from her home and affairs.

Frequently have the military thought to surprise him, but he for a long time was able to elude them, by the vigilance and velocity of his videttes and outposts. The soldiers often found his table at which he a few minutes previously sat, covered with good eating and drinking, and were able if they pleased, to regale him on his marauded provisions. Though Holt, Dwyer and the other leaders are killed off, 'tis certain that a few of their followers still remain to pursue the old scent of plunder and outrage. . . . 'Tis right to observe that before, the deluded

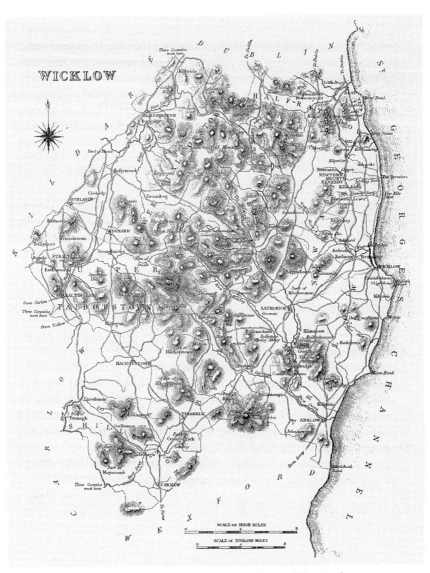

Wicklow County map, published by Samuel Lewis 1837

peasantry, recovered to allegiance and industry, in general detest the
bandities; but from their nightly exposure to them, they must speak
them fair, and afford them shelter.

Michael Dwyer, however, was very much alive, but may have had some
explaining to do to his wife Mary concerning his supposed relationship with
the widow. And as his reputation grew, robberies which took place, even in
the neighbourhood of Dublin city were being attributed to him and the status
of folk-hero has already being bestowed:

> So daring are some of the banditti of whom the noted Dwyer is leader
> that they venture to come very near to the metropolis to commit depre-
> dations. Some hear it, that it was part of that gang who recently committed
> robberies in Black Rock and on the road from it to Dublin. They have
> the audacity to call themselves Dwyer's Fusiliers. Some of them at-
> tempted to plunder houses near Rathfarnham and robbed an eminent
> attorney in Aungier St. on his way to Rathfarhham."[7]

It is highly unlikely that any of Dwyer's men were involved, but a week later
it was confidently predicted that:

> we shall shortly hear of Dwyer and his party being routed from their
> haunts in the county of Wicklow and Dublin by the very active military
> forces. A short time ago that offender and his myrmidons, it is said,
> surrounded a fair in the county and indiscriminately robbed every per-
> son that came out of it possessed of a shilling.[8]

Newspaper coverage of his exploits continued into June, with reports that
one his men, by the name of Dalton, had been shot by yeomen and that the
Inverness Fencibles had killed

> "three or four of the desperate gang". On 8 June, it was further re-
> ported that "a reward of 500 guineas is ordered by the government for
> the apprehension of the noted Dwyer, and a lesser sum for some des-
> peradoes that belong to his banditti. Those of them that have been
> guilty of murder are offered amnesty, provided that they surrender
> within a given time. Dwyer, in his atrocities, progressed through the
> county, endeavouring near the Queen's County [Laois] to induce the
> Colliers to follow his predatory scheme – but fortunately for the poor
> people they rejected his deluded solicitations."

And a fortnight later Col. George Stewart issued a proclamation from his

---

7. *Freeman's Journal*, 24 May 1799.
8. *Ibid.*, 31 May 1799.

camp on Lugnaquilla Mountain to the effect that 30 mountain roads had been opened by the military:

> The possession of these roads, passes and mountains will most effectually open the country and protect the properties of its loyal inhabitants to the King. It will also enable the people to travel with safety and bring provisions to his Majesty's troops there. I will give immediate protection to any of the inhabitants who will assist me, or any detachment of the troops in securing any of the gang of rebels headed by Michael Dwyer.

But while plans to build a military road from Glencree in Dublin across the mountains, and down past Glendalough (Seven Churches) to Croghan Mountain were being formulated, Michael Dwyer's father who had been arrested and lodged in both Baltinglass and Wicklow Jails and was brought to trial in Rathdrum in October. John Dwyer was charged with "treasonable and seditious practice, harbouring rebels, keeping arms for them and carrying intelligence to them" and was sentenced to life imprisonment. He was later sent to New Geneva Jail in Waterford, but in December 1801 a petition was signed by 12 members of the Donoughmore Yeomanry Cavalry, and countersigned by William Hoare Hume M.P. and Morley Saunders of Saunderstown attesting to John Dwyer's honesty of character, and that "instead of committing any injury assisted to the utmost of his power the families of such in his neighbourhood as remained at home."

On 24 October 1800, Lt-Col. George Stewart issued a further proclamation from Rathdrum naming a total of 47 "Robbers, Murders and Deserters now wandering about, and are occasionally concealed by disaffected Persons in the counties of Wicklow, Wexford, Carlow, Kildare, Dublin etc." The vast majority of the named rebels, however, came from Wicklow and the list which contained detailed personal descriptions included:

1st. MICHAEL DWYER, aged about thirty one years, five feet nine or ten inches high, very straight in the back, short neck, square shoulders, a little in-kneed, rather long-legged, with a little rise on the shin bones, very long feet, black hair and complexion, broad across the eyes, which are black, short cocked nose, wide mouth, thin lips, even teeth, but stand separate, very long from the nose to the end of the chin, full breasted and rather full-faced, born in Imaal. Five Hundred Guineas for taking him.

2nd. JOHN MERNAGH, about thirty years old, six feet high, full-bodied, but light limbed, dark complexion, marked with the small pox, black hair, heavy eyebrows, and thick lips, somewhat round-shouldered, born in or near Glen Malur. Two hundred guineas for taking him.

7th. MARTIN BURKE, about five feet eleven inches high, dark hair, rather fair complexion, long nose bending downwards at the point, uneven teeth, long face, straight in the back, but stoops in the shoulders down from his neck, strong legs and thighs, a little bowed at the knees, walks very upright, thirty years old, born at or near Imaal. Two hundred guineas for taking him.

14th. HUGH BYRNE, about five feet eight inches high, freckled, fair face, light or sandy hair, well made, shot through the thigh, twenty four years old.

The proclamation was inserted in newspapers on a weekly basis until the end of the year, but with little tangible results, and there was further alarm in January 1801 when Major Henry Sirr arrested Bryan Early and James Cullen in Francis St. Dublin. They were both natives of Co. Wicklow and "were in the act of casting bullets, preparing it is supposed, to join their predatory acquaintances, Dwyer and his gang."[9] At the end of the month it was reported that a party of yeomen "had pursued Burke and Byrne, two of the proclaimed rebels, whom they shot in the Glen of Imaal. Dwyer's gang is so closely pursued it is not possible for any of them to escape". But once again it proved to be just as false as the March report that "Dwyer, fearing that he cannot possibly escape apprehension, has made an application to surrender. But it is not known whether it will be accepted without his receiving that punishment which the law prescribes for the offences he has committed."[10]

In September 1801, the newly-appointed Lord Lieutenant, the Earl of Hardwicke, accompanied by Chief Secretary Abbott, toured the county of Wicklow and, as part of the ensuing increased military activity, Major Tattam of the Somerset Fencibles submitted a plan to him through his Commander-in-Chief Sir William Meadows "for apprehending certain outstanding rebels in the mountains of Wicklow, it having appeared that they have for some time past frequented the mountain farm at Aughavanagh and the houses of the inhabitants, the Major conceives that all those parts may be minutely searched by the Somerset Regiment, the Yeomanry and the other military posted in the mountains, especially the Duke of York's Highlanders at Fannaneiring, [and] the detachment at Ballymurroghroe, Rathdangan and Imaal." The plan was hurriedly approved by the Lord Lieutenant on 21 December, with Tattam being asked to carry it out with as little delay as possible and, "at the same time His Excellency is not inclined to extend mercy to such of the rebels as shall surrender within a period to be mentioned, upon any other terms than transportation for life."

But Tattam's search proved to be fruitless while Dwyer and his comrades would not consider terms which included transportation. By now Dwyer was the father of three children, Mary Ann (1799), John (1801) and Peter (1801),

---

9. *Ibid.*, 13 January 1801.
10 *Ibid.*, 10 March 1801.

and was still determined to remain in his native county. Likewise, Hugh Byrne was in a similar position, being the father of two children, Philip (1799) and Michael (1800), and given the alternatives being now offered to them, life on the run in the Wicklow mountains, however uncertain, remained their preferred option. And for as long as they remained protected by the people (no-one would still dare to attempt collecting the reward money) they could reasonably hope to avoid capture. They rarely appeared together in large numbers, remaining largely on the defensive, and the account by Dwyer of his life-style in those years reveals that he led a surprisingly solitary existence:

> The way I avoided capture was this; I never slept in a house, always either in a hiding place or in the open air, and by wrapping myself in such covering as I carried I was always able to do so, even in the severest weather. I always had a store of bacon and such of provisions in some concealment to which I never ventured but in the case of absolute necessity. If it snowed I made my way to this place of concealment while the snow was falling, still defacing the marks of my feet as I went. While the snow lay on the ground I never moved. At other times I was accustomed to go to any cottage, always without previous notice, with a cocked pistol in my hand I made the owner to give me full intelligence of all that was passing in the country and to give me such provisions as the house could afford and as I chose to demand. Having done so I went off first saying to the owner of the house, for his own safety, and give immediate information of what he had done. Before any pursuit could be made, by then I would be seven or so miles off. I would live in this manner for many years. For firearms I prefer to use a musket by day and a blunderbuss by night.[11]

The authorities achieved a rare success on 22 December 1801 when a group of eight yeomen from the Rathdrum Cavalry, led by Lt. Tomlinson, discovered the hiding place "of three of the most nefarious of the banditti" at Castlekevan, about eight miles from the town. They were hiding under a clamp of turf in an outhouse belonging to a man by the name of McDonald. They made an attempt to escape

> "during which the rebels kept up a sharp fire, being well-armed and provided with ammunition, and priming and loading with surprising alacrity. Their knowledge of the ground too gave them "the vantage point" as they kept the bogs and heights, which the yeomen perceiving, some dismounting, dislodged them from their strongholds, and after a time Andrew Thompson was killed and John Byrne housed and taken. John Harman effected a most miraculous escape, being now left alone,

---

11. Wickham Correspondence, Hampshire P.R.O.

he betook himself to a constant flight, directing the course to the Seven Churches [Glendalough]. After a chase of upwards of five miles through the country . . . he beat two of the best horses in the troop, 'till the pursuers having lost sight of him in a thick mist on the top of a mountain over St. Cavan's [Kevin's] bed, and night coming on, they thought it advisable to return to the party. This fellow, in his flight, took off most of his clothes, so that at least he was stark naked; this circumstance, the length and hardship of the chase and, and severity of the season, coupled with the consideration of his being wounded in the back of the neck, give room that he cannot survive such a shaking. The ruffian harbourer of these hordes having absconded, his house was consumed, and during the conflagration upwards of 100 rounds of cartridges exploded from the thatch. There were also 46 rounds found on the rebels. . . . Andrew Thomas, John Byrne and John Harman were three of the ruffians proclaimed by Colonel Stewart.[12]

But such encounters were rare and the military forces continued to rely on the construction of the new road through the mountains which for a final resolution of the problem by the end of 1802 had progressed along the top of the Glen of Imaal with a barracks due to be built at Leitrim. But, to the mortification of the authorities, Dwyer was reported as having engaged the workers in conversation during its construction, and it was left to Captain King of the Rathdrum Yeoman Cavalry, in December 1802, to keep pressure on the rebels:

Be assured from the day that Dwyer appeared as a rebel of note I have not ceased by every means I could devise to endeavour to bring him in – I have kept correspondence with two men who were considered friends of the party to whom I have given money . . . in order to gain their confidence – I get a good deal of information from them, but nothing which has enable me to catch any rebel – Dwyer is very cautious and 'tis almost impossible to get acquainted with his movements. [He] seldom comes to this side of the mountains and while he continued in Imaal or the bogs about Rathdangan, he thinks himself – and I have reason to believe he is perfectly safe. It is most confidently asserted that all the Yeomen resident in Imaal, as well as the other inhabitants, make no secret of harbouring him – he walks about in open day, and every man watches for him by day as well as night, and not one man in that whole district would give the smallest information. . . . A jealousy has arisen between Dwyer and Mernagh, the latter thinks himself as good a man and does not like Dwyer assuming the chief command. In consequence

12. *Freeman's Journal*, 11 December 1801.

these gentlemen are seldom together. Dwyer's principal associates are Martin Burke and Hugh Vesty [Byrne] – all the others keep chiefly on this side of the great body of mountains – the resort Aughavanagh, Glenmalure and from thence toward the gold mine and very often come within a mile of this place yet I cannot hear of them until they have removed. Mernagh and his party which is increased to 15 or 16, well-armed, appear often. They were seen at Kinderragh, near Aughrim, about two months ago, by one Smith, whom they forced to drink with them and then beat him severely. All these armed men were then seen in the last week of October at McCredin. You know most of the men in my troop, and am confident you have a good opinion of their steady loyalty. There is nothing they would do or attempt, was there any prospect of getting Dywer, but in truth, while the inhabitants of Imaal continue his protection, nothing can be done there by any man from this side.

On a Sunday evening in the summer of 1803, Dubliner Thomas Thorpe, accompanied by his father and brother, were travelling in the vicinity of the Glen of Imaal when about two miles outside Donard they were stopped by a man carrying a blunderbuss and, as he later aggrievedly reported: "Two other men came up to him likewise. Dwyer was one of them. He was armed with a case of pistols . . . that the party robbed him of three pistols – 17 guineas and a half in cash . . . they were detained for about three hours. Dwyer stated that he was fighting five years for liberty and the sixth would gain it." Thorpe reported his loss to Major Henry Sirr in Dublin who had made sporadic, if largely unsuccessful, forays into the Wicklow mountains over the years in search of Dwyer. The context of Dwyer's final remark to Thorpe would have been regarded by Sirr as an idle boast, but quite unknown to the authorities, an event was about to take place in Dublin which would severely shake the complacency of the Irish administration and would spell disaster also for Dwyer and his comrades. That event was the rebellion of Robert Emmet.

CHAPTER TWO

1803

On 16 March 1803, Alexander Marsden, the Under-Secretary of the Irish administration, based in Dublin Castle, wrote to his immediate superior, Chief Secretary William Wickham who was on business in London. The St. Patrick's Day celebrations were already under way in Dublin and Marsden clearly was in an expansive mood as he penned what was virtually a daily report: "Many of my letters to you are written after dinner, and you know that in Ireland makes a serious difference." Chief Secretary Wickham recognised this truism only too well. Although he had spent many years in Switzerland, ostensibly as a diplomat, but in reality as Britain's chief spy, all of this expertise had still left him unprepared for the vagaries of Irish politics, and he had written in exasperation to Prime Minister Addington claiming that "the system of jobbing and supplanting and calumniating each other is so deeply rooted that I am bound constantly to mistrust the very best."

The relationship between Marsden and Wickham, however, was a relatively cordial one. The Dublin-born Alexander Marsden, the son of one of the city's most prosperous merchants, and a founder member of the Bank of Ireland, had been educated at Trinity College and practised as a barrister before succeeding Cooke as Under-Secretary following the passing of the Act of Union in 1801 which had resulted in the dissolution of the Irish parliament in College Green. His immediate task had been to administer the various emoluments and financial bribes which were scattered about to help persuade various members of the Irish parliament to vote themselves out of existence, and he also inherited a large network of spies which had been built up during the period of the 1798 Rebellion. There was never a shortage of individuals of all classes and religious persuasions willing to help themselves to a slice of the generous secret service funds by providing Dublin Castle with a plethora of largely useless information.

Although the fragile peace between Great Britain and France which had been negotiated at Amiens in 1802 now seemed in the balance, there were few reports of disturbances in Ireland and, on St. Patrick's Day Marsden was able to reassure Wickham that "a drunken holiday has passed off without incident, even in Dublin." But he added, in a more serious tone: "The newspapers are in good training, the *Dublin Journal* and the *Evening Post* do us, I think, credit." Marsden was very proud of the fact that he had managed to buy off the newspapers by means of secret payments and intrepid local journalists sought out the advice of Dublin Castle before rushing into print. Marsden had good reason to feel smug and self-satisfied. He successfully concluded the secret Act of Union deals and the country had settled down again into a sullen acceptance of the status quo. The odd agrarian outrage was still being occurring in the south of the country and there were a number of rebels still holding out in the Wicklow mountains who continued to be a source of embarrassment but Marsden, whose family country home was at Verval outside Bray, was almost alone among the members of the administration in believing that Dwyer posed no real threat.

He was far more interested in the activities of the emigre 1798 leaders, currently in exile in France, and at the end of March he reported to Wickham: "[Robert] Emmet is in Ireland. I did not before suppose, and but for the authority, would still doubt it, but we must expect that a game will be played here and that some of the ex-Irish will be ordered to return. Emmet, however, is not likely to be one of them."[1] The members of the Emmet family would have been well known to Marsden as they lived in St. Stephen's Green and Dr Robert Emmet Sen. had acted as State Physician of Ireland. One of his sons, Christopher, a brilliant young lawyer and a gifted orator, was a contemporary of his but died at a young age in 1799. Another son, Thomas Addis, had been a prominent leader of the 1798 Rebellion and was presently in Paris. But it was Robert, the youngest member of the family, who had recently returned from France, and Marsden could not convince himself that at the age of 24 he would be entrusted with the organisation of a rebellion. But Robert Emmet was already planning to go one step further. He was in the process of organising his own rebellion and Marsden would almost be the last person to find out.

Less than two months later, on a late Sunday evening in May 1803, Ann Devlin, a young Wicklow girl whose family had moved to Rathfarnham, outside Dublin, watched with heightened curiosity as a group of four men on horseback, approached in single file the house in Butterfield Lane where she was acting as unpaid housekeeper to a Mr Ellis, the fictional name being used by Robert Emmet. She was a first cousin of Michael Dwyer, Arthur Devlin and Hugh Byrne, her mother Winifred being one of the three daughters of Charles Byrne, Cullentra. Her father Bryan Devlin had been imprisoned for two years in Wicklow Jail following the 1798 Rebellion while the women in the family had shown a steely resolve in attending public executions of local men, shielding their bodies from mutilation by the yeomanry and giving them a proper burial. Ann Devlin, accompanied by two of Michael Dwyer's sisters, had even disinterred the bodies of Ulstermen Sam McAllister and Adam Magee at night in order to transfer their remains to Kilranalagh Cemetery.

---

1. Wickham Correspondence, Hampshire P.R.O.

When Bryan Devlin was released from Wicklow Jail he surrendered the leases on his farm and rented a small farm at Rathfarnham where he set up a small dairy and hired out his three horses to local farmers. The family were soon making a comfortable living but were suddenly embarked on a disaster course when their cousin Arthur arrived back in Dublin in the early part of 1803. Arthur Devlin had deserted from the British army, but having failed to get to the Continent, joined the navy instead under an assumed name and was acting as a recruiting sergeant in the south of England when he met up with some of Robert Emmet's followers on their way back to Ireland from France. Devlin deserted again and bringing with him a group of fifty equally disaffected Irishmen, arrived back in Ireland, still dressed as a sailor, to become one of Emmet's organisers with the responsibility of setting up various secret arms depots in the city.

Emmet was anxious to make contact with any remaining pockets of resistance in the country, and Devlin was also given the task of approaching Michael Dwyer in Wicklow. But Dwyer, whose natural caution had stood him well over the years, was suspicious of Devlin's sudden reappearance in Wicklow and it took a second visit, and another from the northern weaver Jemmy Hope, who brought some guns to Dwyer, before he would even commit himself to paying Emmet a visit in Dublin. Even then, he would not specify a date and suddenly arrived in the company of Hugh Byrne, John Mernagh and Martin Burke at Butterfield Lane on a Sunday evening in May. They were met by Robert Emmet and Thomas Russell, "the man from God know's where", the ex-British army officer who had been jailed for his part in the 1798 Rebellion, and who had been one of its chief political strategists. Russell's nephew William Hamilton was also present as was Jemmy Hope and his wife Rose, and for three days the brandy flowed as wild schemes for the overthrow of the Government in Ireland were drawn up and wildly optimistic numbers were bandied about concerning their overall support in the country. Hamilton went as far as seeking a guarantee from Dwyer that when the revolution had succeeded, the dispossessed would not confiscate the lands of the settlers and, for his part, Dwyer joined in the spirit of the proceedings, by promising strong support from Wicklow which he must have known could not be delivered by him. A second meeting was arranged, but on this occasion Dwyer was much more circumspect concerning the type of support he could muster and privately committed himself to coming into Dublin, only after it had been in Emmet's hands for 48 hours. As for his opinion of Robert Emmet, he thought he was a fine young man, if only he had a bit of sense.

On the morning of 23 July, Alexander Marsden did not arrive at his office in Dublin Castle until 11.30. Chief Secretary Wickham was attending a session of parliament in London while the Lord Lieutenant, the Earl of Hardwicke, was at the Vice-Regal lodge, his residence in the Phoenix Park. It was Saturday, the end of another working week, and there was no great pressure of work. On his arrival, however, Marsden was immediately bombarded with reports from various spies and Government supporters that a rebellion was being planned in Dublin for that night. But he was in the habit of receiving such reports and was not unduly alarmed. Part of the information indicated that a number of rebels from County Kildare were planning to come into the city but Sir Charles Asgill who was in charge of the Dublin district had recently returned from there and had not discovered any signs of a disturbance. An informer by the name of McGucken had given warning that both Dublin and the North were due to rise on that very day, and that Robert Emmet would be its leader but, even still, Marsden could not contemplate a rebellion being led by the youngest member of the Emmet family, and had continued to downplay even the significance of a gunpowder explosion which had occurred in Patrick St. in the previous week.

But the flood of rumours continued; the town major, Henry Sirr had also received similar information and, at two o'clock in the afternoon, Marsden decided to inform the Lord Lieutenant. Coincidentally, General Fox, the Commander-in-Chief of the army forces, was conferring with the Lord Lieutenant at the time and Marsden sent them a note requesting them to come to the Castle immediately. They arrived at four o'clock and agreed to take preventative action, but without causing any undue alarm. General Fox was instructed to send reinforcements to guard the principal buildings in the city, but to wait until dusk before doing so. The Lord Lieutenant then returned to Phoenix Park while General Fox went to the army headquarters at the Royal Hospital, Kilmainham where he sent out various instructions to his army commanders and requested Sir Charles Asgill to meet him at the Royal Hospital at nine o'clock. Sir Charles had been invited out to dinner and was already in his dress uniform, but he immediately set off by coach hoping, no doubt, that the night's entertainment might yet be salvaged. But when he arrived there he was sent by Fox to the Castle to check on the situation and had supper with Marsden. As there was still no sign of trouble Asgill went home, but being resigned to the fact that there would be no dining out on that night, changed out of his dress uniform. It was approaching nine o'clock when he returned to the Royal Hospital for the meeting with General Fox which also included other district commanders. The consensus was that there was no immediate cause for alarm, although Asgill did venture the opinion that extraordinary things could happen in Ireland.

On that night the streets and hostelries of Thomas St. in Dublin were crowded. It was the feast-day of St. James which was celebrated by the inhabitants of the nearby parish; Saturday was also pay-day, and in that most disaffected part of the city, where town and country intermingled, spirits were high. In a busy workshop, situated in Dirty Lane, which connected Thomas St. and Marshalea debtors prison, Robert Emmet had donned the splendid green and gold military uniform, with breeches of creamy white cashmere, in preparation for the moment when he would lead his men into battle. "Who's the general?", called out Pat Farrell, a somewhat unwilling helper. "How bad you are for knowledge," came the reply from Emmet. But already his military plans had gone disastrously wrong on that day. Several of his Kildare and Wexford followers, dismayed by what they considered his lack of preparedness, had already withdrawn and there was strong pressure on him to postpone the uprising. And there was even worse news as the hackney coaches which were to be used for the attack on Dublin Castle had been stopped by a cavalry officer and the coachmen had driven off in panic. Even at the last moment, Michael Quigley, one of his principal organisers, had rushed in, erroneously claiming that the military were already on the offensive and coming their way.

Emmet at first wavered, but then rallied, and picked up a copy of his proclamation which stated that "our object is to establish a free and independent republic in Ireland . . . we war not against past opinions or prejudice, we war against English dominion." At nine o'clock, as the bells rang out on the Quays, a single rocket was fired over the roof-tops, and Robert Emmet, drawing his sword, and accompanied by the uniformed Quigley and Stafford, and a group of followers, marched out of Dirty Lane onto Thomas St. to call upon some astonished passers-by to join in his revolution. For Emmet, the sublime idealist, but the hopelessly inadequate strategist, his revolution began and ended the moment he stepped out onto the street. Within half an hour the attack had turned into a disorganised rout. As Emmet marched into Patrick St., he called out "Turn out my boys. Turn out! Now is the time for liberty. Liberty my boys! Turn out! Turn out!" With that rejoinder he fired his pistol in the air, possibly his only violent action of the night, and marched in the direction of Kevin St.

While General Fox still remained uninvolved in the Royal Hospital, other military units stationed in the city quickly restored order and, as drunken crowds emerged from sundry hostelries, ready to fight anyone or anything, Emmet, with his rebellion already in tatters, attempted to call a halt and announced to his remaining followers that they should retreat to Wicklow and join forces with Dwyer. But individuals like Henry Howley, with the memory of the atrocities of 1798 still fresh in their minds, were determined to strike a defiant blow and isolated skirmishes continued. At this juncture a carriage bearing Chief Justice Kilwarden, along with his daughter Elizabeth and his nephew Rev. Richard Wolfe, was making its way from his home in Rathcoole to seek the safety of Dublin Castle. As they passed along Thomas St., however, a mob descended on the carriage; Kilwarden was pulled out and piked to death, as was his nephew, But his daughter was unharmed and allowed to run screaming to the Castle with the shouts of the crowd, "God bless you, Miss" ringing in her ears. The skirmishing soon petered out; Emmet and his principal followers managed to escape, but the Chief Justice was dead and when the hysterical Elizabeth Wolfe screamed her way into the yard of Dublin Castle the worst fears of Alexander Marsden had been realised.

The embarrassment felt by the Irish government in the weeks following Emmet's rebellion was acute. But for the murder of Lord Kilwarden and his nephew they might have muddled through, but suddenly all the dire warnings of the Orange faction in the country seemed to have been justified and the conciliatory policies of the Lord Lieutenant were in shreds. Chief Secretary Wickham arrived back from London and let it be known that his family had accompanied him and that the danger was over. But the Habeas Corpus Act was immediately suspended, the Martial Law Bill was enacted and soon Wickham had to reassure the London government which had become even more alarmed when a copy of Emmet's proclamation reached them. Major Henry Sirr had redeemed himself, in the eyes of Dublin Castle, by arresting Emmet and a number of his followers, 14 of whose number, in addition to Emmet, were speedily brought to trial and hanged.

It seemed, initially, as if Marsden would be made the scapegoat for his failure to detect Emmet's plans but Wickham, on his return, declared himself satisfied with Marsden's handling of events on 23 July and soon General Fox was made to shoulder the blame. Soldiers from the Royal Hospital had not been deployed until one o'clock in the morning and, by that time, the rebellion had been put down by members of other individual units. When the Lord Lieutenant was appraised of this, he confronted the general and, following a heated exchange, Fox agreed to forfeit his command and return to England where, to Hardwicke's further annoyance, he was immediately given charge of the London district. The fact that Fox was made the lone scapegoat was viewed with disfavour in many influential quarters, both in Dublin and London, and as he happened to be a brother of James Charles Fox, the Whig opposition leader, this only added to the feelings of resentment. General Fox was succeeded as army chief by Lord Cathcart, but his orders seemed to indicate that he should report directly to the Duke of York, rather than the Lord Lieutenant, a decision which was vigorously opposed by Hardwicke and Wickham on the grounds that it diminished both of their offices.

Pressure was building up in Ireland also – orchestrated by the Orange faction – to have Marsden removed from office, or to have him examined by a secret committee to defend his actions on the day of the rebellion. William Wickham was also on the defensive and promised the Privy Council members that he would "clear the country forever of at least two hundred subordinate leaders of the counties of Dublin, Kildare and Wicklow", while at the end of October Thomas Russell was also hanged in Downpatrick Jail. The Government now turned their attention to Wicklow. Arthur Devlin had been sent by Emmet in the direction of Co. Kildare on the morning of the rebellion and, in its aftermath, had fled to link up with Michael Dwyer who had remained in Wicklow.[2] But the Dublin administration were still convinced that Dwyer had played a leading role in its planning, and with Hardwicke desperately needing a propaganda victory to reverse the adverse publicity he had received, he sent a letter to Dwyer offering him terms of surrender and "a safe retreat from the Kingdom with all his family" and several of his relations. The letter was given to Ann Devlin's mother Winifred (Dwyer's aunt) and she was released from Kilmainham Jail where all of Bryan Devlin's family had been imprisoned since the rebellion. Quite separately, Dwyer had been offered similar terms a short time before by William Hoare Hume, the local member of Parliament, but he rejected both offers out of hand and was still holding out for a free pardon which would enable him to continue to live in Wicklow. He was also under the impression that Government was so preoccupied with the aftermath of the rebellion in Dublin that he would be left alone, but his reading of the current political situation was as far off the mark as their understanding of his military capability.

The business of the monthly meeting of the Privy Council, held in Dublin Castle, was usually of a routine nature, and not very well attended, but there was a full attendance on 7 November as the Government, still reeling from the effects of Emmet's rebellion, was planning to reveal details of a major offensive against, what they believed was a large number of rebels, still holding out in the Wicklow mountains under the leadership of Michael Dwyer. The draft of a proclamation, offering a reward of £500 for his capture, had been circulated in advance of the meeting which was chaired by the Lord Lieutenant who would have to rely heavily on the support of Chief Secretary William Wickham against the verbal attacks of the majority of the Privy Council members who had already publicly accused his administration of laxity and neglect.[3] And pressure was also being kept up in London in anticipation of the new session of parliament which was due to meet in three weeks. The Orange faction had been frustrated in their attempts to get rid of Marsden mainly, as Wickham noted, because "Marsden was the person who conducted the secret part of the Union. . . Ergo the price of each Unionist, as well as their respective conduct and character. . . . Those who vapour away, and vapour in so great a style in London are well known to him. They live in hourly hour of being unmasked." Like many liberally-minded Englishmen before him, the Earl of Hardwicke had arrived in Ireland, determined to create a mood of reconciliation, and to unite the various factions within the framework of newly-created Union between Ireland and Great Britain. He

---

2.   It is impossible to evaluate Arthur Devlin's links with Michael Dwyer in Wicklow in the
       period following Emmet's rebellion. Given Dwyer's original suspicions of him it is hardly
       likely that he would have welcomed his return.
3.   For details of the Privy Council members see *Upon The Mercy Of Government*, pp. 32-32.

attempted to promote Irish industry and to ensure that loyal Catholics would not be disadvantaged, a policy which did not endear him to the Orange faction who were now using the recent rebellion to attack him, even though the rebellion was publicly condemned by Dr Troy, the Catholic Archbishop of Dublin, in an address of loyalty which was read out at all Sunday masses throughout the diocese, and which was principally aimed at what was termed "the lower orders of our communion."

There was little disagreement, however, concerning the issuing of the proclamation against Michael Dwyer, the wording of which was read aloud at the meeting: "Michael Dwyer, late of Imaal in the county of Wicklow stands charged with repeated acts of High Treason and with furthering the rebellion that lately broke out in Ireland." It went on to state that a reward of £500 was being offered for his capture and a similar sum for anyone giving information leading to his arrest. All law officers and yeomen in Wicklow were urged to redouble their efforts and an instruction was given to the officers commanding the military forces "to punish according to martial law, not only Dwyer himself, but anyone assisting or sheltering him." The use of court martials, however, was something which Hardwicke and Wickham had been anxious to limit, believing that prisoners should be tried by the courts of law, despite the recent enactment of the Martial Law Bill. They were consequently reluctant to hand over the initiative in such cases to the new army chief, Lord Cathcart, and Wickham had been careful to point out that while he himself had the right to hold a court martial, he could not delegate this authority, and that the discretionary power was vested solely in the office of the Lord Lieutenant. As for Cathcart, he was anxious to avoid becoming entangled in any procedural squabbles between the administrations in Dublin and London and agreed also to their suggestion that Brigadier-General Beresford should lead the offensive in the Wicklow mountains against Dwyer, with General Sir Charles Asgill, commander of the district having overall responsibility.

But, quite unknown to Hardwicke at the time, William Wickham, despite his outer calm and air of assurance, was undergoing an extraordinary crisis of conscience, brought about by an incident which happened on the day of Emmet's execution. Just before he was taken from Kilmainham Jail to the place of execution in Thomas St., Emmet had asked the sheriff for permission to return to his cell where he wrote a letter to Wickham and handed it to Dr Edward Trevor, the Superintendent of the jail for delivery. Wickham received the letter on that afternoon, after Emmet had been executed, and in the intervening seven weeks he had become so affected by its contents and also by the fact that it was the last letter Emmet had written, that he was critically re-examining his entire philosophy concerning the political relationship between Ireland and Great Britain, and had become so mentally agitated that he was actively considering resigning his post as Chief Secretary and leaving public life. Emmet's letter had contained only a general vindication of his actions and a plea to be given an opportunity to explain his actions, something which he claimed had not been allowed to him in court. Perhaps Wickham imagined that Emmet's delay on the scaffold in giving the hangman a signal that he was ready may have been due to an expectation of him appearing and stopping the proceedings in order to give the opportunity of explaining himself. But Wickham's inner turmoil remained hidden as the Privy Council meeting drew to a close and the proclamation against Dwyer was sent to John Grierson, the Government printer for general distribution and to various newspapers for publication.

In the following weeks, with the new session of parliament looming, Hardwicke sent Marsden to London to brief various members on the Irish government's version of the events surrounding Emmet's rebellion. He was certain that the Whigs, under the leadership of James Charles Fox, would raise the issue of the dismissal of General Fox, in addition to criticising the shortcomings of the Irish administration. But Hardwicke, at least, had the advantage of having his half-brother Charles Yorke in charge of the Home Office in Addington's cabinet and it would be his responsibility to defend the role of the Irish administration in the upcoming debate. But, above all, Hardwicke looked to the forthcoming military offensive in Wicklow to divert attention away from recent issues of dispute.

Winter had set in early in the Wicklow mountains and by the beginning of December, the snow lay several feet deep on the higher slopes. Michael Dwyer, with less than a dozen of his remaining followers, had gathered in an abandoned miner's digging near the Wicklow Gap, in the townland of Oakwood above Glendalough. With him were Hugh Byrne, Martin Burke, John Mernagh, Laurence O'Keeffe (a deserter from the North Cork Militia) and, among others, three soldiers who had deserted from the Royal Barracks in Kilmainham during Emmet's rebellion. Dwyer was already shaken by the events of the previous few weeks for shortly after news of the proclamation had reached Wicklow, a military detachment arrived at his parent's home in Eadestown and arrested his sister Etty and also his married sister Mary Neale whose husband was on the wanted list in Dublin for supporting Emmet.

His mother and father were also briefly arrested as were his wife's two sisters, Catherine and Eily Doyle, all of whom were charged with harbouring him. Mary Dwyer avoided arrest, but over the following days several male relatives were also taken up as was Martin Burke's wife Rachel.[4] They were taken, initially, to Baltinglass Jail from where the women were transferred to Kilmainham and the men to a prison tender, the Hieram, which was an-

---

4.   The question as to whether Rachel Burke was the wife of Martin Burke has been raised by James J. Macken in his book *Martin Burke – The Father Of Pittwater*. Luke Cullen referred to her as his wife in his nineteenth century account, but the mystery remains as to why

chored under the guns of the Pigeon House in Dublin Bay. To add further pressure on the local population, additional soldiers were quartered in selected houses and the owners were followed when they went outside. The new military barracks at Leitrim was fully billeted and, as military preparations continued, the entrances and exits to all of the mountain valleys were manned by groups of soldiers.

This increased military activity, and particularly the quartering of soldiers, was placing a heavy burden on the local population and, for the first time, even some of Dwyer's most trusted supporters were asking him to consider the option of surrender. The local parish priest also wrote a letter to him in the same vein and it was these worsening circumstances which led to the meeting at Oakwood. For the first time Dwyer discussed the possibility of surrender on condition that they should be pardoned and sent to America. His proposal was backed by Hugh Byrne and by Martin Burke who had reportedly offered to join an overseas regiment in the previous year, but John Mernagh opposed it while Arthur Devlin was not present. The meeting ended inconclusively and they all went their separate ways because of the increased military presence. Dwyer had also mentioned the possibility of approaching William Hoare Hume, the local member of parliament and estate owner, but owing to the opposition of Mernagh he delayed – in the event almost fatally.

The new session of parliament began in London on 22 November, but George III, in his King's speech, only made a brief reference to Emmet's rebellion, and it was not until 2 December that Charles Yorke rose to move a continuation of the Irish Habeas Corpus Suspension Act and the re-enactment of the Martial Law Bill. In the course of a low-key speech he attempted to lay the blame for Emmet's rebellion on French agents, and it was not until the following Monday, when both Bills were read for a second time, that the real debate began with Mr Eliot declaring that it was difficult to believe that the Government in Ireland had not been taken by surprise, because if they had any advance information concerning the rebellion it was a pity it was not communicated to Chief Justice Kilwarden. But William Windham was even more scathing in his remarks and asked the government to make up its mind as sometimes the rebellion was being dismissed as a contemptible riot, and at other times as being of such formidable magnitude that it required no less a measure than martial law to put it down.

Both Bills were duly renewed, and on 9 December, Charles Fox made his first intervention on behalf of his brother during a debate on the Army Estimates. The events of 23 July were again discussed in great detail until one

there are no records of her making contact with him following her release from Kilmainham Jail in January 1804.

member, finally losing patience, ventured an opinion that "the Orangemen and Catholics are so full of inveteracy and uncharitableness that an angel from heaven could not settle the unfortunate differences of opinion which agitate, inflame and separate them." The Government of Ireland's attempts to put a brave face on their shortcomings had backfired badly and it was decided that Marsden should remain in London until January. Meanwhile in Dublin, Hardwicke was still fretting about the reporting orders given to Lord Cathcart, and even threatened to resign from office. He wrote a long letter to his half-brother in the Home Office, but received a blunt reply implying that if he felt that strongly about the matter he should carry out his threat. A chastened Hardwicke allowed the matter to drop and waited anxiously for news from Wicklow.

The military offensive under the command of General Beresford began on Saturday 10 December when a general search of the mountains began in very adverse weather conditions, and the military forces achieved an early success on that first day. Martin Burke had called in at the home of a local man, Patrick O'Brien, in the Glen of Imaal, not realising that a group of yeomen were inside drying themselves at the fire. Burke pretended that he had come to the house for a piece of harness, excused himself and left, but their suspicions were aroused and they followed him outside. He tried to escape and some members of the Monaghan Militia who were nearby joined in the chase. The River Slaney was then in winter flood and Burke crossed and recrossed it in a vain attempt to shake off his pursuers. He was finally surrounded in mid-stream but, in a curious example of prevailing local family loyalties, he refused to surrender until a maternal relative of his, by the name of Allen, a barrackmaster at nearby Davidstown, was sent for. When Allen arrived Martin Burke surrendered, was put in irons and sent under escort to Baltinglass Jail where the Allen family ensured that he was not abused in any way.

The capture of Burke on the first day of the military operation was regarded by its leadership as an event of the greatest importance as he was recognised as being one of Dwyer's principal comrades, and soon a flurry of letters were exchanged between Wicklow and Dublin. Beresford assured General Asgill that the reward money for his capture would be paid promptly to the soldiers concerned as a means of encouraging them to further exertions and he asked whether Burke should be sent to Dublin or tried by court martial in Wicklow, adding that whatever the sentence of law was, it should be carried out in the Glen of Imaal.

Lord Cathcart was immediately informed of the arrest and he, in turn, wrote to the Lord Lieutenant seeking instructions regarding Burke. Hardwicke was, no doubt, pleased that Cathcart had contacted him about the possibility of holding a court martial and he sent a note to William Wickham seeking his opinion and, in passing, described Burke as Dwyer's Lieutenant-General.

Wickham consulted with him and they decided not to hold a court martial in Wicklow. In the meantime, Beresford had written again to Asgill, having apparently mellowed in his attitude to Burke, local representations having been made on his behalf: "Of all the gang, if mercy was, or could be extended to any man, he was the most proper object because, never by any account, from the Gentlemen of the County, was there a charge of him being concerned in any murder and, having more than once, prevented the murder of loyal men." But the possibility of court-martialling Michael Dwyer, if he were captured was not being ruled out and Beresford wondered if, in that circumstance, Burke would also be included, while adding

> if, however, as I have reason to believe will be the case, Dwyer should throw himself upon the mercy of Government, it will supercede the necessity of any immediate determination relative to Burke as I shall send them all immediately to Dublin, conceiving that Government would not wish to have brought to punishment any of the inferior agents 'till it had been decided relative to the principals. If, however, Dwyer does not immediately surrender, and that Burke will not give such information as enables me immediately to take him, I am convinced that an instantaneous example will have the most salutary effect upon those who have been his adherents or shelterers, and upon the lower orders of the country in general.

The fate of Martin Burke, therefore, might depend on the actions of Michael Dwyer over the next few days and Beresford's confident assertion that he would surrender was well founded. News of Martin Burke's capture quickly became known, as did the possibility of his court martial. Dywer was on very close terms with his family and direct pressure would have come from them to try and save his life. On the following day Dwyer sent a message to Capt. Tennison, a local magistrate and member of the Glen of Imaal Corps of Yeomen, offering to surrender without any other conditions except that his own and Martin Burke's lives should be spared, and that they should be transported. Capt. Tennison, having consulted with the military, perhaps even with Beresford, sent a message back to Dwyer stating that the only acceptable terms were that he should throw himself upon the mercy of Government. But Dwyer was unwilling to accept terms which, *de facto*, meant that his agreement to unconditional surrender, and with the military pressure ever increasing, he turned to his last hope, William Hoare Hume, whose terms he had dismissed disdainfully a few weeks before.

On the following morning (13 December), three days after the capture of Martin Burke, Mary Dwyer arrived at Humewood and, according to the official report, "surrendered herself to Captain Hume." She had come to make a straightforward offer on behalf of her husband, namely that he would surrender on the sole condition that his life should be spared. William Hume felt it necessary to consult first with General Beresford at his headquarters in nearby Saunders Wood, but Beresford still believed that Dwyer would be soon captured and would only agree that Dwyer should surrender "upon the mercy of Government". But Hume, whose worst nightmare would have been the hanging of Dwyer and Burke in the Glen of Imaal, went one step further and, on his own initiative, gave Mary Dwyer an assurance that if her husband surrendered he would use his influence to persuade the Government to spare his life. That was the extent of the terms negotiated at this time and a fearful but relieved, Mary Dwyer left Humewood to inform her husband who may have been sheltering in the nearby home of a Protestant friend, Billy "the Rock" Jackson. There was little time for protracted negotiations or delaying, and persuaded, no doubt, by his wife and Jackson, Michael Dwyer agreed to surrender. And so, by pre-arrangement, on the evening of Wednesday 14 December, William Hume, taking with him a member of his Corps of Yeomen for reasons of safety, walked out through the back gate of his Humewood estate and waited at the nearby Three Bridges where Michael Dwyer, who was hiding nearby, soon joined him. The surrender terms having been confirmed, he walked back with William Hume into Humewood House, and into captivity. His five-year rebellion had ended.

CHAPTER THREE

1804

On the night that Michael Dwyer surrendered a tremendous storm of wind and rain swept the country from the south-east which continued throughout the next day, causing severe damage, particularly to shipping along the east coast. But in Humewood on that night, while the storm raged outside, Michael Dwyer and his wife Mary were liberally treated with food and drink, and the conversation continued long into the night, with Michael Dwyer regaling William Hume with accounts of his various escapades. Hume also enquired about the whereabouts of the military uniform which Robert Emmet had sent down before his rebellion. It had remained hidden in a local house from where it was later retrieved by Capt. Tennison.

It was during the course of this night also that additional terms were discussed. One of Dwyer's priorities was the release of his own and his wife's relatives while Mary Dwyer would have referred to her desperate plight as the mother of three young children, with no means of supporting them, and with her husband facing a long prison sentence or transportation. Hume promised that he would seek the approval of the government in Dublin to release their relatives and for Mary Dwyer and her children permission to live with her husband while he remained in prison, something which was not unusual at the time, particularly in the case of debtors. Most important of all, Dwyer, accompanied by his wife and children, would be given free passage out of the country. Their final destination, however, would become a matter of controversy as Michael Dwyer was in no doubt that William Hume indicated that they would be sent to America, and that he was advised not to divulge these secret terms to anyone. For his part, Hume made no mention of America to the military commanders in Wicklow in the days following Dwyer's surrender, although he later claimed in a letter to Marsden that he had informed Wickham about them, stipulating only, however, that Dwyer should be sent out of the country. Likewise, there is no evidence to suggest that Hume ever discussed the American option in his later discussions with government officials. In any event, he would have realised that, given their stated policy on transportation, the American government would be highly unlikely to accept a well-known rebel of Dwyer's calibre. But throughout his stay in prison, Dwyer resolutely clung to the belief that America was to be his final destination. He obeyed Hume's alleged strictures with regard to secrecy and manfully tried not to jeopardise the agreement. It is nor clear whether he

believed that the terms would extend to the other rebels and seemingly made
no attempt to negotiate on behalf of Martin Burke on that night in Humewood.

Owing to the adverse weather conditions Hume did not inform Beresford
about Dwyer's surrender until the following morning and Mary Dwyer was
allowed to leave Humewood to arrange for word to be sent to his remaining
comrades concerning the surrender terms. Beresford immediately rode over
to Humewood and, having congratulated Hume, immediately questioned Dwyer
concerning the extent of his operation in Wicklow, and whether he was planning a further rebellion with the help of the French. The Irish government,
with the exception of Marsden, had grossly overrated Dwyer's importance,
being still convinced that he was a prime mover in Emmet's rebellion, and
that he had upwards of 25,000 men on call in Wicklow awaiting help from
France. Beresford was relieved to hear from Dwyer that this perception was
totally false, although he must have been somewhat incredulous to discover
how pitifully small Dwyer's following really was.

Beresford also discussed the surrender terms with Hume who seemed, in
the cold light of day, to fudge the issue completely and their main discussion
centred on the forwarding of Dwyer to Dublin. Beresford presumed that he
would be handed over to his charge, but Hume was anxious to retain responsibility for his safety and requested that his own Corps of Yeomen should
escort Dwyer to Dublin. Given the influence of William Hume in the county,
it is not likely that Beresford had any serious objections and wrote on that
night to General Asgill making some highly interesting comments concerning
what he believed to be the surrender terms which Hume had made:

> I have reason to believe that the assurances given to Dwyer that his life
> shall be spared have been somewhat stronger than there had been war-
> rant, for the fellow does not appear to have any doubt or anxiety on that
> head. Captain Hume, however, tells me that he has thrown himself
> unconditionally on the mercy of Government, he [Hume] promising to
> use his personal interest with the Government to save his life. I cannot
> omit saying that if his solicitations on this head can or will be listened
> to, no-one deserves to be attended to than those of Captain Hume; his
> zeal, activity and exertion have been unremitted and undefatigable. The
> account which Dwyer gives of the disposition of the people is to us very
> satisfactory, and the more so is corroborated by every person with whom
> I have, of late, conversed on the subject as well as by the unasked-for
> declarations of the people themselves.

Dwyer remained in the guardhouse at Humewood during Thursday and
Friday, and Beresford wrote again to the government saying that he would
delay sending him to Dublin only for as long as was necessary "to procure the
necessary information from him to guide us in the pursuit of any others still
at large." A strong oral tradition, rarely aired in public, has survived in the

Wicklow mountains to the effect that, in the days following Dwyer's surrender, a number of houses where he had received shelter over the years were burnt to the ground, the inference being that Dwyer was the informant. In the written records of the military, however, there is no direct evidence to support this claim, although it might be argued that Beresford's statement that they wished to "procure the necessary information from him to guide us in the pursuit of any others still at large" might be construed in the above context. But this was a highly disciplined military operation and it is likely that the burning of houses would have been carried out by individual groups of militia or yeomen, frustrated at being denied a portion of the generous reward money which was on offer. And it is on record that at least one yeeman was disciplined for offences committed during the Wicklow operation. As for the charge that Dwyer had given information concerning the movements of his comrades, the reality was that they had all gone their separate ways since the abortive meeting in the cave at Oakwood, although Dwyer reportedly met John Mernagh on the day before he surrendered but he did not dare mention his intentions to him.

The search for Dwyer's remaining followers continued, with disappointment being felt among the various military groups that the reward money for his capture had been denied to them. But letters of mutual congratulation were still circulating in government circles, with Hardwicke delightedly commenting on his surrender: "It would be a great object at any time, but is particularly important at the present moment." Hugh Byrne was next to surrender, having quickly made contact with Humewood, and on Friday 16 December, William Hume, accompanied by Sgt. Perry of his Corps of Yeomen, went to a named house in the locality where Hugh Byrne gave himself up. He was immediately sent to Baltinglass Jail where Martin Burke was being held, and following Byrne's surrender it was decided to send Michael Dwyer to Dublin on Saturday morning; General Asgill had suggested that he should be sent directly to the New Provost Jail but the government decided to bring him first to Dublin Castle – to satisfy their curiosity if nothing else – and then to transfer him to Kilmainham Jail to await an official examination at a later date.

The propaganda value of Dwyer's surrender was now being exploited and the Dublin newspapers needed very little prompting. Already Martin Burke's capture had been reported in detail, and in the Saturday edition of the *Freeman's Journal* two separate stories appeared, the first contradicting the second, while the leading article in the following issue was simply headed "DWYER" and which separately described him as "the rebel robber", "this daring marauder" and "the Mountain-Robber". In the following weeks the provincial newspapers followed suit and even the *London Times* regarded his surrender as being of sufficient importance to devote a leading article which forecast that the "desperate ruffian's gang are now expected to surrender." All of this coverage must have heartened the Lord Lieutenant greatly as during the same week the *Dublin Evening Post*, showing a modicum of independence, published a detailed account of the recent House of Commons debate on the Emmet rebellion which, from a government point of view, made for dismal reading.

For the journey from Humewood to Dublin on Saturday 17 December, Michael Dwyer was given one of William Hume's best horses and, for his escort of Yeomen, it was a profitable and enjoyable day out as their leader William Murray, later collected the hefty sum of £32 to cover their expenses. They took the usual route through Donard and then on to Blessington where they stopped for refreshments, and the whole affair took on an air of victory, rather than defeat, as people along the way shouted words of encouragement. The majority of his escort would have known Dwyer and his family personally; indeed his surrender represented a valuable loss of income for them. But William Hume remained in Humewood attending the surrender of Hugh Byrne and awaiting the likes of John Mernagh and Arthur Devlin to make contact with him. Hume was regarded as a humane landlord and liberal in his views, but he would have regarded Dwyer as a nuisance and, potentially, a dangerous enemy. His uncle had been killed by rebels in 1799 and although Dwyer was not involved there always lurked in the back of Hume's mind the very real possibility that if any outrage occurred within his jurisdiction by loyalists, or if any of his tenants harboured a major grievance against him, Dwyer had the capability of seeking redress, perhaps by burning down a barn, or even his house. He was also aware that Dwyer was being protected by many of his tenants and workers, and he had recently written to the Government stating that for as long as the people protected Dwyer he would not be able to take him. It was in his own self-interest, therefore, to be in a position at last, not only to be rid of him, but also to be perceived as having acted generously towards him. By offering improved surrender terms he, undoubtedly, saved Dwyer and his comrades from the imposition of harsher sentences, but by holding out the prospect, however vaguely, of a free passage to America for Dwyer and his family he left himself open to the charge of reneging on his word.

Despite the break for refreshments at Blessington, Dwyer's escort made good time and reached Dublin by late afternoon where a newspaper reporter was at hand near the Castle to witness the scene: "Dwyer, the noted insurgent, was brought into town on Saturday evening last between four and five o'clock, escorted by a party of Captain Hume's cavalry Corps of Wicklow. He was dressed in country style, in a white frieze jockey, and appeared to be somewhat inebriated. The noble Captain was much displeased at the mob gazing at him and used some ruffianly expressions [having received some as well.

He has been lodged in Kilmainham Jail." Owing to his inebriated condition it was not possible to engage him even in a preliminary examination at Dublin Castle and he was transferred immediately to Kilmainham Jail where his female relatives were still being held and where one of the turnkeys reported: "Michael Dwyer is just arrived. He is very drunk and by much ado we have got him to bed. He appears to be a most complete villian in his liquor, but I got out of him that he saw his aunt, Mrs Devlin when we sent her to him." Mary Dwyer arrived at the Jail a few days later and was allowed to stay with him, but despite spending his first night in Kilmainham Jail, Michael Dwyer was quite insensible to the cares of the world.

On the following Wednesday, 21 December, Martin Burke and Hugh Byrne were transferred from Baltinglass to Kilmainham Jail. It was Hugh Byrne's second visit there, having been briefly imprisoned in 1799 following his arrest at the home of a relative in Dublin on charges of burning the houses of yeomen in Wicklow and robbing the inhabitants of their firearms. He was subsequently court martialled in Wicklow and sentenced to death, but managed to escape from jail and rejoined Dwyer in the mountains. One of his brothers, however, was hanged in 1798 while his father had also spent some time in prison. Martin Burke had fought at the battle of Stratford during the Wexford rebellion in May 1798, but was captured in Wicklow later that year and brought to Baltinglass Jail from where he also escaped with an iron bolt still fastened to his arm. By the time Burke arrived at Kilmainham his wife Rachel had been released on the previous Saturday. The Superintendent of Kilmainham Jail was the notorious Dr Edward Trevor who received additional payment from the government to eke out information from prisoners while in custody, and who had recently persuaded Michael Quigley, one of Emmet's chief organisers, to become a secret informer. Trevor had kept in touch with the recent developments in Wicklow and had also tried to persuade Arthur Devlin to surrender to himself, rather than to William Hume. Devlin, of course, was known to have been actively engaged with Emmet and was one of the most important of his followers to have evaded arrest. Trevor had written a letter to Devlin offering him terms of surrender and he had released Martin Burke's wife Rachel to deliver it to him in Wicklow, promising terms also for her husband.

As Christmas approached, the military search for John Mernagh and Arthur Devlin continued and James Keogh was charged with harbouring the former. He was tried before a court martial in Wicklow – the military had finally got their court martial – but Hardwicke took the precaution of sending down Prendergast, a well-known barrister, to act as Judge-Advocate. Keogh was sentenced to a term of transportation and Prendergast wrote to Wickham concerning the peaceable state of the county, adding that it was Dwyer alone who had kept that part of the island in a state of disturbance: "The inhabitants rejoice now at his being in the hands of the Government as they are no longer subject to the contributions which he was in the habit of levying previous to his surrender." He was referring to the practice of levying contributions (or protection money) from local firms in the area by the rebels which had caused a lot of ill-will in loyalist circles.

In Dublin, however, Chief Secretary William Wickham would not be taking part in the Christmas festivities. He had injured his knee while attending a shooting party, and it had swollen up again, forcing him to remain in bed over the holiday period. He had now become thoroughly disillusioned with public life; the shortcomings of Irish political figures had always irritated him; he was still smarting at the orders given to Lord Cathcart to report directly to the Duke of York, and on 23 December he had received an unfavourable legal judgement from Solicitor-General Plunkett pointing out that the military establishments of Ireland and Britain were no longer distinct, which effectively meant that the objections of Hardwicke and himself might not be valid. The erosion of the power of Lord Lieutenants in Ireland had already begun. But, above all, Wickham was still deeply troubled by the content and timing of Robert Emmet's letter, to the extent that he was on the point of submitting his resignation. He had in his possession also a copy of Emmet's speech from the dock which had been printed in the form of a pamphlet, and his main preoccupation was vainly trying to comprehend why this young Protestant Irishman, with an upper class background, only 24 years old, and in love with a beautiful girl, Sarah Curran[1] would almost deliberately set out to sacrifice his life in order to establish the independent republic of Ireland.

Wickham became convinced that the first priority of the Government in Ireland should be the disestablisment of the Protestant church and the abolition of church tithes which were levied on all denominations. He could not, of course, approach Hardwicke with these radical policies; indeed he had regarded Emmet's dock speech as being "of a rather mischievious tendency", so Wickham had come to the conclusion that he could not reconcile his position of Chief Secretary with his new beliefs and had written several drafts of a document which he planned to circulate privately among his English friends. But on Christmas Day he wrote to his friend Charles Abbott in England about more topical matters:

> I write to you from my bed where I am keeping a merry Christmas! The surrender of Dwyer is an object of the very first importance, together with the capture of Quigley and his associates, and has set my mind at rest as to the immediate neighbourhood of the capital. And if the French

---

1.   Sarah Curran was the daughter of well-known liberal attorney and politician John Philpott Curran.He was unaware of the romance until his house was searched following Emmet's rebellion.Sarah Curran was the subject of Thomas Moore's ballad "She Is Far From The Land".

would keep away I would vouch for the rest. I cannot doubt that Ireland is the principal object of their preparations.

During that winter the newspapers were filled with such rumours and with anti-French invective. On Christmas Eve a number of Dublin printers were arrested for having published *The Memoirs of Bonaparte* while a carpenter by the name of Kavanagh who lodged in Beresford St was also arrested on a charge of treasonable practices when several seditious papers and the dreaded history book were found in his desk. Even the boatmen on the canal did not escape censure; readers were warned that "there is a party of ruffians and dung luggers on the Grand Canal who call their filthy crafts the Brest Fleet."

Wickham remained convinced that Michael Dwyer had been in close contact with French agents and when he received letters from former informants of his on the Continent who predicted an imminent invasion of Ireland he wrote again to Abbott: "It was a most fortunate thing that Dwyer should have surrendered before any of the late communication from France had reached him. This will make the difference of an army to us. Had his men remained in Wicklow at the time of the landing of the enemy there is no doubt that the most formidable insurrection would have broken out." He went on to speculate that the most likely landing place for the French would be in the vicinity of Dublin, or that they would create a diversion at Killiney Bay and land their main force north of the city. He probably based his assertion on the report of the Duke of Carhampton who came to the same conclusion in 1795. Because of the perceived danger to Dublin, a number of Corsican, or Martello, towers were hurriedly built along the coast stretching from Bray to Ireland's Eye, mainly for cosmetic purposes, to give the appearance, at least, of being well-prepared, but Wickham was quick to add that, in the event of a French landing "then God help us all."

But while Wickham fretted in his sick bed, Christmas for Michael Dwyer in Kilmainham Jail was almost an occasion of happy reunion. His wife had been given permission to join him; he was provided with a clean and reasonably furnished cell; his food was satisfactory and he received a plentiful supply of spirits. He was also allowed access to his imprisoned female relatives whom he expected to be released within a short time and was confident that having spent a short term in prison he would be permitted to begin a new life with his wife and young family in America. Ironically, for the first time in five years, he was able to relax.

Arthur Devlin had spent the period of Christmas in the Wicklow mountains trying to make up his mind as to whether he should also surrender to William Hume. He recognised that his situation was more precarious than the others; not only had he been directly involved in Emmet's rebellion but he was a deserter from both the British army and navy. He was not present at the Oakwood cave meeting as he was on the Wicklow coast planning to escape

from the country. Indeed, it is difficult to assess exactly how much contact he
had with Dwyer since the time of Emmet's rebellion. But on 27 December,
with the military searches still proceeding, he made his way to Humewood
where he was also granted surrender terms by William Hume. It was only
then that he received Trevor's letter from Rachel Burke and, prompted by its
contents (and by her presence) asked for similar terms to be extended to
Burke which was agreed by Hume. Because of Devlin's close links with
Emmet he was sent immediately to Dublin and imprisoned in the Castle
Tower to await an official examination.

On 30 December, Hardwicke wrote a long letter to his half-brother Charles
Yorke in the Home Office in London in the course of which he set out a
detailed account of the military operation in Wicklow to date. He confidently
stated that:

> the dissolution of this gang will not only restore tranquility to, and
> confidence in every part of the county of Wicklow, but will tend to
> discourage and intimidate the disaffected in other places.

But perhaps the most significant section of the letter dealt with his plans for
disposing of Dwyer:

> Though it is certainly to be regretted, on account of the murders and
> other crimes which Dwyer had committed in the course of the last five
> years, that any such expectation should have been held out to him that
> his life should be spared, yet considering the great importance of break-
> ing up this gang which has so long disturbed that part of the county of
> Wicklow, that their exploits and importance have been greatly exagger-
> ated at a distance, as well as the indefatigable exertions of Mr Hume, I
> apprehend it will not be possible to bring them to trial, but we must
> content ourselves with transporting him for life as a felon and a convict.

Hardwicke was obviously unaware of any secret terms negotiated by William
Hume and his decision to transport Dwyer as a felon and convict meant only
one destination, namely the penal colony of New South Wales. Significantly,
the newspapers were soon forecasting that he would join his fellow-Wicklowman
Joseph Holt in Botany Bay, but in Kilmainham Jail, Michael Dwyer remained
convinced that a far different fate awaited him.

John Mernagh was now the only remaining member of Dwyer's principal
followers still at large. He had opposed the notion of surrender at the Oakwood
meeting and had always held independent views. At one period he had acted
independently with a small band of men in Glenmalure, but despite occasional differences with Dwyer concerning the overall leadership, they had
continued to work closely together and he had accompanied Dwyer to Dublin
for the meetings with Emmet. But he too had under estimated the thorough-
ness and intensity of the military operation, and on 9 January 1804 one of his

comrades by the name of Jack Byrne surrendered and informed Gen. Beresford that Mernagh was in a desperate situation and had made several unsuccessful attempts to get to Humewood. It seemed likely that the military search parties, unofficially at least, had cut off the approaches to William Hume's estate, hoping to salvage at least some of the reward money by capturing him. According to the further testimony of Jack Byrne, Mernagh and a few remaining men were close to starvation, having subsisted in the previous fortnight on one small meal, and in the previous three days on a single piece of bread.

The news concerning Mernagh's plight was quickly passed on to Dublin and William Wickham, who had already tendered his resignation, wrote confidently to John King in the Home Office in London that "the last of Dwyer's gang" would be secured within a few days. But the resilient Mernagh, having given up hope of reaching Humewood, tried to break out of the county and still evaded capture. William Wickham remained in office while awaiting the appointment of his successor and although his secretary noted that "Mr. Wickham's spirits are better than they were" his state of mind remained disturbed and he spent night after night writing and rewriting drafts of the document which he intended to circulate in England outlining his radical views for bettering Ireland's relations with Great Britain. The official reason given for his retirement was ill-health and sympathetic noises were made by the administration in Dublin Castle while the newspapers speculated that it was caused by pressure of work following the rebellion. But Wickham was still anxious, before leaving office, to attend the official examination of Michael Dwyer in order to discover the full extent of his supposed involvement with the French. The examination took place on 17 January 1804 and Wickham took his place alongside Chancellor Redesdale and Attorney-General Standish O'Grady. An account of the examination has survived in precis form, to which Wickham later added some footnotes in his own copy.

It promised to be a tricky ordeal for Dwyer as it put him in danger again of being classified as an informer. He realised that he would have to answer some very direct questions and while he would be able to fudge some of the issues which would be raised he did not wish to jeopardise Hume's secret terms by appearing to be uncooperative. His wife Mary was expecting their fourth child in July while his female relatives were still being held in the jail. In addition, Dr Edward Trevor who sometimes winkled information from prisoners with a show of mock friendship, was concentrating his efforts on Dwyer and kept him well supplied with beer and spirits in order to help loosen his tongue. The distinct impression is given from reading an account of the examination that Dwyer was well fortified in this regard and at one stage during his questioning boasted that "if he was let go now all the soldiers in the empire would not take him in six years." But Dwyer had an inbuilt advantage in as much as he knew far less than his examiners believed. He did not have to lie about the French, but he still had to be careful not to place

Arthur Devlin in jeopardy as he was due to be examined immediately afterwards. Indeed, the first questions concerned Devlin's activities which Dwyer
proceeded to answer at length, commencing with an irrelevant story to the
effect that Devlin was on board the ship which carried some of the 1798
prisoners on their release from Fort George in Scotland. He then went into
some detail as to how Jemmy Hope and Devlin had arranged the meeting
with Emmet at Rathfarnham, but that he had dismissed Emmet's plan and
had taken no part in his rebellion. And perhaps realising that he was implicat-
ing Devlin too closely, he hastily added that Devlin had taken no part in the
fighting on the night of 23 July. He further claimed not to know of the names
of the leaders of the rebellion because Emmet and Russell had kept their
names secret and he rejected the possibility of a rising in Wicklow claiming
that the people would not support a French invasion. This statement must
have reassured William Wickham, or perhaps he was disappointed that one of
his pet theories had been so firmly disproven. Dwyer admitted to having
killed three soldiers in Wicklow but did expand on that particular subject
while there was no mention of reprisals, house burnings, robberies or the
levying of businesses. Instead, he went on to regale them with an account of
how he had survived in the mountains and the examination ended with a
curious piece of non-information to the effect that "the key of the letter
which Emmet got from France was in Dowdall's trunk which Major Sirr
opened" a piece of gossip he had picked up in the jail as Dowdall had, by this
time, escaped to America. But Dwyer's most interesting observation came
when he was asked to give the reasons for the outbreak of the fighting in
Wicklow: "In 1798 the people were told that the Orangemen intended to
murder them; the loyal were assured that they were to be massacred by the
people – troops were sent into the country, on their approach the people fled,
the houses were found empty, and thus both parties were confirmed in their
belief. But they have since discovered the truth and Protestants and Catholics
are now as good friends as ever."[2]

The only official reaction to Dwyer's examination came from Under-
Secretary Marsden who, when forwarding a copy to the Home Office in
London, laconically dismissed it as having nothing but curiosity value. The
Government, however, was again careful to exploit its propaganda value and
readers of the Dublin newspapers and the *London Times* were given exagger-
ated descriptions of Dwyer's appearance which contrasted unfavourably with
the drawing made by George Petrie who was granted permission to visit
Dwyer in his cell. On 21 January, however, his sister Etty and his sisters-in-
law, Eily Doyle and Catherine Doyle, were released while his married sister
Mary Neale who lived in Dublin was also released a week later. But Arthur

2.   The most interesting copy of Dwyer's examination can be found among the Wickham
     correspondence in Hampshire P.R.O.

Devlin refused to answer any questions and it is not clear if he was brought before the examiners. Since his incarceration in Dublin Castle Tower, Devlin had received very different treatment because of his close links with Emmet. According to the testimony of another prisoner, Thomas Cloney from Wexford:

> Devlin was ordered to walk around the Castle yard for several days with some well-trained agents of infamy there, in order that I might see him, and another gentleman who was confined in a room in the second floor [Emmet's first cousin, John St. John Mason] should also be appraised of his arrival. The man, whose name was Arthur Devlin, was then made to appear to us in the character of an informer against state prisoners. After keeping Devlin, who proved to be a firm and decided character, among a gang of unprincipled vagabonds for several days to no purpose they sent him to Kilmainham Jail.[3]

The object of that particular exercise was to make Cloney and St. John Mason think that Devlin had turned informer, thus putting additional pressure on them to admit their involvement with Emmet. In that context it is not surprising that Devlin refused to be examined in Kilmainham and, apart from his not wishing to incriminate anyone, he would have to conceal the fact that he had deserted from both the British army and navy. No official action was taken against him, but by the end of March he was complaining that "we are treated worse than dogs in a kennel" and demanded his proper allowance from Trevor, having been granted the status of a second-class prisoner: "I have been given terms, sir, with the Government on my surrender and although you seem well inclined to do so, you cannot alter them." But Arthur Devlin was still in a difficult legal position as, theoretically, the colonel from whose regiment he had deserted in England still had the right to claim him from the civil authorities and, in that event, he would face a court martial and certain death.

The sudden resignation of William Wickham had come as a severe blow to Lord Lieutenant Hardwicke who had come to rely on him for advice and support, and with another House of Commons debate due to take place on the Irish administration's handling of the Emmet rebellion, the resignation could not have come at a more inopportune time. And the real reason became clear when Wickham circulated copies of his radical paper which was headed: "Three reasons for resigning the Office of Chief Secretary to the Lord Lieutenant of Ireland submitted to private friends in the month of January 1804." Wickham argued that the principal reason why differences had arisen between Catholics, Protestants and Dissenters in Ireland was due to the mistaken policy of making the Protestant church an established church but emphasised

---

3. *A Personal Narrative of Wexford* by Thomas Cloney.

that, in the aftermath of Emmet's rebellion, everyone had been brought before the courts rather than court martials. He also quoted Emmet's letter to him in full, adding that it was written "without a blot, erasure or interlineation in a firm and steady hand, and that when he closed, sealed and directed it, he had said, 'I am now quite prepared'." Wickham finally summed up, in an emotional manner, his reasons for resigning:

> No consideration on earth could induce me to remain after having maturely reflected the contents of this letter, for in what honours, or other earthly advantages could I find compensation for what I must suffer were I again compelled by an official duty to persecute to death men capable of thinking and acting like Emmet has done in the last moments for making an effort to liberate their country from grievances, the existence of many of which none can deny one, and which I myself acknowledge to be unjust, oppressive and unchristian. I will know that the manner in which I have suffered myself to be affected by this letter will be attributed to a sort of morbid sensibility, rather than to its real cause, but no-one can be capable of forming a right judgement on my motives who has not, like myself, been condemned by his official duty to dip his hand in the blood of his fellow countrymen, in execution of a portion of the laws and institutions of his country of which his conscience cannot approve.[4]

By any standards it was an extraordinary document to emanate from such a high-ranking government official and, in some respects, his sentiments matched Emmet's own sense of idealism. But on 20 February 1804, William Wickham quietly left Ireland on board the yacht Dorset and effectively retired from public life. But Emmet's letter would continue to haunt him for the remainder of his life.

His successor as Chief Secretary to Ireland was Sir Evan Nepean who, for the previous nine years, had been Secretary to the Admiralty and who was succeeded in that post by Marsden's brother William, the well-known orientalist and numismatist. Nepean had the reputation of being a hard-working official with moderate views, and he had supervised the setting-up of the penal colony of New South Wales in 1788. But during the single year in which he would remain in Ireland we would struggle in vain to comprehend or come to terms with the political situation. One of his first duties was to inform the Home Office of the capture of John Mernagh. Following his unsuccessful attempts to reach Humewood, Mernagh had initially returned to the Glen of Imaal although, according to a letter written by Sir Charles Asgill at the end of January, the military search for him was temporarily halted in order to give him an opportunity of surrendering. But Mernagh failed to

4. *Wickham Correspondence*, Hampshire P.R.O.

oblige and the search was resumed because "it is very evident that he has no intention of surrendering." Information was then received that Mernagh was attempting to reach a friendly house in the area of Rathcoole, Co. Dublin and on the night of 19 February, a group of militia, led by Capt. Clinch of Peamount, surrounded a house owned by a James Doyle where Mernagh was hiding. He rushed out of the house and attempted to make his escape in the dark, but Capt. Clinch followed him on horse back and when Mernagh stumbled into a sandpit, he proceeded to jump his horse on him as he lay on the ground. Mernagh did not have a firearm, but continued to throw stones at his pursuers until he was overpowered. He was taken initially to Naas Jail in Co. Kildare and then transferred to Kilmainham where he emulated the example of Arthur Devlin by refusing to be examined as Nepean reported: "Mernagh would not say a word. He is a very fine young man but hanged he must be. There is no shirking the business like the present." But despite this crisp and ominous statement by the new Chief Secretary, Mernagh remained in Kilmainham Jail and was included in the surrender terms granted to his four comrades.

The ten-week military campaign in Wicklow was now called off and another round of mutual congratulations were exchanged between the military forces and the administration in Dublin Castle, the consensus being that they had rid the country of a highly dangerous gang of criminals. Dwyer's male relatives were released from the prison tender in Poolbeg at the end of the month but, quite unexpectedly, Martin Burke and Hugh Byrne were transferred back to Wicklow Jail to stand trial at the Spring Assizes on foot of a warrant dating back to 1799. But their trial was postponed until the Autumn and they were back in Kilmainham within a week. The charges were subsequently dropped when it was realised that they had agreed surrender terms with the government. Officially, however, Michael Dwyer had been committed to Kilmainham by Wickham on a charge of high treason while the lesser charges of being involved in treasonable practices had been brought against the others. But these charges were being cited for public reassurance as William Hume had confirmed the surrender terms with Wickham before Christmas, but without making any mention of America as the final destination for the Dwyer family. But this was scarcely a viable option for as far back as 1790, Jeremiah Fitzpatrick, Inspector of Irish Prisons, had referred to the practice of the American government of shipping back to Ireland every convict they found, unless they happened to be skilled tradesmen. In 1798 President Adams had instructed his ministers in London to inform the British Government of his determination to make use of the recent powers granted to him by an Act of Congress "not to allow any traitors from Ireland to land in America". And even if Dwyer was not brought to trial he would still be classified as a well-known rebel leader and the American government would have been informed by Charles Wilson, their Dublin consul.

The intentions of the Irish government, however, were quite clear and soon after his arrival, Evan Nepean was instructed to write to the Home Office in London requesting the provision of a ship to transport 140 men and 30 women to New South Wales. It was over 18 months since the last convict ship *Rolla* had left Cork Harbour and the numbers of prisoners in receipt of sentences of transportation at the various assizes throughout the country was building up again. It was Hardwicke's firm intention to be rid of Dwyer and his comrades by the end of that summer.

On 7 March 1804, the motion for investigating the causes of Emmet's rebellion was finally introduced in the House of Commons by Sir John Wrottesley who stated that if the government in Ireland had no advance knowledge it would be "incumbent to address his Majesty to dismiss those persons from the Government of Ireland." This was a thinly-disguised call for the dismissal of Marsden and Hardwicke, and when Lord Castlereagh opposed the motion on behalf of the government he tried to distance himself from the dismissal of General Fox, but unfortunately added that "Lord Hardwicke was not so uninformed as some gentlemen supposed." It was, at best, a half-hearted attempt by Castlereagh who probably believed that the Irish government had been negligent, and who was secretly advocating the return of William Pitt as prime minister while still remaining a member of Addington's tottering cabinet. When the House divided, the motion for an official enquiry was defeated by a margin of two to one and Hardwicke's administration was spared any further embarrassment. To the exasperation of his opponents in Dublin, Marsden retained his post as Under-Secretary, but no sooner had the issue of Emmet's rebellion ended when a new campaign began, with allegations being made of serious abuses taking place in Kilmainham Jail which were directed against its Superintendent, Dr Edward Trevor, from whose brutality, neither Michael Dwyer, his comrades, or members of the Devlin family in particular, would escape.

CHAPTER FOUR

1804-1805

A new jail to serve the County of Dublin had been built at Kilmainham in 1795 at the cost of £16,000. It was situated near the army headquarters at the Royal Hospital, and just one mile from Dublin Castle while the old jail nearby was used as a laundry and to house female prisoners. Even though it was in operation for less than a decade many well-known rebels had already been imprisoned there including Napper Tandy, Wolfe Tone, the Sheares brothers, Thomas Addis Emmet, Henry Joy McCracken and, in the recent past, Thomas Russell and Robert Emmet.

In the weeks which followed Emmet's rebellion the government panicked and, availing of the suspension of the Habeas Corpus Act, indiscriminately arrested anyone they believed to have been even remotely involved. These suspects came from all classes of society, and the jails and prison tenders in Dublin were soon filled. The most infamous of the prisoners were housed in Kilmainham and the existing debtors were transferred to the Marshalsea prison. By the middle of 1804, some of the prisoners had been held without trial for almost a year; in some instances there was insufficient evidence available, and where the government had enough evidence, there was an overall reluctance to bring to light further embarrassing details concerning the rebellion. Many of Robert Emmet's friends and acquaintances from the Dublin Protestant professional classes were among them, and were experiencing prison life for the first time. But the rigid class society structure also extended into the prison system; at the top of the pecking order were the first-class prisoners, usually comprising the upper or professional classes; the second-class prisoners were broadly equated with the middle classes while the third category was made up of members of the "lower orders" who formed the main bulk of the prison population.

Because of his enhanced status as a rebel leader, Michel Dwyer was placed among the first-class prisoners; Arthur Devlin was consigned to the second class, but Hugh Byrne, Martin Burke and John Mernagh, who were initially granted second-class status, were quickly transferred to the felon's side by Trevor, which in Byrne's case was, at least, a breach of his surrender terms. The living conditions and the food allowances of the three categories were also strictly defined and costed; the first-class prisoners were usually given a cell of their own and were entitled to a generous daily food allowance to the value of three shillings and three pence, the breakdown of which amounted to one pound of bread, a half ounce of tea, three ounces of sugar, a half-naggin of milk, and one and a half pounds of either beef, mutton or pork, a quart of small beer and, on occasions, a half naggin of whiskey. For Michael Dwyer however, having spent five years in the Wicklow mountains, it was like moving into a mansion. The allowance of the second-class prisoners was proportionately less, but still generous; as for the prisoners on the felon's side, their allowance consisted of two loaves per week, a pint of milk a day and a supply of water. In addition, they lived in primitive conditions and their bare cells were covered either with wet straw or had no covering at all. Within that overall framework, however, there was plenty of room for manouevre by the authorities of the jail, and for the majority of prisoners held in Kilmainham during this period, life became intolerable owing to the machinations of its Superintendent, of whom the inmates would later testify that "there is not so cruel a monster in human shape than Dr Trevor."[1]

Edward Trevor was born in the North of Ireland and, having served in the army, came to Dublin to seek his fortune and trained as an apothecary. He returned to the North again where he became involved in the cut and thrust of electioneering in County Down. In time, he again drifted back to Dublin, calling himself a doctor, and in 1798 was appointed as medical attendant and Superintendent of Kilmainham Jail. Within a short period he had broadened his portfolio to become medical attendant to the Royal Hospital and the Hibernian School and was also appointed as agent for Transports and principal recruiting agent in Dublin for the army and navy. In this latter capacity he regularly visited prisons and tenders persuading prisoners to enlist in exchange for free pardons.

He was also used by both Wickham and Marsden as their chief spy in Kilmainham Jail and Wickham, despite his qualms of conscience, had no hesitation in granting Trevor a gratuity of £200 before leaving office. At a time when few would have taken on the post of superintendent with any great enthusiasm, Trevor absolutely revelled in the role, and strode along the corridors of the jail, twirling his cane, dispensing favours and issuing edicts in the manner of a feudal monarch. The attendants and turnkeys were his abject slaves, the prisoners dependent on his every whim; this was his empire, his small stepping stone into society, and while he danced to the governor's tune "the reptile crawled to the Castle and was found by the government to be a supple sycophant, crafty and unprincipled." He had a razor sharp mind; he could be equally charming or utterly ruthless; he possessed a gallows-type sense of humour, with an underlying streak of vindictiveness and cruelty, and a complete absence of any kind of morality which, in particular, made the carrying out of his medical duties a ghastly joke.

---

1. Pamphlet *Pedro Redivivus* by St. John Mason, p. 60.

He was particularly valuable to the government in the weeks following Emmet's rebellion when, by appearing to be sympathetic towards them, obtained valuable information from both Russell and Emmet, and was also instrumental in persuading Michael Quigley to agree to become a secret informer. He also tried, unsuccessfully, to bribe Ann Devlin's father: "Dr Trevor often wanted me to turn informer and he offered me money for that purpose; he had taken out of his pocket great quantities of bank notes and offered them saying that he would be a friend to me and to my family all our lives, and when I refused him he was grinning at the same time, 'well you case-hardened old villian you shall be hanged'."

James Tandy and John St. John Mason were the two State prisoners who were mainly reponsible for organising the prisoners into making official complaints against Trevor. Both had been arrested and imprisoned in the aftermath of the rebellion, mainly because of their family backgrounds, although neither were in any way involved with Emmet's plans. John St. John Mason was a first cousin of Emmet's whose mother was Mason from Co. Kerry, and he had just commenced his career as a barrister when he was arrested while on his way to attend a court sitting in Limerick. He was sent to Kilmainham where he was put into a cell measuring ten feet by six. He protested in vain to Wickham and was to remain in solitary confinement until November, although Trevor ensured that he had access to Robert Emmet. Shortly before Emmet's execution he made a futile effort to free him by attempting to bribe one of the guards, which action confirmed the authorities in their belief that he was involved in the rebellion.

James Tandy was a prosperous wine merchant who, far from supporting Emmet, had attached himself to the Lawyers Corps of Yeomen whose members offered their services to Marsden at Dublin Castle on the night of the rebellion. He had served with the East India Company and was well known to Lord Cornwallis. But he was also a son of Napper Tandy, a leading United Irishman, and attracted official attention in 1802 when he successfully opposed Hardwicke's proposal to transport his father to New South Wales. Tandy was owed £150 by a Brabazon Morris and he would claim that Morris had given false information in order to avoid paying his debt. When a warrant was issued for his arrest Tandy arrived in Dublin Castle, accompanied by Sir Marcus Somerville, a magistrate from Drogheda, and they were received by Marsden who was standing with his back to the fire. But a slighted Somerville whispered loudly: "Is this not a pretty thing that this fellow receives gentlemen, warming his backside to the fire, he deserves to be kicked and, for farthing, I would kick him."[2] On hearing this rejoinder, Marsden immediately left the room and, having remained outside for some time, finally returned "with a struggle of composure", being careful no doubt, to keep away from

---

2. Pamphlet "An Appeal To The Public" by James Tandy, Appendix, p. 11.

the fire. This intervention by Sir Marcus Somerville, however, would prove to be very costly to Tandy and, at a later meeting, Marsden bluntly informed him that he could expect no favours from him. This message was undoubtedly passed on to Trevor and Tandy was given the worst cell in the dungeons of the jail where he remained despite the fact that many influential friends were lobbying for him, and having received the promise of an early release from Wickham in the week before he left office.

In May 1804, the administration of Henry Addington finally collapsed and William Pitt was called upon again to form the new government. In France, Napoleon Bonaparte had given himself the title of Emperor of the French and as Pitt attempted to rally the spirit of the British people to renew the war effort against France, it became known that he was opposed to the idea of an early release of the state prisoners in Kilmainham. By the end of June, a group of prisoners, at the urging of St. John Mason, decided to take the initiative themselves; a commission of Oyer and Terminer was taking place at the Sessions House in Green Street and, with some difficulty, the prisoners succeeded in getting a barrister to hand a letter to the presiding Judges on the Bench which stated that "a system of avaricious and malignant severity is practised in this prison which calls aloud for, and might be sufficiently demonstrated by a fair and impartial investigation." The custom which prevailed at the time was that judges were obliged, on the receipt of such complaints, to visit the jail concerned and to interview both prisoners and jailers, but in the case of state prisoners, the government had to be informed first, and the Judges would await their instructions before proceeding.

The prisoners' letter was received by Judge George Daly who was subsequently asked by the government to visit Kilmainham Jail on 7 July where he spoke to St. John Mason and was handed two separate memorials by him. The first was signed by 14 of the first-class prisoners and included the signatures of Mason, Tandy and also two of Emmet's friends, Philip Long, the banker who had advanced him the sum of £1,400 and John Patten, a Trinity College chemistry student. Michael Dwyer did not sign the memorial at this stage as he still had no complaint to make about his treatment. The second memorial was signed by 41 of the second-class prisoners, including Arthur Devlin and Bryan Devlin while 13 further signatures were bracketed together at the end of the list, with the explanation that they had been confined to the felon's side of the prison until a short time before. The last three names were Hugh Byrne, Martin Burke and John Mernagh.[3]

Judge George Daly reported back immediately to the government stating that from his "imperfect investigations the grievances, if they exist at all, are greatly exaggerated in the memorials." He also stated that it was the wish of the prisoners that the memorials be forwarded to Hardwicke who, on reading

---

3.   *Pedro Redivivus*, p. 35.

them, seemed to be genuinely shocked at the allegations which they contained. He would have already been aware of Tandy's complaints, as was Chief Secretary Nepean, as Tandy's wife had recently applied to him for her husband's release and he had naively reassured her: "I am, Madam, a husband and father of a family, and God forbid that I could possibly think of keeping a man in confinement without either bringing him to trial or to the bar." But an embarrassed Nepean had to contact her again with the news that he had been overruled. In response to the prisoners' memorials Hardwicke decided to initiate a high-level investigation concerning conditions in the jail and appointed Chief Justice William Downes to head it, with Judges Osborne and Day acting as his assistants. The investigation would take place in Kilmainham jail over a period of three days (16-18 July) and a decision was taken not to inform the officers of the jail in advance to ensure that the Judges would be able to observe the conditions as they really were, an idle hope with someone as resourceful as Trevor in charge, and given his connections with Marsden in Dublin Castle.

But before the investigation took place, Michael Dwyer had fallen foul of Trevor. With the change of government in London, the prospect of a convict ship being fitted out for New South Wales that summer was fading and Dwyer, in Tevor's eyes at least, was losing his potential value as a source of secret information (and of revenue). On 1 July, without any warning, his allowance of tea, sugar and spirits was stopped and he was ordered into the yard with the other prisoners. He immediately complained to Trevor, asking him in particular not to deprive him of the spirits as he claimed "my health would suffer at being debarred of that to which I had been necessarily accustomed." Dwyer's children had joined him in his cell, in addition to his wife, and they were also ordered to leave the jail during daytime. Mary Dwyer was then nine months pregnant and their fourth child Esther would be born by the end of the month. Trevor warned Dwyer that if he did not obey his orders he would have him transferred to the felon's side but Dwyer asked him again to restore his allowance of spirits saying that he did not deserve such treatment and that it was contrary to the terms pledged to him by William Hume. Trevor then sent for John Dunn, the keeper of the jail, and ordered him to take Dwyer to the felon's side.

Dwyer decided to go quietly with him, but Mary Dwyer immediately complained to Hume's uncle John who lived at Synott's Place in Dublin. A letter was also sent to Humewood and ten days later, John Hume paid a visit to the jail where he spoke to Dwyer in the jailer's parlour. He questioned him about the incident with Trevor and spoke also to John Dunn who confirmed that Dwyer had caused no trouble since his arrival and described him as "a most quiet and peaceable man" while discreetly adding that Trevor was "a most passionate man". John Hume's solution for resolving the situation was surprisingly simple. He suggested that Dwyer should apologise to Trevor, and when he protested that he had nothing to apologise about, at the further insistence of Hume, he was forced to swallow what remained of his pride, and to ask Trevor to be reinstated as a first-class prisoner, and to be reunited with his wife and children. In accepting the apology, Trevor claimed that he had punished him as an example to the other prisoners, and exactly one week before the official investigation was due to begin, Dwyer was back in his cell. But he was effectively reduced to second-class status and began to interest himself in the state prisoners' complaints.

On the morning of Monday 16 July – in what must have been the worst-kept secret of the year – Chief Justice William Downes, accompanied by Judges Osborne and Day, and John Pollock, Clerk of the Crown, arrived at Kilmainham jail. The state prisoners were, naturally, delighted with this development, although it was not completely unexpected; their treatment had dramatically improved over the previous few days and a midnight conference was overheard on the night before during which Keeper John Dunn had instructed the kitchen workers to go out and bring back the best provisions at any cost. Chief Justice Downes decided to interview, separately and under oath, a number of prisoners who had signed their names to the memorials; he would also visit the kitchens and some of the cells, and would finally interview jailers and turnkeys in addition to Dunn and Trevor. A room next to the the sheriff's execution room was set aside for the interviews which were supposed to be confidential, but Trevor placed him strategically in a corridor above, from where he could overhear every discussion.

In all, 30 prisoners were interviewed, including all of the first-class prisoners who had signed the memorial while Dwyer, still smarting over his reduced allowance, had added his name to the list of complainants and asked for an interview. Eight prisoners were chosen to represent the second-class and they gave their testimony under the general headings of food, the reduction and deprivation of their allowances, their close confinement, the capricious confinement of prisoners, privy facilities, the poor treatment of visitors to the prison, and, finally, what they termed "the overall malevolence" of Trevor. Over the following three days a litany of complaints were repeated, including the charge that, on a sudden whim, Trevor would transfer prisoners to the felon's side where they were kept in solitary confinement and were loaded and bolted with four stone of irons. But this was also a mercenary move by Trevor as the savings on their daily allowance of three shillings and three pence would finally accrue to him. In his capacity of medical attendant he was in the habit of prescribing glauber salts for all manners of complaints, including gout, and when the prisoners were administered this all-purpose medicine, they would receive no food on that day, thereby adding, once again, to his profit margins!

When Michael Dwyer was questioned by the judges he recounted the recent harsh treatment he had received from Trevor and, taking the lead from the other first-class prisoners, complained about the quality of food served to him. The judges, surprisingly, agreed to his request that Trevor be brought in to answer his allegations and, having been put on oath, he claimed that Dwyer had become "pert" and so he transferred him to the felon's side. And he proceeded to turn John Hume's intervention to his own advantage by pointing out that Hume had insisted on Dwyer apologising to him. The judges, however, warned Trevor not to tamper again with Dwyer's conditions without good cause.

Hugh Byrne was also interviewed, having been chosen as one of the eight prisoners to represent the second-class. He told the judges that on his arrival at Kilmainham Jail he had been put into the second-class for four days only and was then put on "jail allowance", namely two loaves of bread a week and a daily pint of milk. Apart from his brief transfer to Wicklow Jail he had remained on the felon's side for 15 weeks before being recently upgraded to the status of second-class. Martin Burke and John Mernagh had been treated in a similar manner but Arthur Devlin had remained in the second class since his transfer from Dublin Castle tower. Trevor was interviewed on the final day of the investigation and was at his mercurial best, giving a virtuoso performance of unashamed roguery. No-one could be as concerned about the prisoners' welfare; he had always taken the utmost pains to see that the provisions supplied were of the highest quality and he strongly denied that he had made the smallest profit from any shortfalls. He blamed the recent severe weather for the unsatisfactory supply of vegetables and solemnly promised that hangman Tom Galvin would not be used in future to bring food to the prisoners, which service tended to spoil their appetites. He found St. John Mason to be both irritable and bad-tempered and confided that other prisoners would not associate with him because of his foulness of manner. Their Lordships finally interviewed keeper John Dunn and the prison butcher and baker, and everyone anxiously awaited their report. Given the weight of evidence presented, the prisoners were confident that the abuses would cease and that Trevor would be replaced. Even better, they could look forward to an early release.

The report of Chief Justice William Downes was written and submitted to Hardwicke with almost indecent haste. Judge Osborne was able to be present in the jail on the first day only and, having conferred with Judge Day, and with the assistance of his eponymous notetaker John Pollock, the report was written on that same night by Downes at his house in Merrion Square as he was due to leave in the morning to attend a country assizes. The report noted the great irritation and resentment felt about Trevor but added that "despite this evidence, Dr Trevor, John Dunn and the turnkeys have conducted themselves with humanity towards the prisoners." Some minor criticisms were made concerning the conditions at the jail, but the net result was a complete vindication of Trevor. It was all the more remarkable as Judge Day was a humane judge who would continue to interest himself in the correction of abuses, but it was obviously the report of the Chief Justice Downes who may have been unduly influenced by John Pollock who had often exceeded his role of note-taker by asking questions "which were intrusive and insiduously put" and who was also known to Trevor.

The report was sent to Hardwicke on the following morning who, no doubt, read it with a sense of relief. But Chief Secretary Neapean must have been puzzled, given his knowledge of Tandy's treatment, while Marsden was surely delighted that Trevor had escaped so lightly. The contents of the report were conveyed immediately to Trevor, but the prisoners were not informed of its recommendations, although they sensed from his jaunty behaviour throughout the week, that he was not unduly worried. A week passed and the prisoners, who were still kept in ignorance, organised a mass protest by walking in procession along the corridors of the jail. Trevor was taken aback by this sudden and united show of strength and asked them to return to their cells, promising that he would have an answer from the government concerning the publication of the report. On that night he further announced that no final decision would be taken until the following Monday "when a matter relative to the state prisoners might take place in the intermediate time." On being pressed as to what these matters might be, Trevor professed ignorance, and when he was further asked if the prisoners were to regard his message as being official he replied that it had come from the highest authority "except the Lord Lieutenant". He also asked them not to take part in any other actions until the week had elapsed.

If credence can be given to Trevor's statements it seemed as if some consideration was being given by Chief Secretary Nepean to release some of the State prisoners who had been held without trial for over a year. Many influential people in the country, including Lord Charlemont, were still petitioning for the release of James Tandy, but in advocating such an action Nepean would have been opposed by Hardwicke and Marsden who could ill-afford to be faced with any further plots of rebellion, particularly from released prisoners. On Monday 6 August, Trevor met the prisoners again but gave an evasive answer, claiming that the government was expecting the Court of Chancery to meet before any further comment could be made. If this was the case a hardline attitude could be expected from the Attorney-General and Lord Redesdale, and when Trevor was also unable to give a date for its meeting, it effectively ended the prisoners' hopes for an early release. He was free to indulge himself once more and the instances of cruelty and tyranny increased.

A week later, in an effort to dissuade the prisoners from holding any further mass meetings, Luke White, the county sheriff, arrived without warning as a group of prisoners were taking exercise, and on the pretext that they were investigating some vague plot, soldiers with fixed bayonets forced them back into their cells. At this time also the only musical instrument in the jail, a battered violin, was broken in pieces by a guard, and when it was discovered that James Tandy was feeding tame pigeons they were killed. But on 13 August, the prisoners decided to renew their action and another signed letter was handed to Hardwicke as he was travelling by coach in the city, accompanied by Marsden.[4] Once again Trevor was pilloried and the shocking treatment which had been meted out to Ann Devlin since her arrest was highlighted for the first time. But the letter was ignored by Hardwicke and their only success came in September when James Tandy was released on the advice of Surgeon-General Stewart. Ten months earlier he had entered Kilmainham Jail in perfect health, but he had to be carried out in the arms of two men, with an abcess on his chest and looking like a skeleton.

Lord Hawkesbury had replaced Hardwicke's half-brother in the Home Office and on 10 September, Evan Nepean wrote to him concerning his request to fit out a convict ship for New South Wales. In the meantime, keeper John Dunn had died in Kilmainham Jail, having been administered a pint of castor oil one hour before his death by Dr Trevor, and his successor, a man by the name of Simpson, a drunken boor, was handpicked by Trevor and would make life even more miserable for the prisoners. Hugh Byrne's wife Sarah had joined her husband in the jail, but both Dwyer and Byrne incurred Trevor's displeasure again as another state prisoner, John Galland, recorded: "I have known Trevor to turn out Dwyer's wife and children, and Hugh Byrne's wife who were in Kilmainham with the agreement of the Government out of the jail, late in the evening without dinner, they not knowing where to put their heads; and all this for the alleged offences of their husbands for which Byrne and Dwyer were previously punished."

But while the government waited for news of the convict ship, Trevor dreamt up his own novel plan to get rid of the troublesome Wicklowmen. He had employed two prisoners to act as attendants in the jail, 16 year-old Edward Doyle who had been sentenced to seven years transportation for stealing calico and Edward White who had received a life sentence for robbery. According to the testimony of Patrick Doyle (another Wicklow prisoner) White and Doyle approached Dwyer and some others with a plan to lock up the keeper and escape together from the jail. But when Patrick Doyle climbed onto a window ledge he saw a group of soldiers hiding outside the walls with fixed bayonets. In another version of the same story Edward Doyle is reported as having revealed the plot to Dwyer and, for his pains, was transferred back to the felon's side.

There was disappointment for the government when a decision was taken in London to delay the provision of a convict ship until the spring of 1805,

---

4. *Idid.*, p. 41.

and a furious Hardwicke instructed Nepean to write to the Home Office pointing out that the last convict ship, the *Rolla*, had left Cork as late as the month of November and that the convicts arrived in New South Wales in good health. Already jails throughout the country were crowded with prisoners sentenced to terms of transportation and Hardwicke wished most of all to be rid of the Wicklow rebels in Kilmainham Jail. But the Home Office did not change its mind and with the chorus of prisoners' complaints still getting louder, Nepean decided to pay a visit to Kilmainham Jail on 15 December. Advance notice was given on this occasion and the choicest meat was brought in, only to be returned after he had left. The affable Dr Trevor was, naturally, on hand to give Chief Secretary Nepean, his private secretary Col. Flint and a visiting guest, the Receiver of Excise, a warm welcome. The inspection took place a short time after Trevor had forced James Byrne to strip in order to humiliate him in front of other prisoners, but when he tried to speak to Nepean during the visit, Trevor took the chief secretary aside, whispered something to him, and Nepean turned quickly away. Another prisoner, Edward Coyle, did manage to speak to Nepean, but in a highly agitated manner. Coyle had been kept in solitary confinement for long periods since his arrest and when the visit ended he was immediately loaded with four stone of irons, and when keeper Simpson inspected them he made sure to drop the irons on Coyle's ankles in order to inflict the maximum pain. As for James Byrne, his attempt to speak to Nepean was rewarded by near-starvation and he was placed in an unglazed cell in mid-winter in the company of four hardened criminals who had been condemned for murder and rape. And so Trevor survived again, still protected by Marsden in Dublin Castle, of whom it was alleged that he was his unnamed partner in a bakery concern which supplied bread to the jail.

The year 1805 began with Michael Dwyer's treatment at the hands of Trevor still deteriorating, and he arranged for a long letter to be written to William Hume which he signed in his own flowery handwriting[5] and also thumb-printed. He accused Trevor of calling him a savage and a tyrant, and that he had gone around the jail saying that Dwyer was unfit for any society. And when he protested at what he considered to be an abuse of his terms, Trevor had exploded: "Your terms! Your terms! I know what your terms are better than yourself. You have no terms at all. There is no robber or highwayman could make better possible terms than saving his life, and the capital offence is where you and such people should be." This was the first intimation Dwyer had received that America might not be his destination and he concluded his letter by asking Hume whether the sufferings that he and others had endured were happening with the knowledge of the government

---

5. Michael Dwyer had learned to write at school while John Mernagh and Hugh Byrne learned to sign their names after their arrival in New South Wales.

because he believed they were not. He finally reminded Hume of the promises he had made at the time of his surrender and that he should make sure
that they were honoured.

Mary Dwyer, who brought the letter to Humewood, also gave a personal
account of the manner in which they had been treated and Hume received
letters written in a similar vein by Hugh Byrne and Arthur Devlin. Stung by
their implications, a clearly irritated Hume wrote to Marsden in Dublin
Castle on 19 February:

> There is scarcely a day passes when I am not tormented with letters or
> messages from these fellows in Kilmainham who surrendered them-
> selves to me, viz. Dwyer, Arthur Devlin and Hugh Byrne complaining
> of ill treatment, of being almost naked with various other complaints.
> And yesterday Dwyer's wife came here to tell me that she and her
> children had been thrown out of prison and that he was put in that part
> of the prison allotted for felons and put on the gaol allowance, and she
> says without cause, which I am not certain of the fact. But, although I
> know of no punishment too severe for them, yet it places me in a very
> awkward situation in this country to have these complaints made, how-
> ever unfounded, that the terms I promised them to induce them to
> surrender are not kept. At the time they surrendered I told Mr. Wickham
> that they should be sent out of the Kingdom as soon as possible and
> that, in the meantime, they should not be ill-treated in person, that
> their relatives who were confined merely on their account should be
> liberated and that Dwyer's wife and children should be allowed to re-
> main with him while in prison and sent along with him. And I can
> assure you that it cannot be of any service to the country to have her at
> large here now. I therefore request that she may be confined again with
> her husband in Kilmainham; that if something very particular had not
> occurred to prevent that I know nothing of at present.

At the same time Hugh Byrne forwarded a separate petition to Judge Day in
which he charted the treatment he had received from Trevor since his arrival
in the jail. Byrne had also been transferred to the felon's side and stated that
he was

> struck off the State allowance nor would be permitted to see any friends,
> and compelled to lie on the cold flags where petitioner continued for
> eleven days . . . that his wife and children, together with the wife and
> children of Michael Dwyer were, on a wet and stormy night, without
> their dinner, turned into the streets . . . and that petitioner's wife and
> children are still kept from him, by which they endure great distress.
> That petitioner is confident that these excesses are inflicted by the mere
> authority of Dr. Trevor without the knowledge of the Government . . .

and begs that if your Lordship would please to confront him with Dr Trevor, he would not deny a single assertion made in this petition.

As a result of the representations made by William Hume and Judge Day the entitlements of Dwyer and Byrne were restored and their families were allowed to rejoin them in the jail, but a further hiatus occurred with the resignation of Evan Nepean as Chief Secretary who returned to England with much to ponder upon concerning Irish affairs. Marsden deputised as Chief Secretary in the interim and at the end of March he received a letter from the Home Office in London confirming the recent instruction from Lord Hawkesbury that a convict ship be immediately provided for Ireland. But Dwyer and his comrades still had not been informed of the government's intentions and soon another tragedy occurred in Kilmainham Jail which resulted in Trevor being held responsible for the death of ten year old Jimmy Devlin, the youngest son of Bryan Devlin, and brother of Ann Devlin. Of all those who had been involved in Emmet's rebellion, the family of Bryan and Winifred Devlin suffered most of all. Ann Devlin, who had acted as Emmet's house keeper, was singled out for special treatment but Trevor's mixture of treacly charm, bribery and finally dark threats had no effect on that most single-minded of young women. By March 1805, Ann Devlin and her father Bryan were the only two remaining members of the family still imprisoned in Kilmainham Jail, but their once prosperous business in Rathfarnham was gone. Winifred Devlin and one of her daughters were living in dire poverty in lodgings and were forced to send back ten-year old Jimmy to live with his father in prison. He became very popular with the prisoners and often went up to the old jail where his sister Ann was once again being held. On a cold night in March he was ordered to join his sister there by a prison attendant. His father objected because the boy was recovering from a fever, but the attendant persisted, claiming that he had received direct orders from Trevor. The boy who had neither shoes nor stockings, put on what little clothes he had and despite promises given to his father that he would be wrapped in blankets and carried to the old jail, he was made to walk. On his arrival he told his sister Ann that he was going to die, and his fever having worsened, he died a few days later.

About the same time, another State prisoner, James Camuskey, also died through medical neglect and resulting from these two deaths, and with reports circulating that members of the House of Commons in London had been approached to investigate continuing abuses in Kilmainham Jail, Trevor, prompted no doubt by Marsden, decided on a complete reversal of policy. St. John Mason and Edward Coyle, two of his most vocal critics, were allowed to leave the jail under escort and take warm salt baths in the city. They were also permitted to take the sea air at Blackrock and Kingstown (Dun Laoghaire) and, in what was the most cynical of exercises, Ann Devlin was allowed to visit the Spa at Lucan to improve her health. She set off from Kilmainham in a coach, accompanied by one of her sisters, but Mary Dwyer was initially refused permission to join them. They were, however, guarded by a pair of dragoons and an attendant armed with a pair of pistols. But the trips were soon discontinued, having served their propaganda value.[6]

Michael Dwyer, Hugh Byrne and the engraver John Galland now decided to write to Judge Day concerning their treatment and he contacted the government, indicating his readiness to act. But with news concerning the provision of a convict ship having been confirmed, he received no communication from the government on the matter. By the beginning of April, a ship had been engaged at Deptford in England and was due to sail to Ireland within five weeks. Nicholas Vensiggart had been appointed as the new Chief Secretary, and Marsden was given the task of making all the necessary arrangements regarding the convict ship and liaising with the Home Office. All of the country's sheriffs were contacted and arrangements were made to have prisoners who were awaiting transportation transferred to Cork, the harbour from where the convict ship would leave for the penal colony of New South Wales.

After a gap of over three years, however, there were sufficient prisoners to fill two convict ships, but the authorities were not unduly worried at his early stage. The Napoleonic war was still being waged and there was an ongoing need for recruits in army regiments and navy squadrons. In addition, it was not unusual for a number of prisoners to be given lesser sentences following petitions made on their behalf. As for the female prisoners, in the final analysis, 35 of the healthiest would be chosen. It was the usual practice for sheriffs in the southern counties to send their prisoners directly to Cork under military escort in carts and wagons while the prisoners from the northern counties were first brought to Dublin where they were shaved, bathed and given prison clothes before being shipped down to Cork. This leg of their journey by sea was often very hazardous as the vessels usually were in a poor state of repair, and reeked of fever. As a result it was not unusual for prisoners to die during the short voyage, or even in the holds of the ships while they were still at port.

By the beginning of May, preparations throughout the country were at an advanced stage and on 12 May, Dwyer and his comrades were finally told that they were being sent to the penal colony of New South Wales as convicts, and without any members of their families being allowed to travel with them. The willing Trevor was entrusted with passing on the information and a distraught Dwyer immediately wrote to John Hume at Synott Place: "My solemn conditions are to be violated; the sacred honour of Mr. Hume is set at naught, and my children are to be left without the smallest means of living or protec-

---

6. *Pedro Zendono*, Appendix, p. 111.

tion. This is such a terrible dereliction of everything which, even in an un-civilised life, is held sacred that I know not what to do." He requested John Hume to visit him as soon as possible, warning that "any breach of faith with me will surely be published to the world," and he went on to refer to the "besmirched honour of the Hume family name." William Hume was in London at the time attending a House of Commons debate on a petition presented by some Irish members for the granting of Catholic Emancipation. Henry Grattan, the old warhorse of the Irish Parliament, was making his maiden speech in presenting the petition but, without the backing of Pitt's administration, it was heavily defeated. As John Hume awaited his nephew's return from London, Trevor pressed ahead with his transportation arrangements and, having received point-blank refusals from Dwyer and the others, he resorted to his familiar form of friendly persuasion as Patrick Lynch, another prisoner who was threatened with the same fate, recorded:

> The Deputy Sheriff and Dr Trevor called on me and gave me orders to prepare for Botany Bay, but I refused. In the night, being in bed, both John Mernagh and I were compelled to get up and dress ourselves, and were removed to the capital offence and out among the felons as before, and by their orders we were doubly-bolted with the heaviest irons they could procure, and all this to make us agree to be transported to Botany Bay as was done with Dwyer, Burke, Devlin and Mernagh, which treatment induced them to consent to transportation.[7]

Other state prisoners also refused but, unlike Dwyer, they had not surrendered to the government and had not been charged or brought to trial. Robert Carty from Wexford gave an outright refusal and, having done so, his treatment naturally worsened while two other prisoners, John Kelly and Patrick Doyle were, likewise, removed to the felons' side. But a House of Commons committee ordered the publication of the Downes report and the government were now trying to find a way of releasing the state prisoners, with as little embarrassment to themselves as possible, and even resorted to the old trick of using the newspapers to help sway public opinion. Reports soon were appearing to the effect that "the offender who had been so long in Kilmainham Jail, called Captain Dwyer of the Mountains, had refused to go to Botany Bay. He requests to be sent to America, he and three of his myrmidons with their families, and the expense of such a voyage to be defrayed for them, an audacious request with which the Government will not comply. He is therefore to be tried if he persists and three of his followers. Four of his gang had consented to go to Botany Bay rather than stand trial."[8]

On his return from the House of Commons debate, William Hume was

7.   *Ibid.*, p. 120.
8.   *Freeman's Journal*, June 1805.

faced with an embarrassing, and potentially damaging, situation regarding his personal standing in County Wicklow as news of his supposed broken promise to Dwyer became public. And the prospect, in particular, of Mary Dwyer and her children being left behind, after her husband had been transported to New South Wales, galvanised him into immediate action. He attempted to broker a compromise deal, acceptable to all concerned, and the government, for their part, were well disposed to accept his proposals which would still send Dwyer and his comrades to New South Wales, not as felons, but with the entitlement of free men. They would not be granted pardons, but would be allowed to exile themselves for life. On arrival they would be entitled to receive grants of land which would enable them to begin new lives there and in the case of Dwyer and Byrne, their wives and families would be allowed to travel with them. They would receive the sum of £100 each (Dwyer may have been granted £200) and Hume also promised Dwyer that he would be permitted to say good bye to his father before leaving.

These new conditions were, no doubt, put to the Wicklowmen by the munificent Dr Trevor (he probably took the credit himself) and they were left with little option but to accept. But there were major problems to be worked out by the Dwyers and Byrnes who had very young families, and who were well aware of the risks attaching to bringing them on such a long and potentially dangerous voyage. To complicate matters Sarah Byrne was pregnant again and if she travelled with her husband would give birth during the voyage to New South Wales. They were pressed by the government to give a speedy answer or face the consequences, and when Dwyer finally agreed to the terms Trevor rushed off to the Castle with the good news. But for the Byrne and Dwyer families important decisions had to be made quickly which would influence the remainder of their lives.

CHAPTER FIVE

1805

By the beginning of June the convict ship was already on its way from the Downs to Cork and it was confirmed by Marsden that provisions, clothing and medicine were ready to be put on board. In writing to the Home Office he added, somewhat prematurely, that the prisoners from the various county jails were already in Cork and were being housed in a number of institutions there. The ship's name was the *Tellicherry*, a vessel of 468 tons, 14 guns, and with a crew of 40. It was built in London in 1796 and had previously arrived in Cork in January 1804, bringing the required equipment to erect a series of signal posts around the coast which would as an early warning system in the event of another French invasion.

On arrival, the first task of its master, Captain Thomas Cuzens, was to discharge cargo for some navy transports which were anchored in Cork Harbour and the ship was inspected by Dr Robert Harding, the official medical Inspector of Transports, who was also a part-time government informer. According to regulations the *Tellicherry* had been adapted to accommodate its human cargo and, having completed his inspection, Harding found that the space allocated for the male prisoners was large enough, but not sufficiently ventilated as the ship's scuttles were not well formed. He felt, however, that the female quarters were too small, although he casually added "as they generally sleep in different parts of the ship it is not of much moment."

By 19 June, Marsden was again confidently assuring the Home Office that the convicts from the northern jails and from Dublin had been despatched to Cork, that all of the southern prisoners had already arrived, and that the full complement would go on board the *Tellicherry* when it was ready to receive them. But this was only partly true; indeed, the whole operation was beginning to look distinctly ragged. A group of prisoners had left Dublin on board the *Renown* Wherny, but Nyland, its enterprising master, was obviously in no hurry as he first sailed across the Irish Sea to Milford Haven and then stopped off at Waterford for a few days before finally reaching Cork where he failed even to report to the authorities. And there was a long delay before the remainder of the Dublin prisoners were despatched which was partly due to the long delay in solving the Dwyer problem, but also in dealing with the huge excess in the number of prisoners. The *Tellicherry* had space for 130 male and 36 female prisoners but already 50 women were being housed in Cork, even before the expected arrival of a large Dublin contingent.

In the meantime, provisions bound for the New South Wales colony were being put on board the *Tellicherry* from the Cork Victualling Office, totalling 130,000 of salt beef and the same amount of salt pork, in addition to various household goods.[1] The owners of the *Tellicherry*, Barbe and Company, London had provided a surgeon on board, but Marsden solved another of his problems when he informed Charles Hewitt, the resident agent for Transports in Cork, that the Lord Lieutenant had appointed John Connellan, on the recommendation of the medical board, to be the assisant surgeon on board. But Connellan had a chequered career, having been a prominent government informer during the period of the 1798 rebellion in the Dundalk area and he was now being looked after by the govermnent for servies rendered as it was no longer safe for him to remain in his own neighbourhood. It was mid-July before the Tellicherry was ready to take any prisoners on board, but even then, the second vessel which was due to ferry the remainder of the Dublin prisoners had not set sail and Dwyer and his comrades were still in Kilmainham Jail. The owners of the Tellicherry officially complained about the delay but Marsden, in turn, claimed that it was due to an outbreak of fever on board the *Renown* Wherny which had spread also among the crew and military guard of the *Tellicherry* as Harding reported at the end of July: "I saw a soldier who informed me that he was ill for two days lying in the berths with the other soldiers and women. If they are not more circumspect and cautious about contagion the consequences must be very bad."

In Kilmainham Jail, Michael and Mary Dwyer had come to the painful conclusion not to risk bringing their four young children with them and they would be reared in the Dublin Liberties by Dwyer's sister, Mary Neale. But Hugh and Sarah Byrne had arrived at a separate compromise solution. They would leave behind their eldest son Philip (age six) to be reared also in Dublin by Sarah's parents and would risk bringing their five-year old son Michael and two-year old daughter Rosanna to New South Wales. But the Dwyers now found themselves again at the mercy of Trevor as they endeavoured to ensure that their children would be sent out at a later date. In his capacity as Agent of Transports, Trevor would be responsible for making the arrangements. He seemingly agreed to their request and Dwyer responded by writing a letter of thanks to him on 29 June: "I beg you will accept my warm thanks in return for your kindness towards my children. Nothing lies in my power more than to thank you for your kind and humane assistance, and be assured that I would sooner ask you for that favour than any of my fellow-prisoners, though perhaps you wouldn't think do even if it lays in your power."

---

1.   The general cargo of the *Tellicherry* included 160 gallons of Holland Gin, 10 boxes of soap, 150 dozen bottles of porter, 12 casks of porter, 10 firkins of butter, window glass, mould candles, hats and perfumery.

This was the first of a number of seemingly grovelling letters that Dwyer and his comrades wrote to Trevor before their departure. Once again, on 20 July, Dwyer stated:

> I make bold to return my sincere thanks for your kindness to me, and the consolation you gave me by promising your interest to send my children after me to Botany Bay; and your humane mind will tell you that there is nothing so distressing to the parents as parting of their children, especially me who had to forfeit them and their country. . . . I am sorry to the bottom of my heart for offending so good a government and shall ever exclaim against any man or men if I hear any of them speak or act against the Government. This I declare to be my real sentiments at this moment and will till the hour of my death for I never saw my error till now; as for my children I shall leave it to yourself for it would be too much boldness of me to ask for so great a favour and I so ill-deserving of any. But I sincerely lament for it and still hope for your humanity that I may expect my children and shall find myself happy in earning them bread, and I shall be forever bound to pray for your welfare.

It is scarcely credible that this letter was penned by the same man who had denounced Trevor a few months before, and while it might be presumptuous to suggest that the contents were dictated by Trevor, the reality was that he was in the process of gathering this type of material for future use as James Tandy since his release continued to make public accusations against him. It is also possible that the tone of the letter may have been the result of a cynical decision by the Wicklowmen to wring as many favours as possible from Trevor before their departure. Arthur Devlin had written in similar fashion when asking for help to be given to his aged mother: "Pardon me sir for this application, nor think that if it is not granted, I will be less grateful. No, I will be forever thankful. I am content with any thing you do; because we are all treated by you beyond my expectation."

As the date of their departure approached, Mary Dwyer and Sarah Byrne made their last tearful visits to their families; Michael Dwyer's father is reputed to have come up to Kilmainham from Wicklow[2] but Martin Burke's wife Rachel did not choose to accompany him to New South Wales. There is no report of her having visited him following her relelease from Kilmainham in January 1804, one theory being that she may have suffered a nervous breakdown resulting from her prison experience. On Thursday 25 July, Michael and Mary Dwyer said goodbye to their children, as did Hugh and Sarah Byrne to their son Philip, and on the evening of 25 July 1805, having been

---

2. It is also reported that the Camden cutter landed briefly at Wicklow Harbour where Dwyer reputedly said good bye to his father.

imprisoned in Kilmainham Jail for over 18 months, Michael Dwyer and his group stepped into the waiting carriages which would take them along the Circular Road and down to the Quays where the revenue cutter *Camden*, under the command of Capt. Murphy, was ready to receive them. As the carriages moved away from the front gate of the jail the last person they, no doubt, saw was Dr Edward Trevor and, even then, Dwyer's heart must have sank as he wondered if he would keep his promise regarding the children. The *Camden* was a fast sailing ship, used by revenue officers and smugglers alike in the pursuance of their respective duties and on the following morning they set off for Cork, accompanied by the *Lees Wherny* which was carrying the remainder of the Dublin prisoners. They were soon making their way down the East coast and catching a glimpse of their native Wicklow for the last time. By 1 August, they were entering Cork harbour and must have been astonished to see what appeared to be the entire fleet of the British navy spread across the harbour. The East India Fleet was anchored there and Arthur Devlin, as the only putative sailor among them, no doubt, attempted to identify the various types of vessels.

During the period of the Napoleonic Wars, Cork harbour was of immense strategic importance to Britain, because of its location and also as it was reckoned to be one of the safest and best protected harbours in the world:

> The entrance is safe and the whole of the navy of Britain may ride in it secure from every wind that blows. It is evidently most convenient for the Western world and to what may seem paradoxical, it lies more advantageously for the East Indies than any of the English ports. But the shipping that generally resort here to victual and take in ladling are those bound from Britain to the West Indies and Caribbean Islands.

The *Lees* Wherny had made good time also but Lt. Sainthill and Captain Cuzens, who were supervising the arrival of the prisoners, received a shock when they realised the implications of the terms which has been agreed with Dwyer's group, and an agitated Sainthill immediately wrote to Dublin:

> They say that they shall not be put in irons or put with the convicts, and that their wives and children are to go with them. I hope it is not true as I am sure the Master of the *Tellicherry* could not comply with as the ship is completely filled. He had not room to make such an accommodation, and it would put the safety of the ship's crew in great danger to have such men at large. I shall request Capt. Cuzens not to put them in irons at present. When he is at sea, of course, he will do what he conceives most proper.

Dr Harding examined them on the following morning, but unlike the other prisoners on board, the Wicklowmens' heads were not shaved. Harding was more than compensated for this small loss of earnings as he would charge the

government six and a half pence for shaving each of 170 convicts, in addition
to a guinea a day for visiting a ship, another guinea for visiting a jail and a
British crown for examining a convict.

Assistant Surgeon John Connellan arrived on board at the beginning of
August and was soon writing to Marsden seeking letters of introduction for
use in New South Wales while adding that "Dwyer and his party are behav-
ing themselves very well. " They had, no doubt, assured Capt. Cuzens of
their peacable intentions, but a problem arose concerning their food allowances and there was time for a last lettter to their newly-found benefactor in
Dublin, stating that no orders had been received in this regard and that they
were only receiving a pound of bread and a pound of beef each day. The letter
to Trevor was again couched in terms of the most grotesque flattery and was
signed by all five Wicklowmen, although the final sentence gives the impression that it may have been written more in half-jest than in desperation: "We,
therefore, conclude with every grateful thanks, wishing you and your progeny
all happiness that this life and the next can afford."[3]

A final list of the prisoners to be transported was drawn up and the
problem of accommodating "Dwyer and his gang" was solved when Capt.
Cuzens decided to make the ship's hospital available to them, despite fears
being expressed concerning the possibility of a major outbreak of fever during
the voyage. And in an effort to forestall this the Captan and Surgeon allowed
the prisoners to remain on deck for as long as possible during the day as the
weather was very fine. The excess numbers of prisoners were disposed of
when 23 men enlisted in a Plymouth naval division while a further 17 enlisted
with a Capt. Chilcott. The remaining number of seventeen male prisoners
were deemed to be too old to enlist or were suffering from fever. At least 12
women were left behind in Cork Jail, but the Board of the Female House of
Industry in the city turned down a request to house them. In the meantime,
the *William Pitt*, carrying female prisoners from London, also arrived in Cork
Harbour, and both ships applied to the Master of the *Bellequia*, the flagship
of the East India fleet, for permission to sail with them during the first leg of
the voyage.

But Lt. Sainthill was still complaining at what he considered to be the
over-generous treatment being given to Dwyer's party and added sourly that
he had handed over to them the sum of £350 which had been sent down from
Dublin which enabled Mary Dwyer to go into the city and purchase badly-
needed clothes and also farming implements which would be needed on their
arrival in New South Wales. On 23 August, Marsden returned the list of
prisoners and also provided letters of explanation concerning the status of the
Wicklowmen and Connellan which would be given to the Governor of New

---

3.   Pamphlet – *Dr Trevor's Statement – A Vindication of Himself.*

South Wales on their arrival. On 28 August, permission was granted to the East India fleet to set sail. On the same day Lord Lieutenant Hardwicke and Lord Cathcart were attending a military exercise at the Curragh in Co. Kildare. General Beresford had recently inspected a newly-arrived regiment on Haulbowline Island and would sail with the fleet on board the *Narcissus*. Judge Day was also in Cork attending an assizes while it was just another routine day in Dublin for Alexander Marsden and Edward Trevor.

The imposing East India fleet, bound for the Mediterranean, and comprising three brigades, with a total of 10,000 men, was already in place; at its head were the ships-of-the-line *Terrible* (74 guns), *Diadem* (64 guns) and the flag-ship of the convoy, the *Bellequia* (64 guns). Moored at the entrance to the harbour, they were further reinforced by the frigates *Leda* and *Narcissus*; behind them were positioned the main bulk of the convoy, consisting of 38 transport ships and 19 East Indiamen, and tagging along for protection were the two convict ships, the *Tellicherry* and the *William Pitt*. But the departure of the fleet was postponed when an adverse wind blew up from the west, causing them to put back into harbour, and it was not until Saturday 31 August that a favourable wind helped the fleet on its way. And as the island of Ireland faded out of sight, each prisoner on the *Tellicherry* said goodbye in his or her own individual manner. None of them would ever return to Ireland.

Lord Lieutenant Hardwicke

Postscript

By the end of August 1805, the government was beginning the process of releasing the remainder of the state prisoners from Kilmainham Jail, including John St. John Mason, Edward Coyle, John Galland, Robert Carty, Nicholas Grey, James Byrne, Nicholas Lyons and John Kelly. Bryan Devlin was also released, but not before he was forced to write a similar begging letter to Trevor. One of the last to be released, at the beginning of 1806, was Ann Devlin, and only after the personal intervention of new Chief Secretary Long. On his release, St John Mason demanded £2,000 in compensation from the government to cover the losses he had incurred while in prison, and he had two meetings with Hardwicke who refused to accede to his demands. Following the death of William Pitt in 1806, Hardwicke was replaced as Lord Lieutenant by the Duke of Bedford who was, supposedly, coming to Ireland with considerable powers of redress. Mason drew up another memorial and had it presented by William Hume whom he described as "his excellent friend". But Mason was disappointed again when he was informed that no compensation fund existed. Mason then published anonymously a savage pamphlet against Trevor whom he christened "Pedro Zendono, the Inquisitor of Kilmainham" after a character from the novel *Gil Blas*. The pamphlet was eagerly read by the Dublin public and quickly went into a second edition.

At the same time, James Tandy was taking an unsuccessful legal action against Brabazon Morris and he also published a pamphlet concerning the ill-treatment he had received in Kilmainham Jail. A second pamphlet against Trevor, written by St. John Mason, and using his own name, was then published and it was answered by Trevor's own pamphlet. He had written to various members of past administrations for letters of support and received letters of varying degrees of enthusiasm from Hardwicke, Nepean, Wickham and, of course, Marsden who ventured the opinion that if he had been responsible for any ill-treatment he would not have allowed him to remain in his post for longer than one hour. Trevor's pamphlet also contained unconvincing versions of the death of Jimmy Devlin and, in a final section, Trevor published, as further proof of his innocence, a large number of letters of appreciation, including those of Michael Dwyer, Arthur Devlin, Bryan Devlin and the final letter signed by all five Wicklowmen, from on board the *Tellicherry*.

On the final day of the parliamentary session in July 1808, the playwright and politician, Richard Brinsley Sheridan, moved in the House of Commons for a Royal Commission to inquire into the abuses of state prisoners in Ireland, although he expressed regret that William Hume, who was to support him, was not present that day. As a result of Sheridan's motion, a commission was appointed, and one if its members was Judge George Daly, who had first inquired into the prisoner's complaints. The inquiry began in the Sessions House, Green St., but the state prisoners who had gathered to give evidence were disappointed to learn that it was not a public enquiry and, having also been told that the Commission "could not listen to any matters injurious to Lord Hardwicke's Government" they decided to withdraw. The shutters had gone up once again and they despaired of ever receiving an impartial hearing.

A final effort was made in 1810 by St. John Mason when he published a final pamphlet which he dedicated to Brinsley Sheridan, and which was published by John Stockdale, the printer of Emmet's proclamation, and a former state prisoner. But the issue gradually faded from the public mind; Mason received no compensation while Tandy was also unsuccessful in a further suit when Marsden, who was called to give evidence, chose to hide behind the cloak of government secrecy. As for Tandy's wine business it slumped as loyalists in Dublin continued to snub him. The Waterford-born General William Carr Beresford went on to win fame and fortune in the Peninsular Wars and was victorious at the battle of Albuera under Wellington who described him as "the ablest man I have yet seen in the army." He was later awarded a peerage and died in Kent in 1854. The Earl of Hardwicke, on his return to England, took his seat in the House of Lords and voted for Catholic Emancipation for Ireland in 1829. Ann Devlin, having partly recovered her health, married in Dublin and reared two children. But she had to earn a living as a washerwoman in order to survive and died in abject poverty. Alexander Marsden spent his last years in London and is buried in the same vault as his brother William in Kendal Green. As for Dr Edward Trevor, still unabashed and untouched by accusations and commissions, he continued to stalk the corridors of Kilmainham Jail, dispensing his own particular brand of justice, for many years to come.

In 1835, William Wickham, who was then in his seventies, and living in Geneva, encountered two members of a religious delegation from the Synod of Ulster on the street while they were attending a meeting in the city. He engaged them in a long and bewildering conversation and some weeks later wrote at length to one of them, Dr Armstrong, outlining his plans for peace and prosperity in Ireland, based on the sincere co-operation of all Christian denominations living there. He also enclosed a copy of the letter which Robert Emmet had written to him on the day of his execution 32 years before.

William Wickham

PART TWO

"Thieves, robbers and villians we'll send them away,
To become a new people in Botany Bay"

(Traditional ballad)

"We see in it the beginning of a country which will, in a short time, exceed in power and energy Italy, Greece and Turkey and all those parts of the world that, at one time, held all the rest in subjection."

(*Belfast Newslettter*, 1803)

William Bligh

CHAPTER SIX

1805-1806

The *Tellicherry* was the fourteenth convict ship to have transported prisoners from Ireland to the penal colony of New South Wales; five had been sent out prior to the 1798 rebellion and a further eight between 1799 and 1802 as the scramble to be rid of troublesome political rebels intensified.[1] And a three-year gap to cater for the backlog of mainly petty criminals was being filled with the sailing of a the *Tellicherry*.

Faced with an unwillingness to build expensive penal establishments in Great Britain to house an increasing number of offenders, as laid down by a restrictive penal code, the Transportation Act of 1717 was enacted to ship them instead to the American colonies where they would be far removed from their home environment and, hopefully, re-establish themselves, in addition to providing a cheap labour force for the colonists. But following the American War of Independence in 1775, and the rejection of locations such as Tristan Da Cunha and the coast of Guinea in Africa, the new penal colony of New South Wales was established at the suggestion of Sir Joseph Banks, the President of the Royal Society, who had sailed as a naturalist with Captain Cook in the Endeavour on his first voyage of discovery. In the course of that expedition they had landed at a harbour in New South Wales and, having encountered natives who proved to be curious rather than belligerent, they named their landing place Botany Bay on account of the abundance of hitherto unknown species of plants which were duly added to their collection.

In 1786, the government in London finally agreed to the location and the problems of dealing with the overflow population in prisons and hulks was partly solved by shipping convicts half-way around the world – and at a hefty expense to the exchequer. The First Fleet, as it became known, landed in Botany Bay in January 1788 but its commander, Arthur Phillip, immediately moved further up the coast to a more suitable harbour which was named Port Jackson (Sydney Harbour). No further convicts were subsequently landed at Botany Bay, but its romantic-sounding name caught the public imagination and it continued to become synonymous with transportation:

---

1. The other convict ships were *Queen* (1791), *Sugar Cane, Marquis Cornwall, Britannia*, and post-1798, *Minerva, Friendship, Luz St. Ann, Minorca, Hercules, Atlas 1, Atlas 11* and *Rolla* (1802).

Thieves, robbers and villians we'll send them away,
To become a new people in Botany Bay.

Sir Joseph Banks had recommended New South Wales because he believed that it would be a difficult place from which to escape on account of its
remote location. He was also of the opinion, based on his own observations,
that the land surrounding Botany Bay was quite fertile and that the colony
would become self-sufficient in a very short time. But there were no lush
meadows in the locality and, in the first years, the population came close to
starvation, and had to rely on food supplies which were shipped at irregular
intervals from Britain and Ireland.

The severity of the eighteenth century penal code can be guaged by a list
of over 150 crimes which were deemed to be punishable by execution, and by
an even greater number of lesser misdemeanours subject to a variety of punishments, including long terms of imprisonment, whipping, burning of the
hand, a sojourn in the stocks and, of course, transportation. The rapid growth
of urban populations led to a complementary increase in crime but, paradoxically, it was the gradual trend towards a modicum of leniency in the latter
part of the century which resulted also in the consequent overcrowding of the
prisons and an acceleration in the numbers of those who were sentenced to
terms of transportation. Courts no longer dealt out death sentences for such
outrageous crimes as the shoplifting of goods valued in excess of five shillings,
the larceny of goods from a dwelling-house in excess of 50 shillings, the
stealing of sheep or cattle or that bane of the landed classes, the cutting down
of trees on hallowed demesne avenues. By the year 1795, certainly in Britain,
vocal complaints were regularly aired that this new trend shown by judges to
horse thieves had resulted in the formation of gangs for that very purpose, the
perpetrators being safe in the knowledge that, if caught, they would escape
the gallows.

In the decade prior to 1798, those sentenced to terms of transportation in
Ireland were in the main, petty criminals. A minority had committed serious
crimes, with the original death sentences being mitigated-to transportation for
life. Jeremiah Fitzpatrick, the progressive inspector-general of Prisons, writing in 1790, was of the opinion that only about 30 of the "most atrocious
offenders" should be transported from Ireland each year, but as these were
still executed the main bulk of transportees tended to be those who had
received sentences for larceny, forgery or other petty crimes.[2] But a number
of agrarian offenders were also transported from rural Ireland, members of
secret societies such as the Defenders, peasant farmers who were rebelling
against the iniquities of the prevailing landed system which was so oppressive

---

2. Pamphlet – *Thoughts On A Penitentiary* by Jeremiah Fitzpatrick, Inspector for Prisons
    (1790).

that it even took away their dignity as human beings, and which caused them to retaliate by striking at night, often dressed in outlandish costumes, burning crops and houses, and maiming cattle. Governor John Hunter in New South Wales described them as "horrid creatures" without even wishing or caring to know the reasons why they had been driven to such acts of desperation. But for Hunter and the small military garrison in New South Wales they represented, for the first time among the convict ranks, a potentially dangerous force. A rival Protestant secret society in Ulster at the time, proudly carried a banner, on which was inscribed the pointedly altered Cromwellian motto "To Hell, Connaught or Butney Bay" although, with a curiously enduring double-think, they did not consider themselves as possible candidates for the long voyage. In this belief they were also to be disappointed as sufficient of their numbers had arrived in the colony by 1795 to enable them to form a branch of the Orange Order, proclaiming their loyalty to Crown and Government with the caveat "for as long as they supported the Union".

In the immediate aftermath of the 1798 rebellion the majority of transportees tended to be political prisoners, drawn from the ranks of the United Irishmen, a movement which had drawn support from all classes and creeds in the country, Catholics, Protestants and Dissenters, and which included among their rank, teachers, doctors, clergymen, priesets, surveyors, merchants and master craftsmen. For the anxious authorities in New South Wales the arrival of another potentially dangerous group of politically-oriented prisoners was again viewed with alarm but they quickly, and wisely, put their expertise to good use, and it was left to the unskilled and the more disaffected among them to perpetuate their sense of grievance and to threaten to complete unfinished business in the penal colony if the opportunity arose.

By 1805, however, when the *Tellicherry* sailed with its human cargo fo 130 male and 36 female transportees, the number of political prisoners (apart from Michael Dwyer and his comrades) was negligible. There was a second Hugh Byrne on board, nicknamed 'Hughie the Brander'. He had been captured at Derrynamuck in 1799 but his life was spared when he turned informer. He then moved to County Carlow were he became a leading member of a gang led by James Corcoran of Wexford. A reward of £500 had been offered for his capture in 1803, but the gang which operated also in County Kilkenny was broken up in 1804 following a gun battle in which Corcoran was fatally wounded. Hughie Byrne was captured and would surely have been hanged but for turning informer once again, or to be more accurate, providing the authorities with a signed statement concerning a French ship bearing arms which was supposedly due to land on the Wicklow coast. For this piece of imaginative lying his life was spared and although offering to enlist in an overseas regiment, he was sentenced instead to transportation for life, and was accompanied on the *Tellicherry* by Laurence Fenelon and John Fitzpatrick, two other members of the gang.

Walter Clare was another prisoner in this category who lived in Thomas Court, Dublin, off Thomas Street where Emmet's rebellion had taken place. He was living with his wife in a rented room, and in a typical example of the prevailing crowded conditions, they shared a single room with another married couple and their sick child. Walter Clare worked locally in Roe's brewery and, having spent three hours queuing for his wages on the evening of the rebellion, was later reported to the authorities by a neighbour for having a pike in his hand, but when the skirmishing began the reluctant rebel had rushed back to his door calling on his wife to let him in. Despite the circumstantial nature of the evidence presented in court he was sentenced to death, but while 13 others were hanged soon afterwards, his life was spared because of unspecified information he had supplied to the authorities in Newgate Jail.[3]

Among the other transportees on board, Nicholas Prendergast from Wexford was given a seven-year sentence for "seducing soldiers" to desert; Pierce Condon from Tipperary had received a life sentence for stealing a cow while a further dozen of his countymen, including James and Stephen Halpenny, were convicted for similar agrarian offences. There were 14 Kildare men on board while among the 46 prisoners from Dublin were Thomas Holden and Edward Doyle, convicted on separate charges of stealing calico; Timothy Murphy for stealing 18 bank tokens, 15 dollars and a half guinea note, and John O'Neill for stealing a Bank of Ireland promissory note. James Sheedy, a native of Bodyke, Co. Clare, was another prisoner on board who had narrowly escaped the gallows. A member of the local Kilnoe Yeomen Cavalry, he became involved in a brawl with some fellow-members outside a public house following a Sunday parade in August 1803, during which a yeoman received a fatal blow. James Sheedy was subsequently sentenced to be hanged, but received several stays of execution before his sentence as commuted to transportation for life.[4]

What lay in store for the *Tellicherry* transportees, whose ages ranged upwards from 16 to 65, when they reached their journey's end was something which they understood less than fully; they realised that they would not be confined to prison if they remained on good behaviour; that the men would be assigned to work for the government, or for individual landholders, while the women would become domestic servants or be sent to work at the female factory in Parramatta. In addition, a "ticket to leave" system was in operation for those who showed sufficient initiative or application and which was designed to give partial remission of sentences, leading to conditional and absolute pardons, and entitling them to free grants of land: already a number of former convicts had amassed large fortunes in the colony, But this knowledge would

---

3. *Account of Walter Clare trial – Freeman's Journal,* 3 September 1803.
4. *Feakle – A History,* pp.43-44.

have given scant reassurance to the majority of prisoners on board whose perception of life in New South Wales was far bleaker; for them it was a fearsome journey into the unknown; permanent exile from their native land into oblivion. There was a sense of finality surrounding their departure from Ireland; a sentence of seven years was virtually the same as a life sentence and for married men it meant permanent separation from their wives and families. It was reported in 1801 that a noted swindler by the name of Turley who, with his wife, had been sentenced to a term of transportation, died on his arrival at Cork, having fallen a victim "to his own artifice, in putting tobacco in a certain place to cause sickness, to prevent himself from being sent off."[5]

But for the educated minority in Ireland who had access to newspapers, a more enlightened view was being formalised concerning the rapid development of New South Wales, particularly following the publication of the colony's first newspaper in 1803. When copies of the first issues of the *Sydney Gazette* reached London later in that year the city newspapers published some of the contents which were also reprinted in Ireland. The rapid progress of the penal colony took London by surprise while the reaction of the Irish newspapers was equally enthusiastic, if somewhat patronising:

> There is, no doubt, a disagreeable idea attending the mention of Botany Bay, and there are some whose levity will lend them to look contemptuously on the country, but when we consider that such an establishment is raised from that part of society that was lost to the country and had justly forfeited their rights, how highly ought we to admire the humanity and the policy of those who converted the rigours of justice into so mild a channel, and from the crimes and misfortunes of mankind raised a society that promises to become so respectable and worthy of protection.

The *Belfast Newsletter* also welcomed the publication of the *Sydney Gazette*, regarding it as "an act which gives a sort of unity and character. We see in it the beginning of a country which will, in a short time, exceed in power in a short time, Italy, Greece, Turkey, and those parts of the world that, at one time, held all the rest in subjection and contempt."

By 1805 the colony was just 17 years in existence and the European population still numbered less than 8,000. The principal town of Sydney was still a ramshackle affair, with badly-planned streets and very few public buildings. The General Hospital which was constructed from prefabricated panels, brought out on the First Fleet, was now in a bad state of repair while the majority of dwelling houses were little more than cabins, apart from a few imposing homes built by the successful merchants. There were a fair number of shops and a goodly number of disreputable taverns in the area of the Rocks

---

5. *Freeman's Journal*, June 1801.

on the harbour-front, some of which boasted distinguished Irish names such
as "The Harp" and "St. Patricks", and which attracted a broad, if
undiscriminating, clientele. A number of small settlements had also been
established within a thirty-mile radius of Sydney, at Parramatta, the
Hawkesbury, Cabramatta, the military establishment at Castle Hill, the Government farm at Toongabbie and, further to the north, the newly-established
punishment outpost at Newcastle where the convicts worked long hours quar-
rying the recently-discovered coal seam, making lime from the vast mounds
of oyster shells, or felling the rapidly disappearing stands of cedar and rosewood
trees whose timbers were in great demand. Norfolk Island and Van Diemen's
Land were also being developed, but a further decade would elapse before a
concerted effort would be made to extend the boundaries of the colony to the
interior.

      This was the prospect which awaited the prisoners on board the *Tellicherry*
as, in the company of the East India Fleet, they began the first leg of their
voyage in September 1805 and sailed towards the island of Madeira. And they
were very fortunate to have as their captain the humane Thomas Cuzens. The
history of transportation is replete with stories of brutality, sadism, neglect,
starvation, disease, sexual abuse and death. During the voyage of the *Hercules*
from Ireland 14 prisoners were executed, and a further 30 died on board,
while a total of 65 prisoners perished from the voyage of *Atlas I*. In both
instances the captain was charged with neglect, only to escape a nominal fine.
But now, with an efficient and conscientious captain in charge, the *Tellicherry*
sailed in warm September weather towards Madeira, and for the five
Wicklowmen who had the freedom of the ship it became a welcome change
from the wretched prison conditions of Kilmainham. Within 11 days they had
arrived in Madeira from where John Connellan, still revelling in his role as
informer, reported back to Alexander Marsden in Dublin:

> The Captain has been remarkably attentive and humane to the convicts,
> having taken whole charge upon himself to see that the prison is washed,
> scrubbed and swabbed, and perfectly dry every day and fumigated occa-
> sionally. From the good conduct of the convicts he has taken the irons
> off twelve of them, and all the rest have but one leg in irons. Their state
> of health, in general, is very good but we have not been free of fever
> since we came of board. The greatest discontent among them is the
> want of tobacco which I understand was ordered by you but was ne-
> glected to be sent on board from Cork. But the Captain, always attentive
> to their complaints, went on shore this day and for the purpose of
> buying as much tobacco as will be sufficient for them until we arrive at
> Rio [de] Janeiro. Dwyer's party have behaved very well. The women
> occupy one of the hospitals. The Captain has been remarkably civil to
> them, particularly to Byrne's wife, who is far advanced in pregnancy; he

frequently sends her fresh soup, mutton etc., from his own table. In short, all the convicts, men and women, seems highly sensible of the Captain's humane attention to them, and I hope they will continue to deserve it.[6]

The *Tellicherry* now parted company with the East India Fleet but the *William Pitt*, the female convict ship out of London, remained with the fleet for reasons of safety as it made its own way to the Cape of Good Hope to engage the Dutch. The second leg of the journey usually took six weeks and was the usual route taken by ships on their way to New South Wales, Rio de Janiero being a major port where provisions would be replenished, including fresh fruit, butter, tobacco, rum and wine. By the middle of November they were on their way again, sailing across the South Atlantic, and it was probably during this period of the voyage that Sarah Byrne safely gave birth to a daughter who was named Roseanna. She was assisted in labour by Mary Dwyer and the happy event was duly celebrated by the Wicklow group on board. During the run across the Indian Ocean they encountered some bad weather, and even in the best-run ships there was a certain amount of hardship to be endured by the prisoners who were chained together in the hold. James Sheedy recorded this graphic account of life below decks during the course of a storm:

The worst aspect of our trip out was being chained up at night as this made the night very long. The system of chains being that you had a small chain attached to your wrist and the other end on a ring attached to a round iron bar. There were two of these rings which ran the full length of the hold in which there were one hundred and thirty men. This system allowed you to be able to use the sanitary convenience which was situated at the end of the hold. For instance, if you were number twelve at the bar to use the convenience ahead of you, when any person was violently ill, it meant the unfortunate victim had to have several of his shipmates up all night with him to allow him to use the convenience as it was impossible for these men to pass one another, the ring merely sliding along the rail which often led to complications. However, the worst position by far was when the ship struck a storm as the refuse was usually bailed out by pail through the hatch, but with a big sea running, the hatches were kept closed. This, of course, was essential but try to imagine, if you can, that these men were in chains and violently seasick with the ship tossing like a cork. Most of them had never been to sea in their life and so became so sick that they could not walk or crawl under their own power. The position then was that the

---

6. "Upon the Mercy of Government", p. 135.

men behind them who were able to walk had to carry them forward so that they themselves could use the convenience. On one occasion we were battened down for two days. This was something no human would wish on his greatest enemy.[7]

There was still some sickness and fever on board and a few of the transportees had already died, but for the bulk of the prisoners who remained healthy a lesser problem was how to deal with the boredom which set in during the couse of the long voyage. Over the years in Irish convict ships a certain amount of singing below decks took place while the prisoners on board the Providence were lucky enough to have a piper by the name of Denis Begley on board. And on one particular voyage out of London a group of prisoners regularly held mock trial sessions, grotesquely mimicking the proceedings of the Old Bailey. The English generally divided themselves in to two classes, namely "townies" and "yokels" while the Irish classified themselves as "the Cork boys", "the Dublin boys", "the Northern boys" or "the Scots boys". The Irish prisoners were also known to pray frequently together in the holds "counting their beads" and fervently crossing themselves and repeating their prayers from a book." And some lifelong friendships were struck during the voyage – John Mernagh with James Sheedy from Co. Clare, and Martin Burke with John Clarke, one of the serving soldiers on board.

But while the *Tellicherry* was sailing on unconcernedly, rumours were circulating in London that there had been trouble on board. A British ship, having landed in San Salvador, was informed that a convict ship had run aground to the south of the island and that the captain and crew had been murdered. When local fishermen were asked if the name of the ship was the *Tellicherry* they naturally replied in the affirmative and the story was given further credence (and further complicated) when it was alleged that some of the female prisoners on board had been transferred to the *William Pitt*. The name of Michael Dwyer, inevitably, was linked to the rumours, and he was reported as having escaped and disappeared somewhere on the island. A naval officer logged the entire story and it was reported back to London, and finally Dublin, where it was taken so seriously that an official search began in Wicklow again to ascertain if he had returned home.

But oblivious to all of these rumours the *Tellicherry* was by then nearing the end of its voyage and as the coastline of New South Wales loomed ever closer, new apprehensions began to fester in the minds of the transportees as

7. *Diary of James Sheedy*. The authenticity of this diary (and the whereabouts of the original) has long been a source of puzzlement to historians. The opinion of the author, at least, is that James Sheedy did compile a diary in his lifetime which passed initially into the hands of his brother Michael Sheedy who made selective use of it and added some spurious material. His account was consequently used by Harold Sheedy who supplied his own document to the Mitchel Library. The biggest problem is attempting to distinguish fact from fiction.

to what exactly lay in store for them on arrival. And for Michael Dwyer and his companions there were worries too as to whether the promises made to them in Dublin, and contained in Marsden's letter to the Governor, would be honoured. By Friday 14 February 1806 the *Tellicherry* had arrived outside the Head at the entrance to Port Jackson where the town of Sydney, the main settlement of the colony was situated, and the official despatches recorded their arrival:

> On Friday morning came in a six-oared cutter belonging to the *Tellicherry* with information from Captain Cuzens, apprehending detention from contrary winds, with advice to his Excellency of his approach: and on yesterday morning the ship entered the Heads, with 126 male and 35 female convicts from Ireland, having lost only four men on the passage.[9] In the evening, thirty convalescents were brought on shore and received into the General Hospital, all the others being in good health. At six in the morning boats were now in readiness to take the prisoners from on board, and at seven they left the ship for Parramatta.[8]

The *Tellicherry* had tied up at the King's Moorings, the voyage from Cork having taken 168 days. A number of government officials first came on board, a clerk of the Colonial's office to take charge of the ship's indent, two surgeons to examine the prisoners, and three army officers. The prisoners were then ferried by boats to the colony's second settlement at Parramatta and having been provided with a mid-day meal, the task of assignation began. It was Sunday and the *Sydney Gazette*, having already reported their arrival, a large crowd of expectant settlers had turned up. News of the arrival of a convict ship, particularly from Ireland, was always eagerly awaited as it was certain to contain a number of badly-needed agricultural workers to augment an inadequate labour force in the colony for both government and settlers. The ship would also bring provisions for government stores, news of political happenings in Britain, and in a colony which contained a large imbalance of men, the prospect of a wife, or in earlier years, what were officially termed as concubines from among the female prisoners. When the muster got under way the government had first pick and chose the craftsman and building workers who would join work gangs, mainly in Sydney, which were engaged in various building projects; next it was the turn of the military officers and ex-officer landholders, and finally the small landholders who were, in the main, emancipated convicts. Within the space of two hours the muster was over and two thirds of the transportees had been assigned; the majority of the female prisoners being taken on as domestic servants by the large landholders, but those who remained unassigned (usually older women or women with children) were sent to the Female Factory at Parramatta. The factory was

8.   Fiche 3289. 5/3822 2A (AONSW)

engaged in the making of woollen garments, but consisted of a loft situated above a jail where the accommodation was so poor that the inmates slept on the raw wool at night. The majority of the women who worked there opted instead to find lodgings in the town of Parramatta where one report states: "they cohabit with the male convicts or any other person who will receive them". There is no breakdown available as to how the *Tellicherry* women were originally assigned, but future records would show that they fared reasonably well in the colony.

There seems to have been some initial confusion, however, concerning the official status of the Wicklow men, and one report suggests that Arthur Devlin was assigned; that Michael Dwyer was told by an official that he had been assigned to his wife, and that John Mernagh was given to understand that he would not be considered for government work because of remarks made about him in the ship's indent, labelling him as a troublemaker.[9] But their fate would lay in the hands of Governor Philip Gidley King, a native of Cornwall, a crusty, hard-bitten naval officer who, at the age of 48, was already suffering badly from gout, and who was nearing the end of his long sojourn in New South Wales. He had landed with the First Fleet in 1788 and was appointed soon afterwards as the first commandment of Norfolk Island, a settlement situated in the Pacific Ocean, 800 miles from Sydney which was originally developed for its supposed flax-growing potential and as a supplier of timber for ship-building. Having returned briefly to England, King was appointed as Governor of New South Wales in 1800 and returned to the colony with the dual brief of trying to achieve self-sufficiently and of curbing the undue economic influence of the New South Wales officer clique. He immediately applied himself to both tasks with energy and determination, attempting at first to boost agricultural output, despite his own assertion that he could not make farmers out of pickpockets. But despite his reservations a renewal of public farming began; arrangements were made to have grain bought directly from growers and he established a government store for this purpose which then resold the grain at a reasonable price.

Despite his best efforts, however, Governor King was less than successful in attempting to break the monopolistic hold on the economy by the New South Wales squirearchy. The original convict guard which came out to the colony consisted of marines but in 1789 Major Francis Grose, a veteran of the American War of Independence, was given the task of raising a special New South Wales Corps to replace them, and was also allowed to sell the rank of lieutenancies to the highest bidders. The result was that many of the officers arrived in the colony determined not only to recoup their money but also to create a new ruling landed class which would make full use of the free convict labour. Grose quickly became Lieutenant-Governor of the colony, but a more

---

9. *Diary Of James Sheedy.*

influential figure soon emerged in the person of Scottish-born John Macarthur, the regimental paymaster and Inspector of Public Works. Grose ensured that members of his New South Wales Corps received preferential treatment to the detriment of the civilian population and they were soon monopolising the whole of the infant economy. When an American cargo ship landed in 1793 the hardnosed captain refused to sell the goods on board unless his cargo of rum was also purchased and an irreversible trend ensued as the rum was sold at an exhorbitant profit and soon became, not only the common drink, but an official currency and a means of barter. Soon it was claimed that there were two classes of people in the colony, those who sold rum and those who drank it.

On becoming Governor, Gidley King had taken the bold step of arresting the leaders of the monopoly, including Macarthur, who was sent to London, but the wily Scotsman, with his razor-sharp mind working overtime, soon gained the backing of the royal court with his ambitious plans for the breeding of sheep in the colony, and arrived back in triumph, bringing with him, not only rams from the royal flock, but the right to receive further large grants of land. The hapless King could only remark bitterly that the rest of the colony should now be handed over to Macarthur as he already owned half of it.

But if King had become paranoid about the New South Wales Corps clique he was equally intolerant of the presence of Irish convicts. His term as governor had coincided with the arrival of the bulk of the 1798 rebels, and while the majority led peaceable lives, in the course of his six-year tenure, rumours and counter-rumours were circulated on a regular basis, concerning supposed uprisings among the Irish. Even before the year 1800 there had been instances of prisoners absconding and engaging in futile attempts to find a mythical overland passage through China which would eventually lead them back to Ireland. It may have been a wild and hopeless escapade but it was the only dream they possessed. At the end of 1797, a group of 14 Irishmen, helped by native Aborigines, commandeered a board belonging to a settler in the area of Hawkesbury river and, having killed the crew, made off towards the south before being captured. In 1800 rumours again circulated of a rising by the Irish while in March 1803 15 Irish prisoners escaped from Castle Hill, only to be captured with the assistance of Aboriginal trackers. But the most serious outbreak had occurred a year later when over 100 Irish and English rebellious prisoners (in what became known as the Vinegar Hill Rising) gathered at Castle Hill and marched in the direction of Sydney. Without the benefit of an overall strategy, or competent leadership, the revolt was quickly put down by a detachment of the New South Wales Corps, led by Col. George Johnston, and the surviving Irish ringleaders were quickly hanged.[10]

---

10   "Unfinished Revolution" by Ann-Maree Whitaker, Chapter 5, pp.89-115.

At the time of the arrival of the *Tellicherry*, Gidley King was staying at the Government House in Parramatta and he, undoubtedly, examined the ship's documentation with some apprehension. On the credit side he would have been relieved to find that there had been a low instance of mortality during the voyage; the cargo also included some badly-needed provisions for the government stores, but owing to another mistake at the victualling office in Cork, a consignment of salted beef was included in addition to salted pork; the order had been for pork only because, in terms of the weekly rations allowance, four pounds of pork equalled seven pounds of beef. But this was a minor irritation compared to the shock he received on reading Alexander Marsden's letter from Dublin Castle explaining the terms on which Michael Dwyer and his comrades had been sent to the colony. King's own term as Governor of New South Wales was drawing to a close; he was due to leave for England within a few months and his greatest wish was for a quiet life before retirning peacefully to his native Cornwall. The last thing he expected was the arrival of what he perceived to be five prominent United Irishmen who had been promised the freedom of the colony. Marsden had used all of his lawyer's technical skills in phrasing the accompanying letter but there was hiding in its intent:

> Among the number on board are five men . . . who have been engaged in treasonable practices here and who have requested to be allowed to banish themselves for life to New South Wales to avoid being brought to trial. And as it has been deemed expedient to make such a compromise with them, they are sent there. Not having been convicted they claim the advantage of this distinction the effect of which is not, however, to prevent their being subjected to all the laws and disciplines of the settlement. And that any further indulgence is to be earned by their behaviour of which there has been no reason to complain during the time of their confinement here. Three other men are also charged with treasonable practices, and who have acknowledged their guilt, are embarked from Gaol of the County Carlow. Their names are John Fitzpatrick, Hugh [Brander] Byrne and Lawrence Fenelon – with these there have not any terms been made and they are considered to be of a very bad description.[11]

The last sentence of the letter did little to improve King's disposition either, and although Captain Cuzens vouched for the good behaviour of the Wicklow men during the voyage, the sight of the formidable quintet arriving at Government House only increased his sense of apprehension, while their stated intentions of living peaceably in the colony failed singularly to ease his

---

11. Fiche 3289 5/3822, 2 A (AONSW).

mind as the texts of two official letters reveal. When writing to Lord Camden, Secretary of State for the Colonies, King stated that "the arrival of the five United Irishmen will call forth the utmost attention of the Officers in the colony" while in the course of a lengthy reply to Marsden he stressed his regret that the Wicklowmen had been sent out without any convictions and expressed the pessimistic view that "more than half of the inhabitants are only too ready to renew the troubles of two years before if they were to receive leadership." But despite this gloomy prognosis he also realised that he was obliged to comply with the directive of the Lord Lieutenant in Dublin:

> As Dwyer and his companions are not liable to the restraints placed on prisoners sent here under sentence of law, they very rightly consider themselves entitled to all the rights and immunities of free subjects; but how far they may prove legal ones remain to be discovered by their future conduct. That no plea may be made for them of wanting the means to obtain their living by industry, and well knowing the capriciousness of the Irish character, I have clearly explained to them the footing they are on, and on their promise of being circumspect in their conduct, and not giving any cause for complaint, I have allowed them to become settlers, with the encouragement given to free settlers sent from England. But how far these indulgences will operate on their apparent turbulent dispositions time will show.

At the same time, John Connellan presented his letter of introduction from Marsden and was offered the post of Assistant Surgeon in Norfolk Island which enabled his fellow-Irishman, the colourful D'Arcy Wentworth to return to Sydney.[12] But Governor King was unable to make the position permanent until official confirmation was received from London, which could take up to two years and, in the intervening period, Connellan would not receive a salary. It was the beginning of a long period of financial uncertainty for him, but he had little option but to accept the posting and left immediately for Norfolk Island. There was just time for him to write another letter to Alexander Marsden in Dublin in which he spelt out his misgivings, attempted to enlist his support regarding the sanctioning of his post, and in passing, paid another handsome tribute to the captain of the *Tellicherry*:

> Before I conclude I should feel it a great breach of duty not to notice Captain Cuzens' extraordinary friendship and humanity to all on board, particularly to the convicts who were treated by him not as prisoners, being perfectly free from irons and confinement during the whole pas-

---

12. D'Arcy Wentworth, a native of Portadown, served in the Irish Volunteers as a young man before studying medicine in London. Quite incredibly, he was charged with highway robbery on four occasions before he opted to go to New South Wales in 1790 as an assistant surgeon on board the *Neptune*.

sage, except a few weeks subsequent to our departure from Ireland, and just candidly confess the landing of so many of them here in good health is in great measure owing to its human attention upon all occasions, but in particular towards the conclusion of our voyage when our wine and every other article of nourishment was expended he supplied the ship with wine, porter and sugar etc. very liberally of his own private property on the representation of the ship's surgeon, and also at Madeira he bought tobacco for the convicts, on its being made known to him how necessary it would prove to guard against ulcerated and inflamed throats which they were at the time attacked with.[13]

But Thomas Cuzens scarcely deserved what fate had in store for him. Having discharged his cargo he was hired to deliver a consignment of seal skins and 774 feet of oak to China, and also took on a small number of passengers who had received permission to leave the colony.[14] But he had the misfortune to be shipwrecked in the Straits of Apo in the Philippines and the *Tellicherry* was lost. All on board, however, managed to escape and succeeded in first reaching Manila and later the Chinese city of Canton. Later in the year, the luckless Thomas Cuzens arrived back in the colony aboard the *Admiral Wellesley* which was on route from Penang, but news of the shipwreck was celebrated in Sydney by some of the Irish convicts who, despite the captain's efforts, did not appreciate life in the holds of the *Tellicherry*.

For Michael Dwyer and his comrades, however, the importance of being granted the status of free settlers in the colony became more tangible when they were each granted 100 acres of land at Cabramatta, south-west of Syndey, an area which was in the process of being developed. Their holdings bounded Cabramatta Creek and were close to George's River which flowed into Botany Bay. Given his stated misgivings, it was perhaps surprising that Governor King allowed them to live in such close proximity, but they soon encountered at least one friendly face among government officials in the person of James Meehan (known to the Irish as Jimmy Mane) who would lay out their farms. A native of Co. Offaly, he had been transported to the colony in 1800 following his participation in the 1798 rebellion, but his surveying (rather than teaching) skills were immediately put to use and he was appointed as the Assistant Surveyor in the colony to Charles Grimes. In later life, he would claim to have laid out every farm on New South Wales and Van Diemens Land, but he was now of great assistance to the Wicklow group as they took

---

13. Connellan to King, Norfolk Island Corr (AONSW).
14. The following were given permission to leave the colony on the *Tellicherry's* ill-fated voyage: Thomas Maloy, John Clifton, Charles Bennet, Thomas Roach, James Cooper, Joseph Hibbert, John Holmes, John Thompson, Joseph Gamm, William Miell, William McGinniss, William Beard, Christopher Hughes, James Galway, William Hesketh (*Sydney Gazette*, 4 April 1806).

possession of their properties. As new settlers they were entitled also to draw free rations from government stores for a period of eighteen months and, ironically, to be assigned convict workers who would also be victualled at government expense. Dubliner Walter Clare was soon learning the rudiments of agriculture from Michael Dwyer, in addition to Patrick Mulhall and Laurence Bailey, while Hugh Byrne was also assigned two *Tellicherry* transportees, Denis and Patrick Farrell from Co. Kildare. Myles Dolan was assigned to John Mernagh while Martin Burke also had a convict assigned to him. And there was another surprise in store for the Wicklowmen when they learned that Joshua Holt, a son of their former rebel colleague Joseph Holt, had received a similar grant beside Martin Burke's holding.[15] Holt had been permitted also to bring his wife and children with him to New South Wales, and, having received an early pardon from Governor King, he became a successful farmer before false information was given against him in 1804 concerning his alleged involvement with the leaders of the Vinegar Hill uprising. Holt was arrested and examined in court before a nervous governor who sent him initially to Norfolk Island, and later to Van Diemen's Land where he struck up a friend-ship with Lieut-Governor David Collins who valued Holt's agricultural expertise. He received permission to return to New South Wales and arrived at Port Jackson just ten days before the *Tellicherry* berthed, with King warn-ing him to remain on good behaviour and "to beware of rocks and quicksands". But there would be no reconciliation between him and his former comrades-in-arms, although given Holt's outspoken manner, he may have reminded his new neighbours that their eventual fate was similar to his own.

The Wicklowmen now experienced their first sense of real freedom since the outbreak of the 1798 rebellion and commenced the difficult task of clear-ing their heavily-timbered lands, making it ready to grow crops and erecting homes for themselves. They were initially hindered by high rains, culminat-ing in a deluge at the end of March which had a more devastating effect in the Hawkesbury area where the river burst its banks, drowning a number of settlers, making a number of others destitute, and wiping out the wheat and barley crops. But at Cabramatta, despite the bad weather, the houses were quickly erected, with saplings being used for the uprights and framework, while bark stripped from gum (eucaalyptus) trees covered the roofs which were battened down also with saplings. The timbers were put in rough and chipped all over with an axe to ensure adhesion to a coat of plaster. The houses had a single chimney and a stone fireplace and were divided into four compartments.

All of the principal European vegetable crops had already been intro-duced into the colony; wheat was generally sown from April to June and harvested from the middle of November to the end of December while maize

15. Joshua Holt received his Cabramatta grant early in 1806.

was sown in October and harvested from the end of March to mid-May. The
potato, however, did not fare too well, because of the climate, and was generally grown as a first crop. Agriculture was still in its infancy and the
back-breaking and cumbersome task of clearing tree roots from the ground
became known as hoe-husbandry. Owing to the efforts of Governor King
there had been a steady increase in the numbers of cattle and horses while
large landholders such as John Macarthur and the Rev. Samual Marsden were
experimenting with different strains of sheep to find a breed suitable to the
colony's needs. Pigs were to be seen everywhere, even in the streets of Sydney; there was an abundance of fish both in the rivers and in the sea, and
there was a wide variety of fruit available, including apricots, oranges, lemons
and cherries while peaches were so plentiful that cider was made from them
and they were also used as pig-fodder.

When Joseph Holt was allowed to return to New South Wales he examined his son's farm at Cabramatta and realising that it was a better area for
feeding stock moved there with the rest of his family. He soon built a house
and stockyard and in the first year managed to clear 40 acres which may have
acted as a spur to his neighbours, or as a source of understandable envy, as
they had not the same financial resources at their disposal. One report suggests that John Mernagh worked part-time on the farm of Col. George Johnston
where James Sheedy had been assigned and he also became involved in the
brewing and sale of beer as his name appeared in an account of beer brewed
at Parramatta in 1806. The amount was 30 gallons and a later report suggests
that he was selling beer at a house in Parramatta in the following year.

For some inexplicable reason, however, Joseph Holt became involved in
the distilling of illicit spirits, and he was reported to the authorities by Hugh
Byrne, perhaps to even an old score, or resulting from an official notice which
appeared in the 10 May edition of the *Sydney Gazette* which highlighted the
existence of concealed stills in different parts of the colony "from which a
poisonous and inflaming spirit is procured", and which offered various in-
ducements for information leading to the conviction of anyone involved. In
the case of a settler the reward amounted to "stock of otherwise equal to the
value of twenty pounds Sterling."[16] Holt was arrested but was given bail and
finally bound over for a year on a bond of 400 pounds. The bitterness between the former allies only increased.

As their first year in the colony progressed the Wicklowmen seemed to
have settled into routine domestic anonymity. Sarah Byrne and Mary Dwyer
were both pregnant again; John Mernagh was living with Mary Johnson (age
29) from Co. Meath who was serving a seven year sentence and who had
come out on the *Tellicherry*; Martin Burke had met Pheobe Tunstall (age 39)
who had arrived on the *Nile* from England in 1801 to serve a seven year

16. *Sydney Gazette*, 11 May 1806.

sentence. She had been assigned to Thomas Andrews and had a child by him in 1803. At her prompting Andrews had given up his small holding to take over the operation of a shop in Pitt St., Sydney which was owned by Simeon Lord, the wealthy merchant and emancipated convict. But following the death of Andrews in October 1806, she moved to Cabramatta to join Martin Burke, together with Sarah, her infant daughter.[17] As for bachelor Arthur Devlin, shortly after his arrival he visited the "The Malting Shovel", a tavery-cum-brewery which was a popular resting place for travellers on the road between Parramatta and Sydney. It was owned by James Squire, the colony's first brewer who had originally come out from England as a convict with the First Fleet and had since been emancipated. The beer was served to Devlin by Squire's 14 year old daughter Priscilla, a "currency lass" and the eldest of six children from Squire's liaison with Elizabeth Mason[18] and they were married at the beginning of April, in a Church of England service at Parramatta, just seven weeks after the arrival of the *Tellicherry*.

But the Wicklowman soon experienced their first taste of the volatile and uncertain life in the colony when Martin Burke was arrested and charged "with an attempt to disturb the good order and discipline of the colony [which] prevented [him] obtaining the deeds of his farm. The accusations proving false and malicious [he] was discharged and remained in possession of his farm."[19] The exact nature of the alleged offence, or the identity of the informer were not recorded. On 20 April 1906, the *Sydney Gazette* confirmed the appointment of Captain William Bligh of the Royal Navy while on 10 August his arrival was confirmed, having been received with due military honours by the outgoing governor at Government Wharf. For the new settlers at Cabramatta who were concentrating on developing their holdings and attaining economic viability the news would have been only of passing interest. But their dream of leading peaceable lives in the colony would soon be shattered and the new governor would be largely responsible.

17. *Martin Burke, Father of Pittwater* by James J. Macken, p.30.
18. Elizabeth Mason was a First Fleet convict. She had one son and seven daughters by James Squire.
19. *Martin Burke, Father of Pittwater* by James J. Macken, p.31.

CHAPTER SEVEN

1806-1807

William Bligh is best remembered in history as "Bligh of The Bounty", on account of the mutiny in 1791 when he was cast adrift in an open boat with 18 of his crew in the Pacific Ocean by a group of mutineers led by Fletcher Christian. But they performed the extraordinary feat of navigating without charts, surviving with little food and water for three months, and covering a distance of 3,000 miles before reaching safety. Bligh resumed his naval career only to be caught up in the Mutiny of the Nore, when British seamen attempted to force the Admiralty into introducing overdue reforms and a more humane code of conduct. Bligh had the added misfortune to be ejected from his ship once again, and a number of the seamen who were involved in that particular incident were subsequently transported to New South Wales, including Thomas McCann, a Scotsman who was no friend of the new Governor.

Bligh was next given the less demanding task of surveying Dublin Harbour which he completed in 1800, but when it was suggested that he might publish his findings in Ireland he insisted on a London publication in order to reach a wider public.[1] In the following year he completed a similar survey of Holyhead Harbour in Wales, but he was in trouble again in 1804 when a Lieutenant Frazier, who was serving on Bligh's ship off the Dutch coast, brought charges against him for "tyranny and unofficer-like conduct." On this occasion, Bligh was courtmartialled, but was restored to his command, having been warned to be more careful about his language in future, surely a unique rebuke for a sea captain. As in the case of the Bounty mutiny, Bligh seemed to be more sinned against than sinning on this occasion, but he was correctly described as "a stickler for discipline, and a martyr to naval efficiency; fiery and passionate, subject to outbursts of wrath, accompanied by violent gesture." On occasions, he certainly showed signs of schizoid behaviour; he would savagely abuse an officer and moments later, having calmed down, would invite him to dinner or, having initially terrorised all on board his ship, would then take the trouble of spending an hour talking to a sick seaman in his bunk.

It was Bligh's patron Sir Joseph Banks, the confidential adviser to the British government on all matters connected with New South Wales, who

---

1. *Freeman's Journal*, 31 January 1801.

recommended him as the possible successor to Gidley King. For his part, Bligh hesitated before accepting as he did not wish to be separated from his family for a long number of years. He had six daughters, while his wife Betsy had a dread of the sea and could not face the prospect of the long voyage to New South Wales. But the persistent Banks kept on urging him to accept the post, offering him a salary of £2,000 a year, in addition to the prospect of further promotion on his return, and even making the less than convincing suggestion that Bligh's unmarried daughters would make more suitable marriages in the colony where the population of men far exceeded the women. Bligh finally accepted the post of Governor and, in the absence of his wife, brought with him his daughter Mary and her husband Lieut. Putland who was appointed to his staff. But during the course of the voyage out, Bligh quarreled with Captain Short who was in charge of the two-ship convoy. The autocratic Bligh began to take naval decisions without reference and when he ordered the ship on which he was travelling to change course an exasperated Short ordered Lieut. Putland to fire a shot across its bows. On landing in Sydney, Bligh had Captain Short arrested and sent back to England, thereby ruining his plans of making a new life in the colony and, to add to his misfortunes, his wife died during the return voyage.

Bligh arrived New South Wales with basically the same set of instructions which King had received six years before, namely to stimulate agriculture, to halt the drain on the British exchequer by making the colony self-sufficient, and to curb the power of the monopolists, with particular reference to the control of the rum trade. He was thoroughly briefed on his arrival by Gidley King who remained in the colony for a further couple of months and the new Governor, who lacked even a modicum of common sense, and who had seemingly neither the desire nor the capability to make valid judgements based on his own observations, accepted without questions all of King's grim warnings concerning the New South Wales Corps and the ever-present supposed threat to the peace of the colony posed by the dreaded Irish convicts.

All factions in the colony hurried to present flattering addresses of welcome to Bligh, the first emanating from the unabashed John Macarthur who took it upon himself to represent the views of the colony in general. But his address was quickly repudiated by the worthy citizens of Sydney who directly attributed to him the recent rise in the price of mutton, accusing him of withholding a large flock of wethers until he received the price he wanted. The landholders from the Hawkesbury area also drew up a separate address, objecting also to Macarthur's audacity of speaking on their behalf, and pointing out that the monopolists had recently caused ships to leave Port Jackson, laden with badly-needed merchandise in order to keep goods at highly inflated prices. They also complained about the low prices paid for grain and, above all, about the depreciated currency which was in circulation. It was an impressive document from the Hawkesbury settlers which set the parameters for the future emergence of a democratic state and an independent voice in the colony as they adverted also to the prospect of free trade, the abolition of monopolies, and demanded that allocation of property should be carried out without prejudice, and that the law of the land be impartially administered.

Bligh attempted to meet some of their immediate demands by granting help to those who had suffered most in the recent floods and he also gave notice of his intentions concerning the monopolists when he issued an order banning the use of rum as barter. He also supported Andrew Thompson, one of the biggest emancipist landholders in the colony (and his own farm baliff) when Macarthur demanded repayment from him of a promissory note expressed in wheat at the inflated currency prices. But Bligh's heartening support for the Hawkesbury farmers did not extend to the new Wicklow settlers at Cabramatta whose farms had not yet been officially registered. Hugh Byrne, becoming impatient at what he perceived was an undue delay, went to Government House in Sydney where he confronted both King and Bligh and pointed out that James Meehan had long since drawn up the necessary papers. But he received an evasive answer and, conversely, his visit probably provided another opportunity for King to impress on Bligh the potential danger posed by the Irish rebel leaders in Cabramatta.

In the meantime, five Irish labourers, including James Sheedy and James and Stephen Halpenny from the *Tellicherry*, were charged with stealing cows, sheep and two muskets, the property of John Macarthur. The Halpennys were later hanged but Sheedy was given a late reprieve and had to attend the condemned men on the scaffold.[2] Rumours began to circulate also towards the end of the year that another rebellion was being planned by Irish convicts to avenge the defeat at Vinegar Hill two years before, and while the Wicklowmen at Cabramatta had no intention of becoming involved in such activity, news of their arrival in the colony had spread among the Irish, and it is probable that the name of Michael Dwyer was raised by disaffected convicts as a possible leader. There is plenty of evidence to suggest that Dwyer had worked extremely hard on his holding during the first year. His wife helped to "burn off" the land he was clearing on a regular basis, even late at night,[3] and by the end of the year he had nine acres of maize ripening, in addition to some wheat, while in January 1807, when Bligh sent James Meehan to check on the progress of the Cabramatta settlers, he was asked by Dwyer to calculate how many bricks would be needed to build a barn 40 feet long and 10 feet high.

But there were reports also of a rift between Michael Dwyer and Arthur Devlin; a number of factors could have precipitated it, stretching back to Emmet's rebellion and to their period of imprisonment in Kilmainham. But Dwyer's dependance on alcohol could also have been the principal cause.

---

2.   Reel 2651, p. 321. *Sydney Gazette*, 30 November and 21 December 1806 (AONSW)
3.   Diary of James Sheedy.

During his years as a fugitive in the Wicklow mountains the combination of cold winters and the long hours spent sheltering in various shebeens had led to a situation where the consumption of whiskey had become the norm; he was drunk on the night he arrived at Kilmainham, and during the early period of his confinement he was deliberately supplied with an unlimited supply of alcohol by Dr Edward Trevor in order to loosen his tongue. The colony of New South Wales, with its reputation for the prodigious drinking of rum and other spirits, was scarcely an ideal location to shake off his drinking habits. At the end of 1806, he seemed to have resumed his old rambling ways, travelling up to the Hawkesbury, and visiting Sydney where he frequented the many Irish taverns in the Rocks. At these gatherings he was more likely to be introduced as the great rebel leader rather than a Cabramatta settler and as the drink flowed, and as he regaled the company with colourful anecdotes from the Wexford and Wicklow campaigns, a certain amount of loose talk, however fanciful, began to circulate as the night progressed as to what might transpire if "the Wicklow boys" got hold of some guns or pikes. Given the extremely volatile nature of the colony such bravado was highly dangerous as there was no shortage of informers, particularly among the Irish convicts themselves, who would gladly pass on and embellish such information to local magistrates in the fervent hope that it would gain for themselves a remission of their sentences or the ultimate goal of a free pardon. Such was the nature of life in the colony; Arthur Devlin and the others may have been aware of it but Michael Dwyer seemed to have been oblivious to the attendant dangers.

In the early part of 1807, Bligh became convinced that the arrival of the naval ship *Porpoise* had prevented the outbreak of a rebellion, but that the conspirators were still biding their time, waiting to strike at the next suitable opportunity. Aware of his anxieties in this regard the Hawkesbury settlers, heartened by the support he had given them, presented him with a signed declaration of solidarity, the supposed rebellion having united the various factions in the colony. On 22 February 1807, an order was issued from Government House "that a return be made immediately to the magistrates at the Hawkesbury, Parramatta and Sydney of all persons who have arms of any description – distinguishing the different kinds of which they are in possession, and the quantity of powder, ball or shot which is to be registered in a book to be kept by the magistrate. And the magistrates are hereby directed to enrol the names of all His Majesty's subjects as are ready and willing to defend the country against war and tumult, administering them the oath of allegiance, as is customary on such occasions."[4]

And on the same day the *Sydney Gazette* gave further credence to the supposed plot by printing an account of the plan of action which, no doubt,

---

4. *Sydney Gazette*, 22 February 1807.

was supplied to them by Government House: "They were to have destroyed the Governor, who they supposed would be going into the country as soon as the Buffalo sailed, on his way to the Hawkesbury, and which was to have been the commencement of the general insurrection; the New South Wales Corps were to have been surprised; the leading gentlemen of the colony were to have been seized; and a general massacre was to have taken place." Resulting from this article, and in an atmosphere of growing hysteria, the Hawkesbury settlers felt impelled three days later to present another address to their saviour, signed by over 500 persons, in which they thanked Bligh for "his wise and unwearied solicitude over the public welfare at all times". They wholeheartedly promised to some to the defence of the country and added significantly "we sincerely hope that your Excellency . . . will be graciously pleased to dispose of the ringleaders and principals so as to prevent future conspiracy and restore public tranquillity which blessing of peace and happiness may your Excellency long continue to give and enjoy in your gracious government over us is the earnest prayer of your Excellency's devoted, etc, etc."

It was now incumbent on Bligh to produce the ringleaders, and with a number of informers predictably emerging, and with the grim warnings of Gidley King still ringing in his ears, he ordered a military guard to arrest the Wicklow settlers at Cabramatta. Michael Dwyer was named as the leader of the supposed rebellion and Bligh instructed his son-in-law Captain Putland who was in command of the *Porpoise* which was anchored at Sydney Cove to "keep in strict custody Michael O'Dwyer, a state prisoner, and victual him during the time he may remain in your charge." Dwyer would be kept in solitary confinement while Hugh Byrne, Arthur Devlin, John Mernagh and Martin Burke were lodged in Sydney Jail as was Dwyer's assigned convict, Walter Clare, and also William Morris from Wexford, who was assigned to John Ramsay, and Scotsman Thomas McCann who had acted as a standard bearer during the Nore mutiny when the seamen marched daily through the town of Skegness, and who had helped to eject Bligh from his ship. And following their arrests a meeting took place at the home of Andrew Thompson to prepare a book of evidence for the upcoming trial which was compiled with the assistance of George Crossley, the former English attorney.

The sudden arrests came as a devastating blow to the Wicklowmen and their families who had just completed their first year in the colony. It was particularly heartbreaking for Mary Dwyer and Sarah Byrne who had fought so hard in Ireland to secure a future for their husbands. They had begun to believe that the nightmare years of uncertainty and despair were finally over and were settling into some kind of normal living again. But now, in nightmarish fashion, they were plunged into an even greater crisis for reasons they could not even begin to comprehend. Their husbands were hardworking settlers, not disaffected convicts, and once again their wives experienced feelings of outrage and helplessness when confronted with what they perceived to be the brutal and uncomprehending power of the law. In addition, they were expecting their first children to be born in the colony, while there was the added burden of being left to cope with the running of their partly-developed holdings. And there was similar anguish for Phoebe Tunstall, Mary Johnson and the young Priscilla Devlin who was expecting her first child, and who returned to her father's house in Ryde.

The trial of the eight prisoners was due to commence on 11 May 1807 and they would appear before the Court of Criminal Jurisdiction on a charge of being the leaders of a conspiracy in order to raise a rebellion in the colony; if found guilty they would, in all probability, be sentenced to death. As friends of the accused and witnesses arrived at the courthouse on that morning the main question centred around the quality of the evidence which the prosecution had gathered in the intervening weeks, and whether the prisoners, who would be responsible for their own defence, would be be able to counter it successfully. When writing to William Windham, the Home Secretary for the Colonies in London, shortly after the arrests had taken place, Bligh was less than convincing when outlining the background to the charges:

> In general, we are improving and have every hope that we shall do well, notwithstanding a late attempt to insurrection, which has been preparing for eighteen months past, and was to have been put into execution the date before I arrived, but was prevented by my appearance off the coast, and of which Governor King had an alarm. No arms having been found, or any positive overt act having been committed, our information leading only to declared plans, which were to be put into execution by the Irish convicts, headed by O'Dwyer and some of the Irish state prisoners, as they are called. It appears, to avoid detection, they determined to rest their success on seizing the arms of the loyal inhabitants and in order to affect this, the Irish servants of the inhabitants were on a certain time fixed to massacre their respective masters and the principal persons of the colony, and to possess themselves of their arms. Of this determination I continued to have proof, more or less, when I determined on seizing the persons represented as the ring-leaders and effected my purpose. O'Dwyer I have put on board the Porpoise. Byrne, Burke and some others are in jail for trial and will be brought forward as soon as the evidence are all arranged and prepared.

Judging by the contents of that letter it was obvious that the evidence presented during the trial would be mainly in the realm of hearsay, while in stating that the conspiracy has been in the making for 18 months he conveniently overlooked the fact that the Wicklow men had arrived in the colony only a year before. But their description as being state prisoners, rather than free settlers, would have serious implications during the course of the trial. The court was presided over by Richard Atkins, the Judge Advocate of the colony, with the assistance of six officers, drawn from the military forces. This was its prescribed composition and which gave it the appearance of a court martial. The best known (and most senior) of the officers was Col. George Johnston who had put down the abortive Vinegar Hill rising in 1804 while the remaining members were, Lt. William Minchin, Lt. James Simmons, Lt. William Ellison, Ensign William Lawson and Ensign-Cadet Draffin.

Richard Atkins could hardly be described as the jewel of the legal profession. In fact, he had very little legal background, having arrived in the colony with the New South Wales Corps, and having been appointed as a Justice of the Peace soon afterwards. He quarreled with the New South Wales Corps and became a sworn enemy of John Macarthur which action endeared him to Gidley King who later described him as "a man of abilities and exceedingly clever" while adding the necessary codicil that "he is unfortunately, some time addicted to liquor." But another settler was more forthcoming, describing Atkins as "an infamous drunken character", to which description the soubriquet of womaniser could be added. And Bligh who was never one to mince his words when it suited his purpose stated that "sentences have been pronounced in moments of intoxication, his determination is weak, his opinion floating and infirm, his knowledge of the law insignificant and subservient to private inclination." But despite these reservations he was allowed to preside over a trial during which he would carry out the role of prosecuting attorney, being in possession of the book of evidence which had been drawn up by Thompson and Crossley. Witnesses for the prosecution would be called first, examined by the court on the basis of their written evidence, and the accused would then be given an opportunity to cross-examine them if they wished. When the prosecution case ended the accused would call on their own witnesses to give evidence after which Atkins and the six military officers would retire before bringing in a verdict.[5]

The trial, which would last for over a week, and with over 30 witnesses being called, opened with a surprising prosecution witness, namely James Squire, the father-in-law of Arthur Devlin. His presence in court scarcely pointed to his approval of his daughter's marriage, and it transpired that he had written to magistrate John Harris, having supposedly received information that "the croppies were going to rise", the word croppy being defined in court as "dissatisfied persons opposed to the lawful government of the colony and rebellion against the state." Squire informed the court that his son-in-law Arthur Devlin had asked him for a hogshead of beer to take to the Hawkesbury for the purpose of collecting wheat and he promised also to deliver beer to Squire's customers in Sydney; but that, as he was about to leave, James Kavanagh, an assigned Irish convict who worked for Captain Kent, arrived

5.   Dwyer Trial 5/1149. (AONSW)

and spoke privately to him. Immediately afterwards, Devlin came back to Squire and said: "Father, I want to speak to you . . . I cannot go to the Hawkesbury on Tuesday as I intended, for Kavanagh has been up to Parramatta on Saturday for his provisions and was told there that Dwyer was going to the Hawkesbury with a cask of beef to see what could be done with the people up the country." Squire added that Arthur Devlin had then told him not to take any notice of what he had said, but that he had felt it his duty to report the matter. It might be construed at this stage of Squire's evidence that he was attempting to distance Devlin from Dwyer, but he went on to inform the court that Kavanagh had spoken further to Devlin, but that he did not know the content of their conversation. It was a curious piece of evidence as the incident only seemed to confirm that Devlin did not wish to meet Dwyer, because of their recent quarrel.

The next prosecution witness was Edward Abbott, the resident magistrate of Parramatta who arrested Joseph Holt on the charge of illicit distilling (he would soon fall foul of Bligh when it was discovered that he had imported an illegal still from England!) and he claimed that as far back as the previous August he had received information concerning a rising and that he had been assured in the month of January that "it was the intention of the disaffected to come into Parramatta on a Friday evening and to seize the barracks and its arms while the soldiers were receiving their provisions." Abbott claimed to have forestalled the rising on that occasion by placing extra sentries and constables on duty and that he also received information that the detachment of soldiers stationed at Castle Hill was to be attacked. And his suspicions were further confirmed when the convicts did not apply for their week-end passes on a certain Friday at the end of February.

At this stage of the proceedings Richard Atkins put a leading question to Abbott by suggesting to him that if he had not taken these precautions, and that if Dwyer and the other prisoners had not been arrested, an insurrection would have taken place. Abbott wholeheartedly agreed and added that "it would have been attended with most atrocious proceedings contrary to the peace." Michael Dwyer now made his first intervention by asking Abbott if he had noticed anything suspicious in his conduct since his arrival in the colony and Abbott replied that he had not. But when the court asked if Dwyer's conduct had been peaceable, Abbott replied that he was obliged on one occasion to bind him over to the peace, but for nothing seditious. It became clear that Abbott had bound over Dwyer for being drunk but, for obvious reasons, Atkins did not pursue that particular line of questioning and the next witness was called.

John Macarthur was a surprising witness in view of his recent dispute with both Bligh and Andrew Thompson and, for the only time during the course of the trial, Atkins pointedly addressed him as "sir" and somewhat frostily put another leading question:

COURT: Was you not informed that O'Dwyer made an observation, on seeing a flock of sheep passing by, and on being informed they belonged to Capt. Macarthur what was his observation?
MACARTHUR: "To the effect that they should not continue as they had done, that there was a plan among the Irish prisoners to break out into an insurrection and that Dwyer was to lead it."

Macarthur further agreed, on being asked by the court, "that such an insurrection, had it broken out, would have been attended with the most sanguinary of atrocious proceedings, even to the massacre of all those who were not actuated by their principles", and he stepped down without being asked any further questions.

The next witness was Mr Knight, the superintendent at Castle Hill, but the nature of his evidence was equally unconvincing and revealed more about the lifestyle of the accused than any supposed uprising. He told the court that Arthur Devlin and Hugh Byrne had come to him in February to order two sows and that he kept them in conversation until the sows were delivered as he had been warned by Captain Abbott not to allow them to speak to the assigned convicts. Some days later, Devlin came back saying that he had lost the sow and as the weather was bad he was given permission to stay overnight, even though it was against regulations. That was the extent of Knight's testimony and he was immediately challenged.

DEVLIN: Did you see anything in my conduct to lead you to suppose I came for any purpose than of getting my sow?
KNIGHT: No. I did not.
COURT: Have you seen Dwyer after at Castle Hill?
KNIGHT: Not more than twice and then it was to buy corn of me.
BYRNE: You have known me ever since I came to the colony. What is your opinion of me?
KNIGHT: I have always considered you as an industrious man. You drew your provisions at Castle Hill and I never knew anything improper of you.

Knight gave the impression of being a reluctant government witness. Indeed, the most striking factor concerning the witnesses in general was that, when cross-examined by the accused, they invariably gave them good character references.

Following some inconsequential hearsay evidence by Chief Constable Thomas Oakes and his Irish assigned convict James McCarthy it was the turn of the first of the two main prosecution witnesses to give evidence. Dominic McCurry was a 42 year-old Irish convict who had come out on the *Hercules* in 1801, and his evidence was directed against Michael Dwyer only. He claimed that he had met Dwyer while he was driving sheep up Constitution Hill and that when he commented that he was not a free man Dwyer had assured him that every prisoner in the colony would soon be free, and that he was going up to the Hawkesbury to contact some people in this regard. Prompted by a number of leading questions from the court, McCurry further claimed that Dwyer had told him that a rising would take place a fortnight after the *Buffalo* had sailed and when the governor was on his way to the Hawkesbury, and he also mentioned the names of Colonel George Johnston (one of the sitting officers), Dr Harris, Mr Palmer and Mr Laycock as being other colonists who were to be "checked". On receiving further prompting he also claimed that Dwyer had told him that he could get his hands on 150 pikes and that if he had 50 or 100 Wicklow boys with himself at their head, he would not be afraid of anything. The general thrust of McCurry's evidence seems to have been based on the *Sydney Gazette* issue of 25 February, and he finally claimed that Dwyer had offered to "take on anyone that would run with him" and that, but for his arrest, a rising would have taken place. He finally made the surprising admission that he had heard that Hugh Byrne would have nothing to do with it.

Michael Dwyer then proceeded to question McCurry closely, concentrating on the early part of his evidence, and their supposed meeting on Constitution Hill, and asked him to state exactly when it took place and whether anyone else was present at the time. McCurry replied that they had met a few days before Christmas and that no-one else was present but Dwyer kept on pressing him.

DWYER: Have you ever spoke to me in any person's company?
McCURRY: I never did.
DWYER: Was you ever in conversation with me before?
McCURRY: Yes. Several times, at the lumber yard when you asked me to give you a pint of whiskey which I did at Graham's, which was served by Graham's man, Thomas Bartlett, and after we drank half a pint we separated.

This last statement would be queried again by Dwyer, but the reference to drinking alcohol had the desired effect on the bench; it was three o'clock in the afternoon and the proceedings of the first day were speedily brought to a close.

The prosecution continued to call witnesses on the following morning beginning with the artist J. W. Lewin who testified as to the good character of McCurry, as did two further witnesses, before the second main prosecution witness gave evidence, namely Daniel Grady, an Irish convict who had come out on *Atlas II* and was assigned to Thomas Ramsay, a settler in the Field of Mars. Grady had also reported his information to magistrate Dr John Harris and he claimed that Walter Clare had informed him that Michael Dwyer was going to the Hawkesbury two days before the rising was due to take place, that he intended to lead a rebellion there and that John Mernagh was to take charge of Parramatta. He further claimed that Dwyer and Clare had also told him that they expected to get some pikes at Captain Kent's farm and that it was their intention to take over the ships *Porpoise* and *Lucy*, in addition to seizing the barracks in Parramatta because "they would not be called cowards on this occasion."

The last remark of Grady's probably encapsulated the entire affair, namely the overhearing of some loose talk by some disaffected convicts who were expressing the hope that the arrival of Michael Dwyer and his companions in the colony might provide the necessary spark to instigate another Castle Hill-type incident. Grady was closely questioned by Dwyer as to when he had spoken to him and he replied that it was at Mernagh's house in Parramatta (where he sold beer), but that Mernagh was not present, and that Dwyer had sent Walter Clare down to the wharf for a cask of rum. He further claimed that Dwyer had refused to tell him the date of the rising until he returned from the Hawkesbury, but that if he got hold of the Governor, George Johnston and Captain Abbott he did not care a damn for the country. His evidence almost echoed the previous day's statements made by McCurry, and again Dwyer pressed him as to where this last conversation had taken place. Grady claimed he had spoken to Walter Clare in Dwyer's own home, having been sent to George's River to collect a gun from Andrew Cunningham for his master, and to seek out further information concerning the rising at the request of Captain Abbott and Dr. Harris, and that he had spent the night at the home of Sgt. Stroud who lived beside Dwyer's holding. Grady was also questioned by Walter Clare before standing down and the next witness was his master John Ramsay who gave him a good character reference. Ramsay would later be described by Harris as "a notorious character", but when asked by both Michael Dwyer and Martin Burke to describe their conduct he replied: "Nothing but what was good and proper." This was one of the few occasions when Martin Burke spoke during the trial; in fact, no evidence of any kind was brought against him.

The next witness, Denis Stacey (*Atlas 2*), claimed that Thomas McCann had told him that "good times" were coming, while William Morris had tried to persuade him to go to Castle Hill in order to steal some arms and promised that he would be respected after the rebellion. And when he asked for more information Morris had told him of the proposed rebellion and that Dwyer was up at Hawkesbury drinking at Clarkes. Morris then took out a small book and asked Stacey to take hold of it but he had refused. In the days following Dwyer's arrest Morris had again approached him saying that it was time to get arms before "those people were sent out of the colony or disposed of". Morris did not choose to cross-examine him and it was left to Thomas McCann to suggest that when Stacey approached the magistrate in Parramatta he was threatened with a flogging if he ever concocted such a "cock and bull" story again. And McCann also accused Stacey of sending Grady to George's River to look for information.

A further prosecution witness, the watchman at Castle Hill, confirmed that he heard Morris tell Stacey that the sooner they could get hold of arms the better "for fear those men who are imprisoned are sent out of the colony", but the next witness Mathew Lock, a constable at the the Hawkesbury flatly denied that he had heard of any improper behaviour concerning Dwyer, and George Bear was even more forthcoming.

COURT: Have you heard O'Dwyer speak about any cruelties committed on the Loyalists in Ireland by him and his party?

BEAR: I never did. Thompson put it down wrong.

The prosecution's case ploughed on despite these reversals and the evidence of the next three witnesses centred round an incident which had occurred at a farm on New Year's Day which had little bearing on the case, but revealed that the sectarian differences occasionally surfaced in the colony. The first of these witnesses was William Chawker whose New Year's Day party at his farm did not run quite as smoothly as intended.

COURT: Had you not a good deal of company at your house on New Year's Day and was not O'Dwyer there?

CHAWKER: O'Dwyer was there.

COURT: Did not O'Dwyer among others sing a song?

CHAWKER: Not to my recollection.

COURT: Was not a man by the name of John Hewit in the house at the time?

CHAWKER: He was.

COURT: Did he sing a song?

CHAWKER: He did – several.

COURT: Was not a good deal of disapprobation expressed at one of the songs?

CHAWKER: Not to my recollection.

COURT: Did you see John Hewit knocked down by any person with a pailey?

CHAWKER: I cannot say that I did.

The apparently forgetful William Chawker, who had stalled impressively, was now replaced on the stand by the singing John Hewit, an Ulsterman who had come out on the Minerva, and who was mentioned by Joseph Holt as being disruptive during the voyage.

COURT: Did O'Dwyer sing?

HEWIT: He sang one song.

COURT: What was the tendency of the song? Was it disaffected?

HEWIT: I think it was.

COURT:	You sang a song. Was it a loyal song?
HEWIT:	I sang an Orange song.
COURT:	Did you hear some person say: "Knock him down, the bloody Orange scoundrel!"
HEWIT:	I did but I cannot say who it was. He was drunk.
COURT:	Did you not, in consequence of such an expression, receive a blow from a pailey?

But Hewit was unwilling to answer the question and he was asked to stand down. He was replaced by James Metcalfe who willingly told the court that he was in a neighbour's house on New Year's Day when he heard a commotion, and that when he went to investigate he saw Dwyer and Chalker exchanging blows. But he hastily added that the majority of the revellers were intoxicated. A drunken New Year's Day brawl, however, was hardly the stuff of rebellion, and with that final revelation the court adjourned, the prosecution's case having ended, or rather, having petered out. The court would reconvene in two days when the defendants would present their case.

By any standards, the prosecution case had been a weak one. As Bligh admitted in his letter to Windham there had been no evidence of any meetings held, no discovery of arms, no incriminating documents. Not a single word of evidence had been offered against Martin Burke while the evidence against Hugh Byrne was negligible; there was just a single reference to John Mernagh while the evidence against Arthur Devlin was limited to the testimony of his father-in-law. Evidence against Walter Clare and Thomas McCann was equally vague and the case against William Morris rested on the doubtful evidence of Denis Stacey. The main thrust of the prosecution's case, however, was directed against Michael Dwyer, with the majority of the witnesses claiming that he was to be the leader of the supposed rising. But most of the evidence offered was in the realm of hearsay and had been vigorously challenged by Dwyer himself. Nevertheless, given the prevailing mood in the colony, the disposition of the Judge Advocate and, above all, Bligh's conviction that the prisoners were guilty, their defence would be crucial if a guilty verdict was to be avoided.

At the end of the second day's hearing Dwyer was returned to solitary confinement in cramped conditions on board the *Porpoise* and the remaining defendants to Sydney Jail where they had some access to those who were gathering evidence for their defence. In the meantime, the determined Sarah Byrne and Mary Dwyer were loudly proclaiming the innocence of their husbands and canvassing support for them. Lt. William Minchin, one of the military members of the court, was also a landholder in Cabramatta and regarded the Wicklowmen as hard-working and peacable as did many other settlers in the area. It would be important to persuade some of them to speak on behalf of the defence.

The third day of the trial began on the morning of 17 May, but before the prisoners were allowed to open their defence the governor's secretary appeared in court and produced the letter which Alexander Marsden had sent to Gidley King outlining the terms on which the Wickowmen had been sent out from Ireland. Although the letter stated categorically that they had been sent out without conviction, and had not been tried, the court took the view that they were prisoners for life, rather than free settlers. This judgement went unchallenged but the defence opened robustly when three English settlers who lived close to the Wicklowmen at Cabramatta testified separately as to their industry and and peaceable nature.[6] Having achieved this initial advantage, they concentrated their efforts on refuting the evidence given by McCurry and Grady. Their first witness was Andrew Cunningham who confirmed that Grady had been sent by John Ramsay to collect a gun but, on his return, Grady told him that when he discussed the rebellion in Ireland with Michael Dwyer he replied: "Damm the rebellion! Every time I think of it my mind shudders to think of the desolation it has occasioned so many families at home."

This was a far cry from what Grady had told the court and the first cracks in his testimony began to appear. Surveyor James Meehan was then called and he described the progress made by the Wicklowmen on their holdings since their arrival and confirmed that Hugh Byrne had visited Government House seeking the registration of his land grant. He was followed by Thomas Dargan from Parramatta who had signed the address of the Hawkesbury settlers and he testified that he had been in the company of Michael Dwyer between Parramatta and the Hawkesbury on the day that Grady claimed to have spoken to him. The next witness was Malachy Ryan from Limerick who had come out on the *Tellicherry* and was assigned to Sgt. Stroud. He also contradicted Grady's testimony as did two other witnesses and the day ended with Bryan Donnelly casting doubt on Grady's probity by claiming that he had not honoured his promissory note.

The last of the defence witnesses were called on the following day; Thomas Lynch lived "on the farthest part of the Rocks" and gave evidence of Dwyer coming to his house two days before Christmas for no other purpose than to get some spirits while Michael Howlin confirmed that he had been in the company of Grady at Parramatta, that they drank a pot of beer at Mernagh's and that he had not spoken to any other person. Magistrate John Harris next told the court that he had received information "that something improper was intended among the Irish" and that, on hearing that Dwyer had gone to Sydney, he had asked Chief Constable William Redfern[7] to investigate. Redfern

---

6. The English settlers who gave evidence on behalf of the Wicklowmen were Samuel Higginson, Stephen Share and John Emmerson.
7. William Redfern, a native of Wiltshire, was serving as a naval doctor at the time of the

had subsequently informed him that Dwyer had been seen drinking in various inns but had returned home before a constable was able to investigate. Harris was then asked separately by Hugh Byrne, John Mernagh and Martin Burke if he had heard anything prejudicial against them and he replied that he had not. Captain Laycock was then called, but on being questioned by the court stated that Thomas McCann had boasted in his presence concerning his active role in the Nore mutiny and that he was the seamen who had handed Captain Bligh over the side of his ship. Witnesses for William Morris also testified to his good character and Arthur Devlin recalled John Kavanagh and asked him to clarify the conversation which had taken place between them at Squire's at the beginning of January.

KAVANAGH: You informed me that you were going up to the Hawkesbury
                with a load of beer. I told you that O'Dwyer had gone up
                with a cask of beef, on which you replied that as yourself
                and Dwyer had some differences you would not go.

Walter Clare finally having denied the charges made against him, and the case for the defence having concluded, the court adjourned for four days. During this period Dwyer, Devlin and McCann had papers drawn up proclaiming their innocence which were read out by the Judge Advocate when the court resumed. They immediately adjourned to consider their verdict and reconvened for a final time on the following day when Atkins read out the verdicts to a hushed and apprehensive courtroom.

Michael O'Dwyer – Not guilty.
Hugh Byrne – Not guilty.
John Mernagh – Not guilty.
Thomas McCann – Guilty.
William Morris – Guilty.
Arthur Devlin – Not guilty.
Martin Burke – Not guilty.
Walter Clare – Not guilty.

Various expressions of relief and dismay, no doubt, echoed around the courtroom as the verdicts were read, but silence again descended as Atkins continued:

After the most mature deliberations in the respective testimonies that has appeared before the Court, the Court is fully of the opinion that the charges as set forth in this indictment is fully proved against the prisoners Thomas McCann and William Morris, and the Court, therefore, doth adjudge and sentence the said Thomas McCann and William Morris to receive one thousand lashes and the Court further recommends that

Nore Mutiny and was transported for life for speaking in favour of the mutineers' cause. He was granted a free pardon in 1803 and returned to Sydney from Norfolk Island in 1808.

the said prisoners Thomas McCann and William Morris, being delin-
quent of the most dangerous principles of character, be removed by the
most speedy consequence to a remote place where the baneful influence
of their example, cannot be expressioned nor disseminated among other
ignorant and deluded convicts.

The relief felt by the Wicklowmen and Walter Clare was surely tempered
on hearing of the savage sentence meted out to Morris and McCann, the
irony of the verdict being that the Cabramatta settlers and one of their servants had been cleared. Was this the main consideration which had caused the
members of the court to reach their verdict? From the outset, two separate
trials were going on simultaneously as very little evidence had been offered
linking McCann and Morris with the Wicklowmen. Taken on an individual
basis, Martin Burke, Hugh Byrne and John Mernagh had no case to answer
while it had become clear that Arthur Devlin and Michael Dwyer were not
even on speaking terms. Walter Clare was in court simply because he was
Dwyer's servant, but it was the case against Dwyer which had probably
occupied the minds of the court members as they deliberated before reaching
a verdict. He had been mentioned by a succession of witnesses as the leader
of the supposed rebellion, and though it was hearsay evidence, the witnesses
included some of the leading figures in the colony. But Dwyer himself, by his
intelligent and perceptive line of questioning, had succeeded in demolishing
the evidence of McCurry and Grady, while the forthright answers of his
witnesses also weighed in his favour. It was revealed by magistrate Edward
Abbott some years later that Col. George Johnston was of the opinion that the
main prosecution witnesses had committed perjury and that they should have
been brought to trial. On the same occasion Lt. William Minchin also stated
that each of the court's members was convinced of Dwyer's innocence.

Regarding the guilty verdicts brought against McCann and Morris, it
could be argued that they were merely a sop to placate Bligh who was confidently expecting a guilty verdict which would rid the colony of a group of
dangerous rebels, increase his standing in the eyes of the Hawkesbury settlers
and leave him with a stronger hand to take on the monopolists. It was unfortunate that Morris had not challenged Stacey's evidence while McCann's
boasting of what he had done to Bligh during the Mutiny of the Nore, as
reported by Captain Laycock, did little to help his cause.

The court, however, had demonstrated its independence by bringing in
the not-guilty verdicts; the Wicklowmen were released and some, at least,
went to John Mernagh's house in Parramatta to celebrate. But their ordeal
was far from over as a furious Bligh, on hearing the verdict, lambasted Minchin
and ordered their immediate rearrest. And in a flagrant breach of the law of
the colony, he summoned a Court of Magistrates (perhaps the first kangaroo
court) overturned the verdict of the Court of Criminal Jurisdiction, and found
each of them guilty. It was Bligh at his autocratic worst: "The law, sir!", he

had barked on one occasion. "Damm the law! My will is the law and woe to any man that dares to destroy it." The Wicklowmen, in adddition to Clare, Morris and McCann, were sentenced to be deported in pairs to separate penal outposts of the colony, and Bligh defended his actions when writing to William Windham in London in October:

> Referring to my letter of 19th of March, stating that an insurrection was on the eve of breaking out, and that the leading persons were taken up, I have to inform you, sir, they have been since tried, and the fact, in my opinion proved, yet they were acquited – except two, who were sentenced to corporal punishment; the whole being prisoners for life, I immediately divided the gang and sent two to each of the settlements of Norfolk Island, the Derwent and Port Dalrymple, and kept two here. The two men [McCurry and Grady] who informed me of this conspiracy gave their evidence so steadily as to induce me to give them free pardons, and they remain here without any apprehension of being molested by the disaffected Irishmen.[8]

Bligh rationalised his overthrowing of the court's decision by describing the Wicklowmen as "prisoners for life", and it made the intervention of his secretary on the third day even more significant. Grady and McCurry were the only convicts to be granted full pardons during Bligh's tenure as governor, and his assertion that they remained in the colony without being molested could also be judged as further proof that no conspiracy existed among "disaffected Irishmen." Later in the year magistrate Dr. John Harris wrote to former Governor King stating that he had fallen out with Bligh and gave a far different perspective on his actions: "Two of the men who swore against them, being for life, one of them a servant of that scoundrel Ramsay, and a notorious character, his Excellency thought proper to give them free pardons, and which will be also of the kind he will ever do, as he does not seem to have much of the milk of human kindness about him." But Bligh remained convinced of their guilt and referred to the trial also in a letter written to his wife Betsy. She mentioned it in passing to William Marsden, Secretary of the Admiralty, a brother of Alexander Marsden, who seemingly was acquainted with Hugh Byrne from the time he spent at Verval. And when Betsy Bligh wrote back to her husband she passed on a piece of advice from him: "The idea of the mutiny and the massacre of the convicts terrifies us, but Mr Marsden made light of it, and said it was an impossible thing, and that the informers were the people he mistrusted most. Byrne, he said, he would not believe anything against."

Michael Dwyer was placed on board the *Porpoise* once again and before it sailed for Norfolk Island his wife Mary, with her infant son James, came down to the wharf but was refused permission to say good bye to him. When writing to Captain John Piper, the Commandant of Norfolk Island, Bligh gave strict instructions that the two prisoners should not be allowed to leave without his permission, and cold-bloodedly added that the unfortunate Morris "having received 525 lashes pursuant to his sentence of 1,000, you are required to direct the remaining part of the 475 lashes to be inflicted according to the warrant sent wherewith by the Judge Advocate."

A distraught Mary Dwyer returned to Cabramatta, not knowing when she would see her husband again or how she would cope with the running of the farm. In the midst of the crisis, Sarah Byrne gave birth to a daughter, Catherine Agnes, and now had four young children to rear on her own. But the neighbours who had given evidence in favour of the Wicklowmen during the trial – mainly members of the New South Wales Corps – came to their assistance. They included court member William Minchin who also recalled later: "I know, from the information of officers, that applications were made in favour of Dwyer's family, and that the Governor was very violent upon the occasion towards them."[9] Priscilla Devlin gave birth to a son James during this period and remained at her father's house in Ryde, while it can only be presumed that Mary Johnson remained at Cabramatta or was involved in the running of John Mernagh's beer operation at Parramatta.

In May 1807, Bligh instructed Captain Putland "to proceed with His Majesty's ship *Porpoise* to Norfolk Island, and there put on shore, in charge of the Commandant, two convicts, called Michael O'Dwyer and William Morris, which persons have been sent on board of you for that purpose." Martin Burke and Thomas McCann were set to leave for Port Dalrymple (Launceston) in Van Diemen's Land but there was a long delay owing to the unavailability of a vessel. The *Porpoise* returned from Norfolk Island in mid-July 1807 on its way to Van Diemen's Land with a number of settlers who were being evacuated, and among its passengers also was Fr James Harold, a Catholic priest who had been transported following the 1798 rebellion. According to the later testimony of Martin Burke, he arranged to be married to Phoebe Tunstall on board the ship while it remained at anchor in Sydney Harbour[10] and the witnesses were Joseph Barry, an Irish convict and tailor, and his wife who were travelling to Van Diemen's Land. The wedding, however, was carried out in secret as Catholic priests were forbidden to minister to their fellow coreligionists at the time. It is likely that Hugh Byrne and John Mernagh were sent to the Coal River, the penal settlement at Newcastle, and that Arthur Devlin and Walter Clare were sent to the Derwent in Van Diemen's land. And for as long as William Bligh remained as Governor they fully realised that there would be no reprieve for any of them.

---

9. *A Charge Of Mutiny*, p. 264.
10. *Martin Burke* by James J. Macken, p. 36.

CHAPTER EIGHT

1807-1813

Norfolk Island had not fulfilled the initial high hopes of the government regarding the successful growing of flax or the provision of a steady supply of timber for shipbuilding, but a number of landholders and their families had settled there while a penal outpost was established to house the colony's most recalcitrant convicts. And when the island population failed to become self-sufficient, and had to be partly-victualled from Sydney, a decision was taken in London, initially in 1803, to abandon it and transfer its inhabitants to Van Diemen's Land which had greater possibilities for development. The evacuation, ironically, was due to commence shortly after the arrival of Michael Dwyer and William Morris. For the latter, any hopes he might have entertained of escaping the remainder of this sentence were dashed as Bligh's strict instructions were carried out by the island's Commandant, Captain John Piper: "William Morris received the whole of his punishment as soon as Mr Connellan made his report that he was in a fit state to have it inflicted, which was immediately after the departure of His Majesty's ship *Porpoise*."[1] John Connellan's own position as surgeon on the island had yet to be sanctioned by the government in London and he was engaged in a continuing correspondence with Bligh to improve medical supplies and to obtain the services of an assigned convict to work on his holding, the produce of which enabled him to subsist in the absence of any remuneration.[2]

During the remaining months of the year it is likely that Michael Dwyer was engaged in work connected with the evacuation of the island which continued in November 1807 when the *Lady Nelson* brig, with 15 settlers, 6 women and 13 children on board, left for Van Diemen's Land. A further complement of 182 persons, including Dwyer and Morris, were transferred by the *Porpoise* on 17 January 1808, but at the same time, quite unknown to the inhabitants of Norfolk Island, a major confrontation was looming in Sydney between Bligh and the New South Wales Corps faction, led by John Macarthur, which culminated in Bligh ordering his arrest on a series of charges, ranging from sedition to the illegal possession of a still, and for resisting arrest. Macarthur was granted bail and spent the week before his trial drumming up support and loudly proclaiming to all and sundry that Judge Advocate

1. Piper to Bligh, 15 September 1807, Norfolk Island Corr, pp. 145-148 (AONSW).
2. *Ibid.*, Connellan to Bligh, 23 December 1806, pp. 113-115.

Atkins had already pronounced him guilty.

On 22 January 1808, a few days before the trial was due to begin, the wily Macarthur asked Bligh's permission to inaugurate a mess dinner for the New South Wales Corps, and the unsuspecting Bligh consented and even contributed a gift of wine. The dinner went ahead on the night before the trial, with the six military members of the court in attendance, although Macarthur was content to walk up and down outside. The main topic of conversation during the dinner was the upcoming trial and the wine (including Bligh's) flowed so freely that Col. George Johnston fell from his carriage on his way home.

At the commencement of the trial Macarthur attempted to disrupt the proceedings by questioning the impartiality of Atkins, and he was given at least tacit support by the military members of the court. The trial broke up in confusion and, as a highly-charged atmosphere developed, Bligh ordered his Provost-Marshal to arrest Macarthur on the following day. He also summoned the six military court officers to Government House where he intended charging them with treason, but they refused to attend and George Johnston, who had already refused to assist Bligh, released Macarthur from prison on a warrant which he signed as Lieutenant-General of the colony. With the encouragement of Macarthur, and with the regimental band striking up "The British Grenadier", a military party, accompanied by a drunken rent-a-crowd, marched to Government House where they were met by Bligh's daughter, the recently-widowed Mary Putland, who barred their way and shouted: "You traitors, you rebels, you have just walked over my husband's grave and now you come to murder my father!" Bligh had some advance notice of their intentions and decided to hide before attempting to make his way to the Hawkesbury to enlist the support of the settlers, but he was discovered hiding under a bed by a group of soldiers and was placed under house arrest while George Johnston took over as interim governor.

News of Bligh's arrest was greeted with acclamation in Sydney and the occasion was viewed with genuine delight and astonishment by the convict population in general as they witnessed the overthrow of a governor, not by the actions of the disaffected Irish, as had been long feared, but by his own military forces. As they relished this delicous irony there were frantic celebrations in the streets; bonfires were lit; the taverns did roaring business; George Johnston was declared to be the saviour of the colony, and one enterprising Irishman, John Reddington from Roscommon, was later reported as having adopted the sign of the harp without the crown outside his tavern.

Lt. William Minchin was a leading member of the military group which had confined Bligh to Government House, and when news of his overthrow reached Cabramatta, the equally delighted and surprised Mary Dwyer and Sarah Byrne immediately began to petition for the release of their husbands. As both Minchin and Johnston were military members of the court during the Dwyer trial (whose verdict had been set aside by Bligh) it was in their

own interest to highlight such cases and to cite them as glaring examples of
Bligh's abuse of power and his disregard of the law. They readily agreed and
Mary Dwyer, together with her infant son, were allowed to travel immediately to Van Diemen's Land to be reunited with her husband. Hugh Byrne
was among the first to return home and, as part of his efforts to restock his
farm, immediately applied for cows on credit from the Government herd.[3]
But George Johnston, having reflected on the enormity of what had taken
place, and anticipating the inevitable backlash from London, sent a message
to Lt.-Col. William Patterson, the veteran ex-administrator of the colony, and
presently the commanding officer of the New South Wales Corps in Van
Diemen's Land, to take over as governor until a new appointment was made.
But Bligh also wrote to Patterson ordering his own reinstatement and while
the latter dithered and remained in Hobart, Col. James Foveaux, the former
Commandant of Norfolk Island, who had returned from leave in England,
took over the control of the colony from Johnston. In the meantime, Bligh
continued to bombard London with letters of complaint concerning the conduct of the leaders of the new regime, including their release of the Wicklowmen.

> The chief of this conspiracy, Dwyer, who had been banished to Norfolk
> Island, and was to have been left at the Derwent, has been sent for by
> the present rulers – an extraordinary circumstance, for which no reason
> can be assigned unless they purpose by their indulgence to him hereaf-
> ter to unite with his old party in an opposition to Government should
> they feel his assistance necessary.

Despite Bligh's wild speculation, Michael and Mary Dwyer remained in
Hobart until the end of the year, more than aware that Bligh was still en-
sconced in Government House, and preferring to remain at a safe distance in
the event of his returning to power. This eventuality, however, was becoming
more unlikely as Foveaux had sided with the New South Wales Corps on his
return and tried to persuade Bligh to return to England. But he was singularly
unsuccessful as Bligh, who could afford to lose a ship but not a colony,
resolutely refused to budge until he had received orders from London and the
stand-off continued. Foveaux then surprisingly dismissed John Macarthur
who had been acting as Colonial Secretary, and both Johnston and Macarthur
prepared to leave for London to explain their actions in person to the authorities there.

The ailing William Patterson finally arrived in Sydney on board the
Porpoise in January 1809 to take over as temporary governor, almost a full year
since the Rum Rebellion had taken place. Michael and Mary Dwyer travelled
back on the same ship, having presumably received guarantees concerning

---

3.   Macarthur Papers, Vol. 1, p. 1159 (A 2897), Rowland Hassal papers A.859, p. 289.

their safety, and bringing with them the latest addition to the family, their one-month old daughter Bridget. Martin Burke was also on board and once again the five Wicklowmen were in possession of their farms at Cabramatta. But Burke's personal life had been complicated by the remarriage of his erstwhile spouse Phoebe Tunstall to soldier John Butler at St. Philip's Church, Sydney in the previous August. The redoubtable Phoebe, however, took it all in her stride, promptly dropping her new husband, and returning to Cabramatta with her young daughter.[4] But almost immediately Martin Burke suffered a serious setback when his house caught fire as was reported in the *Sydney Gazette*: "Late on Tuesday night, or early on Wednesday morning, a fire broke out in the farm-house of Martin Burke, at George's River; which owing to the roof being thatched, scarce gave the persons, consisting of Burke, his wife and child, time to escape; but not a single article of wearing apparel or other property could be saved, by which the sufferers are reduced to extreme distress."[5]

His Wicklow comrades, no doubt, came to his assistance, and the task of building a new house commenced. The ailing William Patterson remained as interim governor throughout the year 1809, although the real power lay with Foveaux who embarked on a massive spree of granting large landholdings to his friends and supporters, to the chagrin of former Provost-Marshal William Gore who wrote to Bligh's wife in London concerning what he believed to be the slide towards anarchy in the colony:

> Free pardons and emancipations have been indiscriminately granted to almost all of the atrocious criminals that have been transported to this colony – all the principal Irish rebel chiefs have been pardoned, many of whom conscious of the invalidity of these instruments, are now hastily quitting the country for Ireland previous of the expected succours.

But Gore would be disappointed in his expectation of help from Britain. The Napoleonic War still being fiercely waged and news of the overthrow of a governor in a far-off penal colony by his own officers, had created few anxieties in either government or public circles. And there appears to be very little evidence to support Gore's assertion that Irish rebels were quitting the colony in any great numbers, although one surprising departure was Fr Peter Dixon who had been given permission to return to Ireland in 1808. And Bligh also continued to give vent to his ongoing dissatisfaction at what he perceived to be the preferential treatment given to the dreaded Irish:

> Col. Patterson has become very lavish in his favours to a great number of persons in order that when reforms take place it may produce as

---

4. Martin Burke, *Father of Pittwater*, p. 39.
5. *Sydney Gazette*, 15 January 1809.

much discontent as possibly he can effect. Among their iniquities and designing acts, they have been lavish in their gifts and indulgences to some of the worst characters, particularly to the Irish rebels, Dwyer, Holt and other principal ones, and the Romish priest is now following his functions where before he kept within proper bounds and must again be limited by wise and mild measures.

Bligh may have been referring to Fr. Harold who had continued to keep a low profile in the colony, but he left for Ireland also soon afterwards and was appointed parish priest of Rathcoole, Co. Dublin. As for Patterson and Foveaux, they were still unsuccessful in their efforts to persuade Bligh to leave the colony. Following protracted negotiations he agreed to quit Government House and take possession of the *Porpoise*, but having sailed out of Port Jackson he headed for the settlement at Hobart in Van Diemen's Land where he was initially welcomed by Lt-Col. Collins before he received an order from Patterson to have no further contact with him. The irony of the fact that Bligh was floundering about in the *Porpoise* would not have been lost on Michael Dwyer, and there was further welcome news for the Wicklowmen when they were granted full pardons. The official registration of their farms at Cabramatta was also sanctioned, with the usual reservations being included, namely that the timber on their properties could be used for naval purposes by the Crown. The registrations were signed by William Patterson, and counter-signed by the Clare-born Lt. James Finucane who had arrived in the colony as secretary to Foveaux.

About this time a notice appeared in the *Sydney Gazette* that a number of letters were awaiting collection at the Post Office, including one for Michael Dwyer which came from No. 3, Browne St, the Earl of Meath's Liberty in Dublin city where his four eldest children were being reared. The question of their being sent out to the colony may have been raised, but as their ages ranged from six years to ten, they would have to be accompanied, and it was becoming clear that, after a gap of four years, Dr Edward Trevor would not keep his promise that the administration in Dublin Castle would arrange for their passages. So the Dwyer children remained in Ireland, although further letters continued to arrive over the years. The fate of John Mernagh's beer operation in Parramatta is also unclear and in 1809 his name appeared among a long list of people who were due to sell their holdings to Henry Kable.[6] These sales, however, were not regisered and Mernagh retained ownership of his holding at Cabramatta as did Arthur Devlin whose wife Priscilla and their infant son had rejoined him.

Patterson and Foveaux continued to lavish large grants on all and sundry,

---

6. Land Titles ffice (1810) No. 269. Transfer by several settlers of their farms to Henry Kable bearing the date 14 August 1809. John Mernagh [Marnagh] appears among 60 names, but the deeds were subsequently not registered.

ut as the economy began to stagnate news arrived from London concerning the appointment of a new governor to replace Bligh. But as the colony awaited his arrival the old anxieties must have returned to the Wicklowmen as they pondered what the future might bring. There would have been immense relief that Bligh was being replaced, but he was still sulking at Hobart and it was possible that he might have the ear of the new governor rather than Patterson and Foveaux.

On 31 December 1809, a small convoy of ships, bringing the new governor and his entourage, arrived in Port Jackson and anchored off the Governor's Wharf at Sydney Cove. On that night bonfires blazed and they were answered by the firing of festive rockets from the ships in the harbour. On New Year's Day, a large crowd watched with more than passing interest as the new Governor Lachlan Macquarie assumed office on the Grand Parade in Sydney when he broke the wax on the Patent and handed the Great Seal to incoming Judge Advocate Ellis Bent who immediately displayed it to bewildered onlookers. Members of Macquarie's 73d Regiment and the New South Wales Corps stood guard as ceremonial volleys rang out and bands played "God Save The King". Macquarie then addressed the crowds in his rich Scottish accent, stressing that his intention was to exercise the authority invested in him with strict impartiality, and expressing his optimism that "all of the dissentions and jealousies which had, unfortunately, existed in the colony for some time past would now terminate for ever, and give way to a more becoming spirit of reconciliation, harmony and unanimity among all classes and descriptions of inhabitants." The government in London had intended that Bligh should officially remain as the legal governor until that day, and that he should receive Macquarie as his successor in Government House, but Bligh was still in Hobart, and Macquarie, having consulted his Judge Advocate, proceeded without him.

Lachlan Macquarie, a 49 year old army officer, was a native of the island of Ulva in the Inner Hebrides, and a member of the poorer of two septs of the Macquarie Clan who owned a castle in Mull. His father died when he was young and his uncle became responsible for his education. Following the outbreak of the American War of Independence, he joined the British army and later spent many years in India where his first wife had died. Some years later he married Elizabeth Campbell, from Airds in Scotland and she readily agreed to accompany him to New South Wales where their only son would be born. Macquarie had been originally offered the post of Lieutenant-General in the colony, but when the designated governor became ill Lord Castlereagh quickly offered him the post, with the promise of a full pension if he remained in New South Wales for eight years.

There were two interesting Irishmen among his staff; Lieut-General Maurice O'Connell, a debonair member of the famous Kerry family who had the typical background of an "Irish Geese"[7] officer of the period. He was the younger son of John O'Connell of Ballinabloun, a tall strapping lad who was first intended for the priesthood until his famous uncle Daniel O'Connell arranged to have him sent to the military college in Paris. When the Irish Brigade was taken into British pay in 1794 Maurice O Connell was appointed captain and, having adroitly conformed to the Church of England, served in a variety of exotic locations until his appointment to New South Wales. By contrast Macquarie's secretary, John Campbell, was a sober and efficient Unionist from Newry who had previously worked in the Bank of Ireland and was a founder member of the Bank of the Cape of Good Hope.

For Macquarie, his unexpected appointment as governor would become the great challenge of his life, and he relished the prospect with an almost child-like enthusiasm. He was indeed the right man man for the job and, above all, he came at the right time; down-to-earth, bluff and filled with reforming zeal, he possessed a great deal of common sense as well as a keen organisational ability while his no-nonsense upbringing in Ulva meant that he lacked the artificiality of manners, pomposity and hideous class consciousness of so many of his contemporaries. As Bligh had remained as governor in the eyes of the British government until Macquarie's arrival, all of the grants and pardons issued by Patterson and Foveaux were declared invalid, and there was consternation in the colony when a proclamation was issued ordering that all such documentation should be returned to Secretary J.T. Campbell.

The alarm partly subsided when it was further explained that Macquarie would reconfirm the majority of such grants and pardons, and the exasperated Wicklowmen at Cabramatta had no option but to hand them in at Government House where they were assured that the grants would be reissued. At the same time, they submitted individual petitions outlining their changes of fortune since arriving in the colony; Martin Burke stating that he had arrived in the colony "with the same privileges as free settlers", and Hugh Byrne describing himself as a free settler, and outlining the savage treatment meted out to him and his family by William Bligh:

> During this period he [Hugh Byrne] had to lament the misfortune of his wife and five [three] children who were left unprotected, and their pitiable state during that period will, no doubt, be felt by your Excellency, although almost surpassing description – deprived of every indulgence, his men [assigned servants] taken from him, and his property exposed to the merciless world, by which he was under necessity of incurring debts that he has not yet surmounted.

Hugh Byrne asked for two assigned convicts to help with his farm and that they should be victualled from government stores, "and in the meantime

---

7.   The Wild Geese were members of Irish battalions who fought on the Continent of Europe in the decades following the signing of the Treaty of Limerick in 1691.

you will be pleased to confirm the title of his land and allow him to return to the enjoyment thereof." The massive administrative task of re-registering farm grants resulted in long delays and Michael Dwyer, Martin Burke and John Mernagh presented a joint-petition to appraise the government also of their situation:

> That your Excellency's petitioners hold each one hundred acres of land from Governor King, with the promise of free pardons and deeds of grant, and have made considerable improvements on their farm by clearing and cultivation. That the late Lieut. Governor Patterson realised the promise of Governor King, by giving them their pardons and deeds of their farms, which agreeable to your Excellency's proclamation they delivered into the Secretary's office, with their respective memorial, praying confirmation which your Excellency was pleased to promise. Petitioners now most humbly carve your Excellencie's confirmation of their respective pardons and deeds of grant, which they will study to merit by a continuance of that industry which has hitherto distinguished them, and in duty bound, they will ever pray, etc.[8]

Their land grants were duly registered and backdated by Macquarie to 1 January 1810, the witnesses being H.C. Antill and James Meehan. The registrations were counter-signed by J.T. Campbell, but the free pardons granted by Patterson were not renewed and they would have to earn them, in the eyes of the authorities, by their future conduct. As for Bligh, on his arrival back in Sydney on the leaking *Porpoise*, he immediately alienated his successor with a series of demands, and when he finally left for London, determined to indict Johnston and Macarthur, an exasperated Macquarie wrote to Castlereagh stating that he found Bligh "certainly a most disagreeable person to have any dealings or public business to transact with; having no regard whatsoever to his promises or engagements, however sacred." And Bligh had to leave without his widowed daughter Mary Putland who had fallen for the dashing Kerryman Col. Maurice O Connell. Despite his initial opposition to the marriage, he attended their wedding shortly before his departure.

The colony was soon feeling the brunt of Macquarie's reforming zeal, and there was general unease at his insistence on the observance of the Sabbath, particularly as he instructed constables to arrest anyone found working on Sunday. He ordered all couples who were living together to marry and Mathew Hughes, a Protestant teacher from Co. Down, and who had been a corporal in a militia regiment before being transported, was asked to open a charity school at the settlement in Windsor. The Catholic population in the colony, however, still lacked the services of clergy to attend to their religious

---

8.   Fiche 3003 4/1821 No. 96. (AONSW)

needs. The new governor also turned his attention to the colony's innkeepers whom he described as "in defiance of all law and decency, scandalously kept open during the night, the most licentiously and disorderly houses, for the reception of the abandoned of both sexes, and to the great encouragement of dissolute and disorderly habits." He proceeded to curtail the number of spirit licences which had multiplied during the interim period and encouraged the growing of barley so that beer might partly replace the drinking of rum. This was obviously good news for brewers such as James Squire, while Arthur Devlin also took advantage of the new policy and was granted a beer license at George's River in March 1810 which meant that he would be allowed to sell beer without having to incur the expense of running an inn which would legally bind him to provide accommodation for travellers.

Macquarie also revelled in his self-appointed role of town planner and quickly set to work on improving the appearance of Sydney; streets were regulated; sidewalks were built; cattle drovers were warned about their straying herds, and pigs were banished from the streets. His popularity dramatically rose when he allowed horse racing to take place in Hyde Park while his equally down-to-earth and sensible wife Elizabeth became equally popular with the Irish when she gave a dinner on St Patrick's Day for almost 60 assigned Irish convicts and overseers who were working on various Government projects, the first recognition of the national day in New South Wales.

But it was Macquarie's enlightened attitude towards the convict population which marked him out as the Governor who would determine the future shape of the colony when he stated that "long-tried good conduct should lead a man back to the rank in society that he had forfeited and do away and, as far as the case will admit, all retrospect of former bad conduct." It would be the cornerstone of his reforming policy during his 11 year tenure as governor and one which, almost inevitably, brought him into conflict with the less enlightened view which prevailed, namely that convicts should always remain subservient to their masters, and that even when they became emancipated, the middle and major offices in the colony should always remain the preserve of the so-called exclusives. The fact that this latter policy was echoed by government officials in London only added to his problems.

He also set about reorganising the administration of the colony and promoted D'Arcy Wentworth who had been acting as medical officer at Parramatta since his return from Norfolk Island. He was also a prominent business man and landholder, while their mutual friendship with the Fitzwilliam family in England linked him to the new governor. Wentworth was appointed to the posts of Principal Surgeon, Chief Police Magistrate of Sydney, and Chief of Police in quick succession, and was one of the main contractors that undertook the building of the Rum Hospital in Sydney, although this latter venture did not prove to be as profitable as anticipated. Macquarie's reorganisation of the police force included the appointment of new constables in the outlying settlements, and it came as a surprise in Irish circles when, on 25 August 1810, Michael Dwyer was named as one of the three new constables to serve at George's River.[9] There was a settlement in the local area of Bankstown called Irishtown which, as the name suggests, was inhabited by various Irish ticket-of-leave convicts. The area was known to be a trouble spot, so the choice of the former rebel leader to deal with his countrymen was a stroke of genius by the authorities. As for Dwyer it was not quite a case of taking "the Government shilling"; indeed he had very little option but to accept as it would present him with the opportunity to demonstrate his peacable intentions to the new administration while a refusal might have been misinterpreted. His wife Mary would also have urged him to accept. It would provide the family with a badly-needed sense of security and finally remove the threat of sudden arrest; they would feel protected from the crudities of a legal system which had dogged them since their arrival in the colony. Mary Dwyer would no longer have to flinch at the sight of a military uniform. And there was also the economic advantage of being victualled from government stores although the salary of a constable at this time remained illusory.[10] On the debit side Michael Dwyer would have to justify his acceptance of the post to a number of his fellow-countrymen who still regarded him as "the Wicklow chief"; the singing of rebel songs at Clarke's in the Hawkesbury, or at Lynch's in the Rocks would not be feasible, at least in the short-term. The man who had steadfastly refused to wear the splendid military uniform provided by Robert Emmet in 1803 now found himself stoically donning the constable's blue coat with the red collar, taking charge of such intimidating weapons as a whistle and rattle and heading grimly in the direction of Irishtown.

Confirmation of Dwyer's newly-gained status soon became apparent when Governor Macquarie paid an official visit to the area around George's River, having decided to develop the various outlying settlements of the colony, and the inveterate diarist made the following entry:

FRIDAY 9TH: I had sent Mr. Meehan early in the morning to lay out the ground for the town of Liverpool, which deprived us of his services as a guide, and good honest Mr. [Thomas] Moore had never before explored that part of the country in which we had lost ourselves that morning. We must have rode at least twenty miles before breakfast. After resting ourselves and our horses for a couple of hours, I set out to explore the remaining farms in the Minto district and to look once more at the site of the intended town of Liverpool, leaving Mrs M. [Macquarie] to follow and meet me in the afternoon at Dwyer's farm along with Captain Antill; it being our intention to return again in the evening to Parramatta, and therefore, now took leave of

9. Reel 6038, pp.181,2,4. (AONSW)
10. *Ibid.*

your kind hostess Mrs Moore from where I set out with Mr. Moore etc. etc.,
at 1 o'clock crossing the river in the boat to meet our horses on the opposite
bank.

 We proceeded first to Liverpool, where having marked out the square for the
church etc. etc. I continued my tour to the adjoining farms belonging to Holt,
Burn [Byrne] Devlin etc. etc. , and ended up at Dwyer's where I found Mrs
M. [Macquarie] and Captain Antill waiting for us."[11]

The five Wicklow settlers received conditional pardons in July 1811 and were
also granted stock from the government herds. In his capacity of constable,
Michael Dwyer was given the use of a cottage in the newly-built town of
Liverpool, although he continued to live at his own home which was just one
mile away. But his worst fears were realised later in the year when a warrant
was issued to search the home of Arthur Devlin in connection with a charge
of larceny, and he was obliged to execute it.
    Joseph Marcus was a Jewish settler who lived on a farm about a half mile
from Devlin's. On 2 March 1811, he left for the town of Parramatta early in
the morning, but when he returned that night his farmhouse door had been
forced open and a large number of household items, including clothing, a
musket, flour, beef and six shillings in copper money had been stolen.[12] He
immediately reported the loss to local magistrate Thomas Moore and on the
following morning went to the home of his neighbour Arthur Devlin to
inform him of the robbery. In the course of his later evidence, Marcus would
state: "I have never harboured any bad opinion of him, but always thought he
was a friend of mine. I had no suspicion of him at all."
    Two days later, on 4 March 1811, Marcus again left for Parramatta early
in the morning and when he returned before five o clock the door of the
house and barn were again forced and 26 pounds of beef was missing, in
addition to a quantity of flour and a further number of household items. He
suspected another neighbour Thomas Handlestack of the theft and received a
warrant from magistrate Thomas Moore to search his house. He was accompanied by an unnamed constable [possibly Dwyer] but nothing was found. In
the course of his evidence in court Marcus would again state that "at this time
I did not suspect the prisoner [Devlin] nor hardly suspect him now."
    Marcus did not pursue the matter any further at the time, but six months
later, when he visited the new town of Liverpool to conduct some business
with magistrate Thomas Moore, constable Michael Dwyer and Thomas
Handlesack were also present. Handlestack was still smarting at the searching
of his house and had undertaken some investigations of his own. Marcus was

11. *Bigge Report*: Oral evidence – interview with D'Arcy Wentworth. Also HRNSW (1810)
     Police regulations, pp. 479-483.
12. Reel 2393 5/1146 p.447. Reel 2390 5/1120 pp.70-78. (AONSW)

shown a shawl, a jacket and a bedgown which looked similar to those which belonged to his "woman", but he could not be certain. Moore then advised Marcus to go along with Dwyer and Handlesack to search Devlin's house, and it transpired that "Dwyer had before this time got a search warrant, searched the prisoner's home and found the things there which he showed me."

The trio proceeded to Devlin's house, bringing with them the disputed garments. Arthur Devlin was not present and having found nothing they were about to leave when Priscilla Devlin followed Marcus and produced some of his stolen property, including a knife (which he positively identified) and which she offered to him on condition that he return the bedgown to her. Marcus agreed, but later that evening, "thinking that she was making a fool of me", had Arthur and Priscilla Devlin arrested and put in jail at Parramatta. He then went to Cowpastures, accompanied by constable Harry McCudden and acting on further information which had been given to him by Priscilla Devlin, accused his own Government servant John Neal, who had been assigned previously to Devlin, of carrying out the robbery. Neal denied the charge but, having received assurances that he would not be prosecuted if he told the truth, returned with them to Liverpool where Marcus again contacted constable Michael Dwyer. Neal then directed them to an area on Devlin's farm where the stolen musket was buried, Priscilla Devlin having also indicated its location. Neal subsequently informed the court that Marcus had expressed "a very strong desire at the time to hang Devlin and his wife" and that Priscilla Devlin had offered him a quantity of meal and wheat to take responsibility for the robbery, and he further claimed that Arthur Devlin had been responsible for burying the gun.

Priscilla Devlin had been released without charge before the trial took place but Neal also told the court that on 4 March 1811 (the day of the second robbery) he was working on stubble ground when Arthur Devlin asked him to stand guard outside Marcus's barn and to whistle or make noise if anyone approached. When Devlin emerged 15 minutes later he was carrying a bag over his shoulder and he later saw Devlin and his wife examining its contents in their kitchen, including women's clothing, a knife, and a cotton shirt which Devlin gave him in lieu of two of his own which had been burnt by accident. And he also claimed that Devlin had told him he had "done the Old Jew curse" because he had been cheated in some transaction involving Mary Ann Tree, the woman who was living with Marcus at the time, and who had been a frequent visitor to Devlin's house. At the conclusion of Neal's evidence Arthur Devlin accused him of acting out of spite, resulting from a dispute between them over wages, and that Neal had threatened to "bring an old house about his ears". Neal denied the charge but finally added that he had not seen the stolen articles being taken out of the sack by Devlin.

Michael Dwyer was called as a prosecution witness and he confirmed that, on foot of a warrant issued by Thomas Moore, he had searched Devlin's house with Thomas Handlesack, and found a woman's bedgown and a shawl which he later showed to Joseph Marcus who could not confirm their identity. And he concluded: "I was very careless of the search from the good opinion which I had of Devlin. I would not believe Neal on his oath." In the course of his evidence Thomas Handlesack said that his suspicions were aroused when he heard that Priscilla Devlin was wearing a bedgown "said to have been stolen from Marcus's barn", and that he had begun to investigate, although he did not believe that Devlin was the perpetrator, but might have purchased the stolen property in error. He confirmed that the bedgown had belonged to Mary Ann Tree, and that it had been given to her, not by Marcus, but by another man in Handlesacks's house, and had formerly been a pair of trousers! When he first went to Devlin's house his wife was wearing the ubiquituous bedgown, but on his return with a search warrant (which Dwyer read out) Priscilla Devlin was wearing a different bedgown. He found the missing article, however, hidden in a meat cask which contained a quarter of pork.

Magistrate Thomas Moore finally gave evidence that he had known Devlin for about 18 months "and always considered him to be a very honest man. I considered him as an industrious man. I do not consider that Neal is a man whose oath can safely be believed." This was a decisive intervention and Judge-Advocate Ellis Bent found Arthur Devlin not guilty and he was discharged. On this particular occasion, however, he could scarcely quibble at the verdict. Whatever the motivation behind the thefts was, there seems little doubt that Devlin was the prime mover and he was exceedingly fortunate to be able to return home to his wife and children.

But Hugh Byrne had not the same good fortune. Since his release in 1809 he had concentrated his energies on raising cattle and also looked after a herd of 80 cattle belonging to John Connell which "ran" with his own. In November 1812, however, he lost five of his own herd of 19 cattle as a result of a flash flood,[13] a devastating blow as the cost of purchasing replacements from the government at that particular time was set at £26 each. Shortly afterwards he happened to meet Limerick-born Patrick Moloney, a stockman with the government herd who suggested a cheaper alternative and the temptation to accept his offer must have been overwhelming. Hugh Byrne would later claim to have been deceived by Moloney, but the sequence of events, as outlined in the trial which followed, began on 26 December 1812 when James Parker, the overseer of the government stockyards in South Creek, and who had charge of 500 horned cattle, met James Moloney on the road near his home. They walked together for some time until they met Hugh Byrne who was accompanied by two other Irish stockmen, Richard Berry and John Mahony (Marney).

13. *Sydney Gazette*, November 1812.

The latter had been hunting for kangaroos with dogs and Parker invited all of them to dinner in his house which consisted of two wild ducks shot by Boyre, an Aboriginal boy who also joined them.

After dinner (according to the testimony of Parker) Hugh Byrne brought him outside "and asked me what I thought of that business". And when Parker professed ignorance Byrne told him that Moloney was "letting him have some cattle". It transpired that Mahony had already informed Parker, and that Mahony and Byrne had already looked at the government herd that morning and picked out two cows each. Byrne then inquired about the cost of the cows and Richard Berry, claiming to be the eldest, set the price at £10 each "and Byrne made answer that he would not offer less himself". They agreed to meet on the following Tuesday when the four cows were taken from the government herd and joined Byrne's. They then discussed payment and Byrne told them that he was going into Sydney on the following Thursday. Parker agreed to meet him there and, as they were parting "Moloney said he hoped he [Byrne] would act like a man, as to paying the money."

Parker arrived in Sydney on Thursday and met Hugh Byrne that night at Cribb's butcher shop as he was due to receive some money from the sale of a bullock which, in turn, he had bought from a Tom Bird in exchange for a heifer – a perfect example of the barter economy which still prevailed in the colony. Parker met him again on the following morning when he was on his way to financier Simeon Lord's house to borrow some additional money and Parker accompanied him there but remained outside. Shortly afterwards they went to Mrs Graham's inn, facing Pitt Row, and drank a pot of porter before Byrne paid him the £20 for the cows – and also insisted on paying for the drinks. Parker returned to Parramatta and divided the £20 between himself, Maloney and Berry.

All of this came to light in March 1813 when Patrick Moloney, Richard Berry and other individuals were brought to trial on a number of separate charges concerning the illegal sale of government cattle, on the information of James Parker, the main prosecution witness, who had turned informer to escape prosecution. The trial began on 8 March and continued by adjournments until 25 March, and by the time that Hugh Byrne's case was heard both Berry and Moloney had already been sentenced to death twice while Parker's evidence would again prove to be conclusive. Magistrate William Cox gave evidence that he had examined the prisoners and gave details of Mahony's version of the transaction to the effect that Byrne had received the four cows from Parker, but that he had no money to pay for them. He also explained that the cattle had been turned out on the road following the prisoners' arrest and before constables from Parramatta were sent to look for them. Cox was then questioned by Hugh Byrne as to the admissibility of a written statement signed by Mahony which was not read back to him and which he had repudiated on the following day.

As the four cows had been found wandering on the road by a constable over 12 miles from Byrne's property the case against him was circumstantial and the cows also lacked the distinguishing government mark or brand which had supposedly worn off. Parker's evidence to the effect that he could recognise each cow in the herd individually was not convincing while John Moffat, an assigned servant, gave evidence that he had been in charge of Byrne's and Connell's cattle since Christmas and that Hugh Byrne could not have met Parker without his knowledge. Thomas Moxam finally told the court that he had shingled Byrne's house during the first week of January and that Hugh Byrne had been present all of the time, assisting him with the work. But the verdict of Judge-Advocate Ellis Bent was quite specific, namely that "Richard Berry, Patrick Maloney, Hugh Byrne and John Mahony guilty, be severally hanged by their necks until they are severally dead."

Within a few days, however, Hugh Byrne had been granted a reprieve by Governor Macquarie: "And whereas on account of some favourable circumstances in mitigation of his offence I am induced to extend grace and mercy unto him and to grant unto him a pardon for the said crime on the sole and express condition that he shall continue to reside as a convict in the said territory of New South Wales during the term of his natural life and to be kept at hard labour . . . which pardon shall be null and void if the said Hugh Byrne be ever found at large out of this territory or its dependancies contrary to the the express tenor, meaning and conditions thereof."[14] Secretary J.T. Campbell added a brief explanatory note at the side of the document, to the effect that Hugh Byrne had arrived under sentence of transportation on the *Tellicherry* in 1806, that he had been tried at Dublin [untrue], and that he had been granted a conditional pardon in July 1811. Within a few weeks, Hugh Byrne was on his way back to the penal settlement of Newcastle to begin serving a life sentence with hard labour. He was also accompanied by Patrick Moloney and James Mahony both of whom had also been reprieved on the same conditions. For the second time in five years Sarah Byrne, who was expecting her seventh child, was left to cope without her husband and to rear her family, the eldest of whom was still only 13 years old. And once again the prospect of an early release for him seemed remote.

---

14. Reel 6070 6/7020 No.19 (AONSW)

CHAPTER NINE

1813-1825

A subscription list for building a courthouse in Sydney was published in July 1813 which included the names of Michael Dwyer, John Mernagh, Arthur Devlin and Sarah Byrne (in the absence of her husband), all of whom pledged the sum of £1 sterling to the fund. It was further proof, if needed, of their commitment to the development of the colony, although none of them could scarcely afford even such a relatively small amount. The omission of Martin Burke from the list might be explained by the fact that he had leased a tavern in Sydney, having sold his farm at Cabramatta in December 1812 for £190 sterling to Bernard Burn, Pitt St. Sydney, a native of Co. Roscommon who had come out on the *Minerva*.[1] Although Martin Burke had worked in a brewery in Rathdrum before the outbreak of the 1798 rebellion the impetus for the leasing of a tavern in Sydney probably came from Phoebe Tunstall who had previously worked in a shop there. In March 1813, Burke took over the lease of the "Hope and Anchor", 74, Pitt St. for the sum of £75 sterling[2] from James Cullen who had also come out on the *Minerva*. The move away from Cabramatta by the Wicklowmen had begun.

Michael Dwyer continued to make solid economic progress and was soon appointed as poundkeeper in Liverpool, in addition to his post as constable. But his main interest continued to be farming and in October 1813 he borrowed £70 from Thomas Moore to purchase a mare.[3] He also reputedly joined forces with John Mernagh and James Sheedy to rear and sell cattle, the latter having helped to look after George Johnston's estate while he attended the court-martial in London in connection with Bligh's overthrow. He was found guilty but allowed to return to the colony as a civilian, as was William Minchin, and they both concentrated on running their estates. There followed a very harsh period for the farming community in the colony as the usual March rains failed to materialise in 1813 and by August the situation had become desperate. But the dry spell continued and by October more than 500 sheep and 1,000 cattle had died. There was also a shortage of grain and Macquarie was forced to write to the Governor of Bengal for emergency supplies. And the economic situation was not helped by the action of some

---

1.   Land Titles Office No 858.
2.   *Ibid.*, No. 985.. p.224.
3.   *Ibid.*, No. 135, p.281.

speculators who began to hoard their remaining stocks of grain in anticipation of a steep rise in prices. The drought persisted in 1814, with the result that many of the smaller landholders were forced out of business while some of their assigned servants turned to bushranging in preference to reverting to the discipline and drudgery of the government work gangs. It became increasingly dangerous to travel the roads of the colony, particularly at night, and the *Sydney Gazette* warned its readers to travel always in groups so that they could defend themselves more easily. The whole landscape became parched; springs and rivers had run dry and there was no relief until 1815 when the rains finally came.

During this period Hugh Byrne remained as a prisoner for life at Newcastle penal settlement, his petition seeking a reprieve having been rejected by Governor Macquarie in April 1814. It had been forwarded to Sydney by Lieut. Thorpe, the Commander of Newcastle, and the note of rejection included the phrase "lately punished by you."[4] And Hugh Byrne was in trouble again in November 1815 when the monthly list of punishments at Newcastle included a sentence of 50 lashes which had been administered to him for the curious offence of "acting as a constable and principal in a robbery." In the meantime, his wife Sarah had to cope with the worst of the period of drought and, perhaps, forced by debt, applied for a grant of land in the newly-developed area of Airds to the south of Cabramatta, the allotments for which had been measured by James Meehan in 1811. She received a grant of 70 acres beside the Bow Bowing brook in June 1816, but news of this development, and of the proposed sale of the farm at Cabramatta, did not obviously please her husband in Newcastle who gave a notice to a returning convict Myles Leary in September, with instructions that it should be inserted in the *Sydney Gazette*: "The public are hereby cautioned against purchasing a farm of any description, or anything appertaining to within, from Sarah Byrne, without first obtaining the permission of Myles Leary or Michael Dwyer at Liverpool who are appointed agents by the undersigned, Hugh Byrne."[5] And to add to the confusion, Sarah Byrne is believed to have given birth to a daughter, Sarah, in 1816 which meant, if the date is correct, that the child was illegitimate.

The sale of the Byrne farm did not take place at this time, but further correspondence probably took place between Hugh and Sarah Byrne (with Michael Dwyer acting as mediator) after which a further notice appeared at the end of May 1817: "To be sold by private contract, 100 acres of land of the township of Liverpool, 40 acres of which are cleared and neatly fenced, with a neat and commodious dwelling house thereon, having three good rooms, a

4.   Fiche 3213, 4/1864 p.54-54g (AONSW)
5.   *Sydney Gazette*, 14 September 1816.

barn, an excellent peach orchard and a creek of good water, on the east side of Hosking's farm [Devlin's] and in front of Cabramatta Creek, and lies on the borders of 3,000 acres of beautiful common pasture, the whole of which is rented for £30 per annum. Half of the purchase price will be taken in horned cattle. Apply to Hugh Byrne, Airds."[6] The farm was bought by John Hosking, who operated a Methodist school, having been brought to the colony by the Rev. Samuel Marsden. And shortly afterwards, Hosking signed a deed poll in which he agreed to sell 50 acres of land to Hugh Byrne.[7] These transactions took place while Hugh Byrne was still at Newcastle, but in September J.T. Campbell wrote to Captain Wallis, the new commandant of Newcastle, concerning the shipment of a batch of prisoners on the Lady Nelson, and the final paragraph of the letter read: "The Governor is pleased to direct that you permit Hugh Byrne, now a convict with sentence of life, and at this time at Newcastle, to proceed hither for a period of two months in order to his arranging some family concerns."[8] However strained relations might have been between Sarah and Hugh Byrne, his return home after an absence of four and a half years was surely an occasion of joy for the whole family which was heightened when his ticket of leave was extended indefinitely. In December, William Chawker purchased 50 acres of land which the Byrnes owned at Bringelly,[9] and to complete the land deals undertaken by the family, as they moved permanently from Cabramatta to the district of Airds, Michael Byrne, having reached the prescribed age of 17, applied to Macquarie for his grant entitlement of 50 acres.[10]

Arthur Devlin had also sold his farm at Cabramatta to John Hosking in January 1817[11] and settled instead with his growing family at Ryde where he had received a separate grant. He continued to make a living from the rearing of cattle and his name appeared on a nunber of occasions as supplying meat to the government stores.[12] John Mernagh also suffered from the effects of the drought and was forced to mortgage his farm on the suit of Darby Murray, one of the *Tellicherry* transportees, to whom he owed £30.[13] In May 1817, the newly-established Bank of New South Wales also lent him £25, the sum to be repaid within two years. But John Mernagh was unable to redeem the mortgage and his farm was cheaply forfeited. Ironically, his name appears as the second depositor with the Bank while Darby Murray is next on the list.[14]

---

6.   *Ibid.*, 24 May 1817.
7.   Land Titles Office, Book B, No.514.
8.   Reel 6005 4/3495 p.500 (AONSW)
9.   Land Titles Office, Book B. No.615.
10. Fiche 3042. 4/1828. No.37 (AONSW)
11. Land Titles Office.Book B.No. 605.
12. Reel 6031 4/7028 A p.33; Reel 6038 s2759 p.213 (AONSW)
13. Land Titles Office. Book A, No.135, p.265.

Mernagh then concentrated for a number of years on renting various landholdings on which he reared cattle He was in possession of 550 acres in both 1818 and 1819 but this figure had shrunk to 50 acres in 1822.[15]

Apart from the effects of the drought and their bad fortune, the Wicklowmen had always suffered from an initial lack of capital. This indeed was a common complaint among the vast majority of the smaller landholders whose plight was well summed up in the report of J.T. Bigge, the English government official who had been sent out to inquire into the state of the colony, and who analysed the failure of the class of emancipated convicts who became farmers: "They constitute the middle and lower orders of settlers in the colony and having began with very limited means, they have been obliged solely upon the produce of the land. . . . Many of the original grantees are now either reduced to a state of dependance upon their creditors, or are seeking for opportunities for redeeming themselves by removing to more productive tracts near the rivers Nepean and Hawkesbury."

Martin Burke, however, decided to try his hand again at farming in 1817 when he leased 500 acres of land at Bringelly, to the west of Cabramatta, from explorer John Oxley at a fee of £30 per annum. His decision may have been taken because of a falling off in profits at the "Hope and Anchor" tavern resulting from keen competition in the area of Pitt St, but Phoebe Tunstall remained as licensee, in the short term at least. Bringelly was then a notorious hiding place for bushrangers, and D'Arcy Wentworth, a large landholder in the area, in addition to being Chief of Police, persuaded Martin Burke to take up an appointment as constable there. Burke would later be accused of not having arrested a single bushranger but the post, at least, provided him with a modest income and free rations. By 1820, however, he was unable to pay the arrears on his lease and was sued by Oxley for the sum of £90.[16] Burke acknowledged the debt in court and was ordered to pay the balance of £50, together with interest and costs before October 1821, but once again he had to default and 30 acres of land which he had bought in the area of Pittswater was confiscated and sold for £36 to cover part of the debt. On the advice of surveyor James Meehan he had been among a number of settlers who had applied for land grants in 1813 when a peninsula to the north of Sydney at Broken Bay – and which separated Pittwater from the ocean – was about to be developed. He received a grant of 50 acres and later bought an additional 30 from fellow-Irishman James McNally. But the titles for the grants were not registered until 1821 and the area remained undeveloped. In April of that year

---

14. The page containing the signatures of John Mernagh and Darby Murray is reproduced in *Australia: The Pioneer Years* by R.M. Younger.

15. Mayberry Mss.

16. Judgement Book No. 2 (1817-1828) 9/922 No. 476 (AONSW)

James Meehan drew up his land holding again and Martin Burke moved there permanently, having resigned his post as constable, and bringing with him Phoebe Tunstall and her two daughters.[17] D'Arcy Wentworth had bought a 700 acre holding at Pittwater from Robert Campbell, the original grantee, and in July 1822 it was advertised for letting. Despite his recent failure with the Oxley farm, Burke leased the entire holding, having sold his own grant of £35 and was also appointed as a local constable by Wentworth. Taking on such a large holding again appeared to be a brave (or foolhardy) move, but it proved to work out satisfactorily and he entered into the most rewarding and stable part of his life.

By the beginning of 1819 Michael Dwyer was the only one of the five Wicklowmen still living at Cabramatta and it seemed, on paper at least, that he was the most successful as reports showed that he had increased his landholdings while he was tendering regularly for the supply of fresh meat to government stores. In June 1819 he attempted to expand in a different direction when he paid an obviously hard-pressed Timothy Laughlin of Liverpool the sum of £40 for "all the goods, household stuff and implements of a household", and also for his boat which was lying at Liverpool wharf. And Laughlin further agreed to "continue to labour in the employ of the said Michael Dwyer and ply up and down George's River from Liverpool Wharf to Botany Bay . . . to bring shell lime within the Bay and deliver the same at the lime wharf at Liverpool for the sum of four pence per bushel as delivered to me at the kill [kiln]".[18] And in the following year Dwyer received payments for supplying lime to a number of government buildings in the area.

Dwyer was named as one of the largest emancipated landholders in the Liverpool area, according to the commission of enquiry carried by out by J.T. Bigge, with an acreage of 620 acres, of which 200 acres were cleared.[19] While later events would put these figures into some dispute, he signed articles of agreement in March 1820 with Andrew White, a neighbouring farmer, to purchase 200 acres of land for £50,[20] but whereas comparable landholders in the area were heavily stocked with cattle and sheep, Dwyer's livestock consisted only of 120 pigs while his attempt to breed horses seemed to have failed. In May 1820 he was appointed as Chief Constable of Liverpool, although having charge of just three constables, and he continued to live at his farm outside the town which was a source of continuing disquiet among the population.

17. Little is known of Phoebe Tunstall's second daughter whose father was presumably John Butler whom she married in 1808.
18. Land Titles Office. Book C.No.41.
19. Bigge Appendix. Bonwick Transcripts. Box 25. cy 1298.
20. Land Titles Office. Book C No.276.

Despite his move to a new holding in Ryde, Arthur Devlin still had not achieved economic viability. His sixth child Martha was born in 1819, but he was in trouble with the law again in the following year when an order was issued by the Court of Magistrates in Liverpool: "Whereas Arthur Devlin of the district of Botany Bay stands charged with felony, these are to charge all constables and others to apprehend and lodge the same Arthur Devlin in one of His Majesties gaols, and all persons are directed not to harbour the same Arthur Devlin upon the pain of prosecution, to the utmost rigour of the law." Devlin had originally received bail, but when he went missing Dwyer was again placed in the embarrassing position of having to organise the search for him. A preliminary hearing had taken place in late July in Liverpool court, chaired by magistrate Thomas Moore, at which Devlin was charged with theft, and the case was referred onwards to the Court of Criminal Jurisdiction in Sydney.[21] Following the usual pattern the case was brought forward on the evidence of an informer, on this occasion a Thomas Hoosam, alias Cunningham who also implicated George Stevens, a small landholder who was named as Devlin's accomplice. It was alleged that early in the morning of 1 January 1820, Devlin and Stevens had stolen a cow from the herd of George Johnston which they immediately shot dead near the Old Canterbury Road, close to Four Mile Bush, and removed the carcase, hidden under straw, in Steven's horse and cart. James Bryan (O'Brien) was also charged with complicity, the implication being that they were part of a gang trading in stolen meat. Patrick Doncey was also named as an accomplice and it was stated that, on his return from Newcastle penal settlement, having originally been sentenced to death in Sydney, he "became a companion of Devlin's and has pursued that service under his apprehension."[22]

But Arthur Devlin was never brought to trial, having died in unexplained circumstances in the latter part of 1820 – one report suggests that he was killed by a falling tree. He was aged about 40 and was buried in Botany Bay cemetery. His wife Priscilla was left in straitened circumstances, with six young children to rear, the eldest being just 13 years old. She transferred her late husband's beer license to her own name, but was still unable to make a living and applied to have two of her daughters accepted into the orphanage at Parramatta. Her request was initially turned down, but they were accepted a few months later, and in the following year she married Thomas Small, publican, farmer and timber merchant, and they settled also in the area of Ryde where she reared a second large family.

The trial of George Stevens went ahead in Sydney in November 1820 when the charge read that he "with force and arms at Liverpool, assisted and

---

21.   Reel 6023, x 920, p.291. Court of Criminal Jurisdiction Papers Nov-Dec 1820 SZ 792.pp
      564-565. Case papers COD 542c. Nov-Dec 1820 (AONSW)
22.   Fiche 3052, 4/1753, pp.117, 119 (AONSW)

aided Arthur Devlin, since deceased, to steal, take and carry away one cow of the price of five pounds of George Johnston on 1 January, two hundred weight of beef, value 50 shillings, part of the carcass of same." And in the course of a deposition Thomas Moore stated "as Devlin has departed this life I have curtailed and extracted such evidence as I consider were useless, but either of the charges suffice to convict him." William Bowen gave evidence in August that he had lodged at Steven's house and overheard him say to his wife and another person "that Devlin was away and that he was very sorry for it, and that it would be a bad job for him when Devlin was taken as he was the man who supplied him with the means for which he was out from bail, and that if he knew where he was he would come and assist him." And another local settler, William Ikin, told the court that Stevens had delivered a load of timber to his house at the time of the robbery and asked for straw (which was used to conceal the carcase) and which he delivered to Devlin's house. George Stevens was found guilty and sentenced to transportation for life to Newcastle. The evidence also referred to a number of live cattle in Devlin's yard which may also have been stolen from George Johnston's herd. It was a sad end to the chequered career of Arthur Devlin and it would be left to his descendants to make their mark in the colony.

About the same time, a similar trial was taking place which involved Denis Molloy, a close friend of both James Sheedy and John Mernagh, and who was also known to Michael Dwyer, although none of the latter three were implicated. On 15 June 1820, Molloy was charged with the theft of five cattle from the herds of Thomas Palmer, Col. Maurice O'Connell (29) and D'Arcy Wentworth – even the chief of police did not escape the depradations of the cattle rustlers. He was further accused of selling the cattle to Francis McGowran, who was described as the agent of a gang which included David Bell, Annesley McGrath and George Crawford who were, likewise, charged with the theft of cattle, heifers and a black mare. The five were found guilty and sentenced to death and, on 25 August, Molloy was hanged in Sydney along with James Ruse and Thomas Ford (alias Ward). It was reported that the latter two had confessed their guilt on the scaffold but that Molloy had remained silent. After his death Molloy's two children were reputedly looked after by John Mernagh and Mary Johnson (and in the short term by Michael and Mary Dwyer) but there appears to be no factual basis to the theory that their youngest daughter Eliza was one of Molloy's children.

The death sentence passed on Molloy seemed to have triggered off a sustained bout of drinking by Michael Dwyer, and matters came to a head less than two months later, in October 1820, when Thomas Moore, the local Liverpool magistrate, asked him to resign his post as Chief Constable. Dwyer angrily refused and asked Moore "if there was any crime against him to bring forward".[23] But Moore persisted and Dwyer was summoned to appear before the Magistrates Court in Liverpool, charged with being an unfit person to remain in the post of Chief Constable, owing to appearing in a drunken state in public. The charge was heard by magistrates William Redfern and Richard Brook and took place in Liverpool Courthouse. As usual, there was no short-age of witnesses willing to testify, and William Klensendorlffe, owner of the local Elephant and Castle Inn, claimed that Dwyer had told him that Thomas Moore had refused to lend him money because he was not a horse dealer. Having unburdened himself of that piece of irrelevant information he contin-ued: "I have seen Mr. Dwyer so beastly intoxicated on the day of Tuesday the 29th of August last that he was obliged to be taken away from my door in a cart, being totally incapable of walking unprotected."[24] He further claimed to have seen Dwyer repeatedly drunk during that period and that, earlier in the year, he had been in the company "of Denis Molloy, Higgins and other very improper people derogatory to his official situation as chief constable, particu-larly on Saturday the 29th of April, when Molloy, himself and others were drinking and singing until near nine o clock, for which payment Mr. Dwyer became responsible." And Klensendorlffe further claimed that Dywer was so drunk on another occasion that he lost some official letters which he was supposed to distribute. He was finally cross-examined by the Bench concern-ing a remark which Dwyer reportedly had made, namely that he had been "robbed by Mr. Moore in the payment of £5-7s-6d."

John Cutler, a schoolmaster in Liverpool, confirmed that Dwyer had been taken home in a cart from Klensendorlffe's Inn and that he had seen him sitting on the ground in a drunken state in mid-September, while Richard Guise added that he was sometimes led home by constables Bradley and Morgan, and that whenever Dwyer was in the company of Molloy and others they generally went into the parlour by themselves. These meetings had occurred shortly before Molloy's arrest and, no doubt gave rise to infinite speculation. Cutler also specified a number of instances when Dwyer was drunk, adding that Mary Dwyer, and McNally the watchman, occasionally had to lead him home and that he had never known Dwyer to attend the military camp in the evenings, apart from one occasion on a Sunday evening when he ordered the constables to arrest anyone who had not obeyed the curfew.

Constable Bradley was questioned by the Bench concerning the witholding by Dwyer of part of a sum of money owed to him for the sale of cedar, and the next witness was Andrew White, whose neighbourly act of ferrying Dwyer home in his cart had not been appreciated by his wife Mary who blamed him for making her husband drunk and shut the door in his face. Dwyer had apparently drank five glasses of spirits at the barracks on that night, before arriving at Klensendorlffe's, but White attempted to defend Dwyer by claiming that he was able to walk into his house unaided and that he was always capable of riding a horse or of walking home after a visit to an inn. The next witness was Elizabeth Neal who repeated much of White's evidence while Klensendorlffe's wife Elizabeth proved to be much more circumspect than her husband in describing Dwyer's drinking habits.

Dwyer then asked Thomas Moore if he had ever seen him so intoxicated that he was unable to carry out his duties and Moore replied that he had seen him in "that state you ought not to be in." Complaints by the inhabitants of Liverpool concerning Dwyer residing outside the town were also raised and, in the course of addressing the Bench, Dwyer denied ever having been drunk while on duty, the sole exception being the occasion when he was taken home in Andrew White's cart. But he claimed that there had been mitigating circumstances as he was suffering from a cold. He finally referred to the withholding of proceeds from the sale of the cedar, claiming that it had been his intention to give the balance of two pounds to the constables, although the money belonged to himself.

The two magistrates quickly reached a decision that "having minutely examined the evidence in support of the charges brought forward by Thomas Moore on the complaints of the inhabitants of Liverpool, we are of the opinion that Mr Dwyer, from his unfortunate propensity to drunkenness, and his not residing in the town, is an unfit person to fill the situation of Chief Constable in the town of Liverpool." And a week later an official notice emanated from the civil department in Sydney which referred to his dismissal "in consequence of irregular and improper conduct." Apart from his drunken behaviour, it could be deduced from the evidence that Dwyer was not very diligent in carrying out his duties, but the main question to arise, and which went unanswered, concerned his exact relationship with Molloy, whether their meetings at the Elephant and Castle were purely social occasions. And why had Molloy's execution had such an adverse effect on him?

Dwyer was so incensed at the manner of his dismissal that he made an official complaint to J.T. Bigge who was proving to be more than willing to give credence to each gripe, however far-fetched from every malcontent in the colony. Bigge instructed his secretary to obtain the depositions attaching to the trial but the verdict was not reversed and William Ikin, the settler who had given evidence in the Devlin trial, was appointed as the new Chief Constable of Liverpool. According to Dwyer, however, Bigge assured him that "he would not forget him on his arrival in England" but the only tangible result of his complaint was the inclusion of a transcript of the Liverpool Courthouse hearing in the index of Bigge's enquiry report.

One factor to emerge from the trial was Dwyer's lack of finance, and a more tangible example occurred in December 1820 when he was brought before a governor's court on the suit of William Davis for a debt amounting to £16. The bringing of the case was surprising as Davis, the former blacksmith from Co. Laois, and a successful farmer and business man in Sydney, was one of the foremost agitators for the official sanctioning of Catholic clergy in the colony and secretly founded the Council for the Protection of the Blessed Sacrament, in conjunction with Dwyer, Hugh Byrne, John Lacey and stone mason James Dempsey. The debt was incurred "for goods sold and delivered by the deponent to the said Michael Dwyer at his request" and Davis was awarded a total of £30.[25]

Pressure for the official sanction of Catholic clergy to administer in the colony had been renewed following the unauthorised arrival of the maverick Irish Trappist priest Fr Jeremiah O'Flynn who reached Van Diemen's Land on board the *Duke of Wellington* in 1817, despite having been refused permission by the Colonial Office in London. When he arrived in Sydney he was given a frosty reception by Governor Macquarie and when O'Flynn asked him to recognise the fact that there were a very large number of Catholics living in the colony, without the benefit of a priest, Macquarie jocosely replied that he wanted to make them all Protestants while his secretary J.T. Campbell added that one religion was sufficient for any State and that he realised only too well the consequences of the differences of religions for 20 years in Ireland – Protestants knocking the brains out of Catholics, and Catholics knocking the brains out of Protestants and all, supposedly, for the pure love of God. Macquarie decided to deport O'Flynn immediately and, showing the same degree of prejudice as his predecessors, even expressed the fear that some of the Irish convicts "might be worked upon by a designing priest, so as to excite a spirit of resistance."

But O'Flynn's flouting of officialdom was not in vain and further petitions were sent to London to sanction the appointment of Catholic clergy. Dr Edward Slater had been appointed by the clerical authorities in Rome as Vicar-Apostolic for the vast region which stretched from the Pacific to the Cape of Good Hope and he travelled to Ireland in search of priests willing to volunteer for service in New South Wales. Fr O'Flynn, on his return, also kept up the pressure and, having met with Fr John Joseph Therry, a young Cork priest, mentioned his name to Dr Slater who wrote to him and Fr Therry readily accepted his proposal. Fr Richard Connolly, a native of the North of Ireland who was working in Co. Kildare, also volunteered and their applications were vetted in London by the Prince Regent and the Earl of Bathurst before official permission was sanctioned, an annual stipend of £100 each being granted to them.

They duly arrived on board the convict ship *Janus* in May 1819, but were initially tolerated rather than encouraged by the authorities. This attitude caused some of the leading Catholics in the colony, including Michael Dwyer, to petition J.T. Bigge in May 1820 seeking "free admission to the blessings

---

25. Land Titles Office. Book D. No.120.

and benefits of our religion and our clergy . . . we want no more than to participate in religious liberty which our Protestant colonists so happily and freely enjoy".[26] Macquarie had issued detailed instructions to Frs. Therry and Connolly as to how they should proceed regarding the celebration of Mass, the keeping of a parish register and the quarterly return of marriages. They were forbidden to conduct mixed marriages between Catholics and Protestants, or to make converts from members of other religious persuasions. And although Macquarie insisted that "you will ever find me to advocate and support the religious beliefs of your flocks", Fr Therry found an unlikely ally in the person of J.T. Bigge, to whom he complained of the prevailing unhelpful official attitude towards him, and bewailed his departure, claiming that his difficulties would increase "when I shall have no longer a powerful and beneficent protector to look upon."[27]

Both the Dwyer and Byrne families became friendly with Fr Therry from the outset and Mary Dwyer, along with her children, Bridget, James and Eliza, acted as sponsors at a number of baptisms when he visited Liverpool in 1821. These included a number of Aboriginal children as Fr Therry's register for 27 January shows:

> John, of Limabunna and Murragarva – Sponsor: Mary Dwyer
> John Chrysostom, of Ghendel and Boogandoo – Sponsor: Bridget Dwyer
> Elizabeth, of Coaman and Nelly Oulougga – Sponsor: Eliza Dwyer
> Christiana, of Ardengaul and Cawan – Sponsor Bridget Dwyer.
> Agnes, of Byan and Sally – Sponsor: Mary Dwyer.[28]

The first fund-raising meeting to build a Catholic chapel in Sydney was chaired by Fr Connolly and a committee was formed, with James Meehan acting as chairman, while the surprise choice of treasurer was J.T. Campbell (perhaps wearing his Bank of New South Wales hat). Contributions were also received from a cross-section of the Protestant population, including a donation of £20 from Macquarie who agreed to lay the foundation stone and who observed that it was an unusual ceremony for an old Freemason to undertake. An initial list of subscribers was published in November 1821 (and updated in May 1822) which included: "Michael Dwyer £10, Mrs Mary Dwyer £1, James Dwyer £1, Bridget Dwyer £1, Eliza Dwyer £1; Hugh Byrne, Airds £5, Sarah Byrne £1, Anne Byrne 10s., Catherine Byrne 10s.; Martin Burke £1, Phoebe Tunstall £1."

---

26. Bigge Appendix Vol. 127 (3935-3943).
27. Bigge Appendix, Bonwick Transcripts. Box 27.
28. Bigge Appendix. (Vol.138) Fr. Therry's register of baptisms and funerals 1821.

The ability of Michael Dwyer to contribute so generously to the fund could be attributed to the fact that he had been granted a license to open an inn at his home in Liverpool. Ownership of inns had proved to be financially rewarding to a number of emancipated Irish convicts,[29] and the name that Dwyer chose was the Harrow Inn, an attempt perhaps to exorcise the memory of his stint as constable, and in memory of a decisive victory achieved by the Wexford rebels in 1798. In order to provide the requisite sleeping accommodation, the house was extended to ten rooms and he proceeded to borrow the hefty sum of £1800 from Sydney financier Daniel Cooper and a further £300 in October 1821 from Robert Campbell the Younger, the latter debt being liable for repayment after two months. And he also purchased a number of cattle, horses and rams to boost his livestock numbers. Given his personal reputation, and the large Irish population in the area, it should have been a profitable venture, but there were ominous signs from the outset. James Sheedy, who was present at the opening of the Harrow Inn, recorded that Dwyer, having ceremonially opened the front door, in an extravagant gesture, took the key in his hand, walked to a nearby well and threw it in while declaring that the door of the inn would never be closed again. The resulting cheers, no doubt, could be heard a mile away in the town of Liverpool, and the Harrow Inn was soon described, with very good reason, as being the liveliest in the colony. All of this should have augured even more for its financial success, but it also became known that anyone who was short of money was not pressed to pay for either drink or lodgings, and with 15 year old James Dwyer and 14 year old Bridget helping their mother to cope, and with the proprietor being one of its best customers, the ghost of constable Dwyer may have been well and truly laid to rest, but the financial consequences of such bad management would surely follow.

Michael Dwyer, nevertheless, felt confident enough about the success of the Harrow Inn to present an official memorial in 1822 for the renewal of his license for a further twelve months:

> That your memorialist is the proprietor and occupier of the Harrow Inn, near Liverpool, on which has been lately expending considerable sums of money to render it commodious for the reception of travellers. That your Memorialist is induced to hope that his conduct during the term of his former license has been such that his Worshipful Bench will grant him a license to sell spirituous liquors for the ensuing year.[30]

---

29. Successful Irish innkeepers of the period included Andrew Doyle, "Lord Nelson"; Farrell Cuffe, "Macquarie Inn"; Patrick Cullen, "Ships Fame" and Hugh Kelly, "Halfway House (between Parramatta and Windsor).
30. A. 765, cy 727, p.189 (Mitchel Library).

He was granted the renewal in March 1822, but already the unravelling of his complex financial affairs was beginning. In May, a notice appeared advertising for sale the farm he had bought from Andrew White while in June he sold a 50 acre grant which he had taken only in the previous year, to John Lake, a local farmer in the district of Cabramatta.[31] In August, his former neighbour Ann Stroud, the widow of Sgt. John Hawley Stroud, who had moved to Sydney following his death in 1813,[32] brought a legal action against him concerning the illegal renting of part of her land. A warrant was issued to Provost Marshal J.T. Campbell summoning Dwyer to appear before the Supreme Court of Civil Judicature to answer the complaint of John Doe, who was acting on the instructions of Ann Stroud. The charge originally was brought against Richard Roe for having ejected John Doe from Stroud's farm, and for the recovery of what was described as "four messauges, four barns, four stables, two orchards, and one hundred and sixty acres of arable land, one hundred and sixty acres of pasture, one hundred and sixty acres of furze and heath, and one hundred and sixty acres of wood, situated, lying and being in the district of Bankstown at Liverpool, and now in the possession of the said Michael Dwyer."[33]

It transpired that over a three-year period from 1819, Dwyer had illegally let the (admittedly) idle land for £30 a year, but that in May 1822 Ann Stroud had leased it to John Doe for a period of seven years. On the day after Doe had taken possession of the property, however, Richard Roe, acting on the instructions of Dwyer had, "with force and arms entered into the premises, and then and there ejected, drove out and removed him from his said farm, and hath kept out and still doth keep him out from his possession."[34] The charges against Roe, who was described as Dwyer's tenant, were subsequently dropped and he was released from prison, but the case against Dwyer continued until mid-December, and though he pleaded not guilty to the charges, damages amounting to £100 were awarded against him and John Doe regained possession of Ann Stroud's property.

The imposition of the fine was a further blow to Dwyer's financial standing and he suffered an even greater reverse at the same time when he was charged with "buying Government slops [clothes] and provisions from prisoners of the Crown."[35] The complainant was Bridget (Biddy) Garrigan who had come out from Ireland on the *John Bull* in 1819 and the hearing com-

---

31. Land Titles Office. Book D.No.53.
32. John Hawley Stroud died in 1811 and his widow Ann moved into Sydney. In 1813 she mortgaged her farm at Cabramatta (called Warwick Farm) and her house in Sydney (76, George's St.) for £40 sterling to Alexander Mitchell.
33. Supreme Court of Civil Judicature (9/909) 1817-1824.No.562 (AONSW)
34. *Ibid.*, No. 594.
35. Reel 6058 4/1769 p.p 40-40j (AONSW)

menced at Liverpool Court House before Justice Barron Field, Thomas Moore
and Henry C. Antill and continued by adjournments until 24 December.
William Ikin, the new Chief Constable of Liverpool stated that he had received information from Bridget (Biddy) Garrigan, a government servant
assigned to Dwyer, "that her master has on his premises Government sacks
and blankets, the property of the Crown." She further stated on oath that she
had been in the service of Dwyer for eight months and that "scarcely a week
has passed over my head but that her mistress, defendant's wife, has bought
either eatables or wearables and various other property from individuals who
all appeared from their dress to be prisoners of the crown."

She went on to claim that two assigned convicts, McPherson and Thomas
Bradley, brought quantities of flour and beef to the Harrow Inn for sale and
received no payment, apart from a supply of rum from Mary Dwyer, and that
a week before they were flogged for robbing the King's stores at Liverpool,
they had brought in two bags of flour. Bridget Garrigan also stated that
another assigned servant, Patrick Leary, had sold four government blankets to
Mary Dwyer and that he frequently brought in small quantities of flour and
meat which were paid for with rum. It was alleged that bed ticks, blankets
and frocks were also bartered. Mary Dwyer was not in court, and when
Bridget Garrigan was asked whether Michael Dwyer was aware of these
transactions she replied "not to my knowledge". And when pressed by the
court members she added "he was generally tipsy; and when sober, out on his
farm." Two bags of flour were next produced as evidence and Bridget Garrigan
further claimed that Mary Dwyer instructed her to hide some Government
blankets in a pond because she was afraid that a man called Fluskey, who was
then in custody, might give some information about them. And she finally
told the court that she had helped Mary Dwyer to remove red government
marks from 13 blankets.

Thomas Fluskey, a member of William Cordeaux's clearing gang, then
gave evidence that he had lodged at the Harrow Inn for a month while
working in the area and confirmed Bridget Garrigan's evidence concerning
the sale of meat and flour, but added that they were also paid for with tea,
sugar, tobacco and money, that the transactions usually took place on Satur-
days, and were generally made by members of Michael Ryan's clearing gang
and other prisoners who sold their rations.

Michael Dwyer then called Michael Lawler, another of his assigned servants, to give evidence on his behalf, and he told the court that Mary Dwyer
had bought blankets at Sydney Market three months before and denied having tried to persuade Bridget Garrigan from giving evidence. Dudley Hartigan,
a Liverpool constable (who was dismissed shortly afterwards) gave inconclu-
sive evidence that he was present in the Harrow Inn when Bradley and
McPherson brought in the bag of flour and had even helped to weigh it, but
the whole tenor of the case changed dramatically when Dwyer recalled Bridget

Garrigan and questioned her concerning her motives in bringing the case:

DWYER: Was you ever promised any reward to prosecute me or my wife?

GARRIGAN: Never in my life.

DWYER: Did you ever say you was?

GARRIGAN: As I did in fun to Billy Lynch.

DWYER: What was the contents of your joke?

GARRIGAN: Billy Lynch met me going home from the Court House, how could I do such a thing against Mr. Dwyer. I said perhaps I might get my liberty, and what do I care what anyone says about me.

DWYER: Who did you say was to get your liberty for you?

GARRIGAN: No-one at all. I mentioned no names.

COURT: Did you ever tell anybody else you were to get your liberty for swearing against Dwyer?

GARRIGAN: No.

COURT: If a thing of that kind had happened it could not escape your memory?

GARRIGAN: No.

DWYER: Did you ever conspire with any person previous, to come and swear against me?

GARRIGAN: Never.

COURT: Was it your own voluntary act to come forward as you have, or was you asked to do so by anybody?

GARRIGAN: It was my own voluntary act.

Dwyer next called Patrick Scott, an assigned servant of Patrick Garrigan, a Sydney victualler, and he stated that he had seen Patrick Fluskey and Bridget Garrigan together in his master's house, and that he overheard Fluskey "say to Biddy that anything she would say, he would swear to, for he had a good man William Ikin who would back him." This put a different perspective on the case as Bridget Garrigan had brought her complaint to Ikin.

Patrick Garrigan was sworn and told the court that "some time since, Bridget Garrigan was ordered to Sydney by the Rev. R. Connolly and came to his house, who said he was surprised at her coming down, for she knew perfectly well that Fr. Connolly was gone to the Southwards [Van Diemen's Land] and, at any rate, if he had been there he could do nothing for her, owing to the reports circulating against her." It transpired that Bridget Garrigan had become romantically involved with Thomas Fluskey while he was staying at the Harrow Inn and that she left in the middle of the night and came into Sydney without receiving the required pass from her mistress. Patrick Garrigan further claimed to have overheard Fluskey say to her: "You have come down without a pass, and you will be treated like I was, for they thought to send me to the Coal River, so whatever you swear against Mrs. Dwyer I will back." On the following morning Michael Dwyer had come into Sydney to look for her but matters were scarcely helped when he proceeded to hand her over to a constable and also wrote to William Ikin to do likewise if she was ever found in Liverpool again. Patrick Garrigan also stated that Mary Dwyer had temporarily left some blankets in his house which she said had been bought in Sydney market, some of which had black broad arrows on them, but he could not recall if there were any government marks on them.

Bridget Garrigan was recalled for a final time and denied having made a threat against Mary Dwyer or that William Ikin's name had been mentioned, and the members of the Bench "having maturely considered all the circumstances of the case adjudged Michael Dwyer guilty of having broken the Colonial Regulations in buying government property and do therefore fine him in the full penalty of £20 and costs – that his license be taken from him and the government property found on his premises to be given up to the Crown. Court House, Liverpool, 24 December 1822."

The verdict was a devastating blow to the Dwyer family on Christmas Eve and, in their defence, it should be noted that the system of barter was still widely used in the colony and that it was not unusual for assigned prisoners to exchange goods or rations for drink at week-ends. It is likely, however, that Mary Dwyer was not too particular as to the origin of some of the merchandise offered to her, but the case for the government, as presented in court, was faulty and depended on the testimony of an assigned servant with a grudge who had absconded from her service and who was hoping, by her own admission, to gain her freedom by bringing the charge. The fact that Dwyer was appearing before the courts on two other charges at the same time did little to help his cause; the mutual antipathy between himself and the sitting magistrate Thomas Moore may also have been a contributory factor while the attempt to accuse William Ikin, the new Chief Constable of Liverpool, of maliciously bringing the charge, also backfired.

While Michael Dwyer might have survived the imposition of the £20 fine, the cancellation of his spirit license proved to be the final blow which triggered a disastrous sequence of events. Even before the outcome of the trial Robert Campbell had made an application to the Court of Civil Judicature to obtain judgement against him for the sum of £300, "altho' often required did not repay or any part thereof" – or the additional £30 he had borrowed in September 1822.[36] The judgement having been granted, Dwyer managed a payment of just £80 and Campbell was back in court three days later before Justice Barron Fields who directed Provost Marshal J. T. Campbell that a further sum of £220 be levied against "the goods and chattels, lands and

---

36. Supreme Court of Civil Judicature (9/909) 1817-1824. No.593.

tenements of the said Michael Dwyer."[37] The floodgates were now open; Robert Cooper, his other main creditor, moved against him to recover the sum of £1,900, and with the damages awarded to Ann Stroud still outstanding he effectively declared himself bankrupt with the help of attorneys James Norton and Frederick Garling. His declaration was notified to the Government by Campbell, Cooper and Stroud, and on 9 January 1823, an official notice from the Provost General's office appeared in the *Sydney Gazette*:

> Campbell v Dwyer.
> Cooper v Dwyer.
> Stroud v Same.

> By virtue of several writs of Fieri Facia to me directed in the following cases, I will put up for sale by public auction at the places and times hereafter mentioned, the property of several defenders in said case. In these causes I will sell at the Market Place, Liverpool on Saturday January 25th, 64 head of horned cattle, 5 horses, 7 rams, 20 pigs, 1 cart, 1 chaise, 20 gallons of rum, 2 casks of wine, without household furniture and other property. Also a farm of land containing about three hundred acres, all fenced in, in nine paddocks, in possession of the defendant and situated about a mile from the town of Liverpool, with the erections therein, a good house and several outhouses, with a good garden attached, unless the several executions theron be previously discharged.

While the expenditure on the Harrow Inn accounted for the greater part of his debts, the notice also revealed the extent of his livestock numbers in comparison to the statistics included in the Bigge enquiry two years before when he was credited with neither sheep nor cattle. He approached Daniel Cooper, and with the mediation of Patrick Garrigan, attempted to arrive at a settlement which would allow him to retain some of his possessions. A separate notice appeared in the following two issues of the *Sydney Gazette* and which, paradoxically, appeared beside the original notice from the Provost Marshal's office:

> Liverpool – to be sold by private contract 100 acres of ground, more or less situated within a mile of Liverpool on which there is a neat dwelling place, barn stalls etc. There was been lately £1000 expended in improvements. The land is subdivided into nine paddocks and fenced in, and well watered in the driest season, it being bounded on the North by Cabramatta Creek, the same being too well-known to need any particular description, it having for some time being a licensed house and

---

37. *Ibid.*

would also answer for a private residence for a genteel family. The house contains twelve rooms. One, two or three hundred acres can be given if agreed upon. Also in the town of Liverpool eight allotments of ground with tenements thereof, known by Holt, Smith, Marquis Love, and Dwyer's allotments, the whole included with paling. Application to be made to Mr. Michael Dwyer, Liverpool, the present proprietor, or to Mr. Daniel Cooper and Mr. P. Garrigan, George's St., Sydney. Six months credit will be given for the dwelling house and the land attached there to, and cash for the town allotments.

Once again this notice illustrates the acquisitive or entrepreneurial nature of Dwyer, although one is tempted to speculate as to the exactness by which they were negotiated. And while the multiplicity of allotments (he also owned two in Sydney and another in Parramatta) might have indicated a source of hidden wealth, property values at the time were low, particularly in Liverpool, and leases were granted solely on condition of erecting dwellings on them. The office of Provost Marshal, however, was not impressed by the notice and went ahead with the scheduled sale of Dwyer's property at Cabramatta on 25 January 1823 when the buyer was Alexander McLeod from the Newcastle settlement. But the purchase price of £575 fell far short of the amount of his debts and a further notice appeared in the 30 January issue of the *Sydney Gazette*:

> On Friday February 14th, at my office in Hunter St, Sydney at 11am, all the right title and interest of the defendant Dwyer, of, in and to the several allotments thereafter mentioned all situated in the central part of the town of Liverpool, and known by the names and descriptions following viz. Dwyer's allotment – 6 1/2 acres, Morgan's allotment 11/2 acres – subdivided into four parts, Smith's allotment – 11/2 acres. Each of the above (except Dwyer's) being well-enclosed and having a dwelling house thereon, Love's allotment, with a brick house of two rooms, and one house with four rooms unfinished. [Also] fifty acres of land at Cabramatta, known by the name of Newman's Grant; thirty acres known in the name of Dove's Grant. And in the same causes I will sell on February 8th next, on defendant Dwyer's premises near Liverpool, his household furniture of all descriptions and the remainder of his stock in cattle unless the several executions thereon be previously discharged. J.T. Campbell, Provost Marshal.

There was a further delay as Alexander McLeod was unable to raise the money and the sale of the farm fell through. But Dwyer was allowed to remain in possession of his house and, although the remainder of his assets were sold off, the farm at Cabramatta was not put up for sale again until the end of July when a final notice was published in the *Sydney Gazette* listed as

Dwyer v Cooper. On 8 August, the farm was bought by John McQueen, Sydney for the much lower figure of £320 and he promptly resold it to John Ovens for £412. In December, Ovens, in turn, sold it to Thomas Moore, the biggest landholder in the area, and the magistrate who had brought the proceedings leading to Dwyer's dismissal as chief constable of Liverpool three years before. As Moore was more interested in the land, rather than the inn, Dwyer at least had the consolation of coming to an arrangement which enabled him to retain possession of his house. In the meantime, he sold a piece of ground in Bathhurst St, Sydney to victualler John Williams whose own premises bounded it, and in the following month another property, 2 Market St. to Patrick McHugh. In the latter indenture Dwyer was described as a labourer and living at that address which, if true, meant that he left his Liverpool home for a period.[38] At the end of July he also sold a 50 acre holding in Airds, to the Sydney stonemason and fellow-Catholic activist James Dempsey, but in that particular indenture he was again described as a Liverpool farmer.

Lachlan Macquarie's 11 year tenure as governor had now ended, having by his own admission laid the foundation of transforming the colony from a prison camp to a new country, but having failed in his attempt to integrate the emancipated convicts fully into the mainstream of life. His final battle on his return home would be to counter the charges made against him in Bigge's inquiry but his successor, Sir Thomas Brisbane, was also a reformer and he introduced an assisted passage scheme which enabled relatives of the colony's inhabitants to be brought out from Britain and Ireland. Despite their desperate circumstances, the Dwyers considered sending for the remainder of their children who were still in Dublin, but in the meantime, Michael Dwyer, whose resilience in the face of adversity could never be questioned, petitioned the new governor for a grant of land to enable him to support his family, and also to provide grazing for a small stock of horned cattle which he still had in his possession. He received a reply in February 1824 which stated "as soon as you obtain any stock, in proportion its amount, land will be allowed to you on the terms of a ticket of occupation."[39]

In November 1823, it was his own turn to seek redress from the courts when he brought an action against his former ally Patrick Garrigan claiming that he was "possessor of divers horses, mares and geldings – one horse valued £100, one mare valued £100, one gelding valued £100". It seemed that the horses were "casually lost" and came into the hands of Garrigan who refused to hand them back. Whether Dwyer owed money to Garrigan was not made clear or, indeed, why they had not been sold off to recover part of his

38. Fiche 3063 4/1834 B. No. 97 (AONSW)
39. Supreme Court of Civil Judicature (9/909) No. 593 (AONSW)

debts. Dwyer claimed £100 in damages from Garrigan but the case was
finally withdrawn in August 1824. The award of £100 damages to Ann Stroud,
however, was still outstanding. Provost Marshal J.T. Campbell had returned
(rather wearily) to the Supreme Court in February 1824 to state that "he
could not find any property whatever belonging to the said Michael Dwyer,
whereupon to levy the debt and costs."[40] But the corollary of this statement
was the following directive: "Whereupon we command that you take the said
Michael Dwyer, if he be found, and keep him safely so that you have his body
before the Supreme Court on Monday May 2nd to satisfy the said Ann
Stroud of the said £140-1s-4d. [including interest and costs], and by reason of
the non-performance of certain promises and undertakings made by the said
Michael Dwyer to the said Ann Stroud as to her costs."

He was duly consigned to the debtor's section of Sydney Jail, and in what
became similar to the situation which had arisen in Kilmainham Jail 20 years
before, he became involved in prisoners' complaints concerning living conditions and "the want of sufficient food". The complaints were forwarded to
the Chief Justice, and the private secretary to the governor instructed sheriff
John Mackaness to visit the jail "including the part assigned to prisoners for
debt, and whether a more convenient arrangement can be made for the safe
keeping of such persons in some other place of confinement as the gaol is too
limited a space and too crowded to allow a proper division of the several
classes of persons."[41]

Michael Dwyer became ill in November 1824 and wrote to Colonial
Secretary Frederick Goulburn "for an order to the principal surgeon to leave
me into the General Hospital."[42] He was received into hospital on the same
day by order of Surgeon Bowman but was returned to jail once again in the
early part of 1825. He still lacked then means of paying damages to Ann
Stroud and would have remained there but for availing of a recent regulation
which put the onus on those who committed debtors to prison to pay for their
upkeep. In May, he wrote to Chief Justice Forbes stating that he was unable
to maintain himself, and asked that an order be made for Ann Stroud to do
so. But she was unable, or unwilling, to comply and three weeks later he again
wrote to Justice Forbes:

> That petitioner lately received from Your Honour an order of mainte-
> nance which was duly served on the plaintiff, directing a weekly allowance
> of one Spanish dollar to be paid to your petitioner on, or before, two o
> clock on Monday the 23d. Plaintiff wholly unattended to and neglected
> Your Honour's order, and therefore your petitioner entreats Your Hon-

40. *Ibid,*.
41. Reel 6064 4/1788 p.132 (AONSW)

our will direct petitioner's liberation from gaol according to the usual custom in such cases, and petitioner will ever pray etc. etc.[42]

Michael Dwyer, Sydney, May 24th 1825.

For one final time he signed his name to an official document, but with a very shaky hand, and he was released from jail. For perhaps the first time in his life justice had rallied to his side but, ironically, when he appeared to be in the wrong. Michael Dwyer returned to his home in Cabramatta which he continued to hold on sufferance, and died there barely three months later, on Tuesday 23 August, at the early age of fifty three, surrounded by his grieving wife, his 18 year old son James and his two daughters, Bridget aged 17, and Eliza aged 13. Five days later he was buried without ceremony in the Irish burial grounds, his death certificate indicating that he had died from dysentry which was reckoned to be one of the two most prevalent causes of death at the time in New South Wales and which, for the most part, was "greatly exaggerated by the excessive use of spirituous liquors to which the mass of the colonists are unfortunately addicted." The Sydney Gazette reported his death in a single line: "Deaths: At Liverpool, Mr. Dwyer formerly Chief Constable." It was not the description he would have preferred.

Watering cattle on the Wollondilly River

42. Reel 6016 4/3516 p.25 (AONSW)

CHAPTER TEN

1822-

In the years following the move to the district of Airds, Hugh Byrne managed to support his ever-increasing family by concentrating on building up his herd of horned cattle and, to a lesser extent, on the growing of cereal crops. In 1822, he supplied wheat to government stores while in 1825 he successfully tendered to the Commissariat Office to supply 200 bushels of wheat at 9 shillings per bushel. In common with other settlers in the area he availed of the services of clearing gangs to assist in the reaping of wheat on contract, but when he was cited for reputedly owing Owen Meehan's clearing gang the sum of £1-2s., he was quick to point out that when there had been a risk of wheat shedding on a neighbouring farm, he willingly transferred the men who were working on his son's farm in order to avoid disaster.[1] As he struggled to achieve economic independence the need to borrow money was ever-present, and in 1821 he appeared in court to answer an action of debt brought by William Crowe, a Clare-born soldier who had arrived in the colony with Macqaurie's regiment, and who worked a grant of land at Appin, in addition to building houses in the area in conjunction with his brother Edward.[2] Hugh Byrne had borrowed £11 from Crowe in 1818, at a rate of interest of 8%, and the final judgement against him came to £25-11s.-2d.[3]

As the size of his herd increased, Hugh Byrne came under increasing pressure to find suitable grazing land to sustain them and he gave vent to his frustrations in a memorial written in August 1822 to the new Governor Sir Thomas Brisbane:

> Residing on a 70-acre farm memorialist has a wife and 11 children to support, whose chief support is by the produce of his stock consisting of 70 heads. Part of his ground is a small purchased farm, adjoining a large tract of Government ground, which ground is, one side, bounded by that of Mr. Redfern's. That your memorialist's stock has been feeding thereon for some time past uninterrupted, except by Mr. Redfern who about two years ago impounded them, asserting the same ground to be his in consequence of a seven-year lease granted by the late Governor,

---

1.   Reel 6058 4/769, p.159c. and Reel 6010, 4/3508, pp.401-402 (AONSW)
2.   "Ripe For Harvest" by Angela Young.
3.   Governor's Court, No.31. (4/7865) (AONSW)

and which has long since expired. I made applications to the Commissions of Enquiry [Bigge's] who desired me to apply to you for redress. On this day Mr. Redfern's agent again impounded but released them on condition that they would be removed within eight days. The Agent told me that Mr. Redfern has been promised a grant of an additional 500 acres and in consequence of this promise he assumes a title to the Government ground. Memorialist appeals, in humble hope, you will take his care and that of his large family by granting him redress and also to have the goodness to allow his eldest son Michael Byrne to have a grant of 100 acres (given by his late Excellency) located to him convenient to your memorialist's said purchased ground.[4]

This was followed by a separate memorial from Michael Byrne (who was now 23 years old) applying for a grant of land, and his claim was certified by Thomas Moore who added: "I think worthy of the indulgence." Michael Byrne had received a grant of 60 acres at Ilawarra, but his father remained in a difficult situation; as a settler he was assigned government servants but, officially, he was still regarded as a ticket-of-leave convict since his release from Newcastle in 1817. This anomaly prompted him to address another lengthy memorial to Governor Brisbane, in which he gave his own version of his fateful transaction in 1812, and that claimed that he regarded Moloney as "a fair, honest character but that, unfortunately, the cattle proved to be the property of the Crown for which Hugh Vesty Byrne was tried and sentenced to death . . . but on account of his good character was changed to transportation for life to Newcastle." He further stated that while he remained classified as a prisoner he could not earn "that comfortable or independent livelihood he otherwise could as a free man" and asked for a conditional pardon.[5]

But his only tangible success, in the short-term at least, occurred in 1824 when he was sanctioned to occupy 700 acres of government land for depasturing cattle in the recently-opened area of the Burragorang, situated in the direction of the Blue Mountains. Individuals who received tickets of occupation were required to build a stock yard in the centre of their licensed areas, to provide a sample of their brands and register the name of their stockman. The scenic area of the Burragorang with its mountains, deep valleys, rivers and lakes must have reminded Hugh Byrne of his native Wicklow while the rich pasture land on the banks of Woolindilly River provided ideal grazing for his herd. For the remainder of his life he would alternate between the two areas but, given his trouble with William Redfern, he immediately applied for a grant of part of the Burragorang land and he repeated his request in a further memorial written in 1825:

---

4. Fiche 3042 4/1828, No. 37 (AONSW)
5. Fiche 3122 4/1840 C. No. 99. pp. 548-552. Fiche 3081 4/1836 B. No. 151, pp. 699-702 (AONSW)

Petitioner about three months ago presented a petition for a grant of land. Since then saw on the *Sydney Gazette* of November 8th a public notice asking applicants to amend their applications. Has in his employment the under-mentioned convicts [Patrick Beatty, Minerva – 4 years, John Lynch, Countess of Harcourt – 2 years, Michael Rutledge, John Barry – 3 years.] whom he has supported free of expense to the Crown. He asked the Government to make a grant to him, being possessed of a large herd of cattle, and adequate means to bring the land into cultivation. Further asks to grant to him part of the land which he holds now on a ticket of occupation in Burragorang on which he has made various improvements, and that Government extends to him, thereby securing those surrounding him from any inconvenience that otherwise might arise from his cattle.[6]

This memorial was, interestingly, certified by Rev. Thomas Reddall J.P., assistant clergyman, who stated "he is a prudent, honest and industrious man and deserving of Your Excellencie's good consideration." Thomas Reddall, a clergyman and educationalist who specialised in the Madras system, came to the colony with his wife and family in 1820 and, at the suggestion of Governor Macquarie, opened a private school, having rented James Meehan's house at Macquarie Fields. It is possible that some of the younger Byrne children many have been taught by him and his recommendation gives credence to the lack of sectarianism which prevailed at the time. The Byrne's were staunch Catholics and supporters of Fr Therry; they contributed handsomely to the building of the church in Sydney, and also to St. John's Church in Campbelltown while Hugh Byrne's name appeared (along with Mary Dwyer) in 1824 as one of the persons from whom Catholic religious books could be obtained.[7] The endorsement of Thomas Reddall had the desired effect as he received a grant of 100 acres at Burragorang in 1825 in addition to a conditional pardon. In the meantime, Rosanna Byrne who had been born on the *Tellicherry*, married William Craft, a neighbouring settler, in Airds in 1821, but she died tragically four years later, at the young age of 21, and Sarah Byrne agreed to rear her two infant children. And in 1821 also Catherine Byrne married John Keighran who would become one of the most successful businessmen in the neighbouring Campbelltown.

But the fortunes of John Mernagh seem to have waned in these years. Even though his name still appeared in 1822 on the list of settlers to whom convicts were assigned his holdings of rented land remained at 50 acres. But he remained uninvolved in any unlawful dealings nor he did not contract any debts; he continued to live with Mary Johnson and their two daughters and their lives seemed to be increasingly inter-linked with James Sheedy, who

---

6.   Fiche 3213 4/1864, p.54 (AONSW)

owned a holding at South Creek, and who had reputedly married Jane Black following the execution of James Molloy. But in common with most small landholders, Sheedy was forced to borrow money and in 1820 had appeared before the Governor's Court at the suit of Robert Campbell Junior when a judgement of £39 (including costs) was entered against him.[8] In 1824 John Mernagh also resorted to the familiar device of forwarding a memorial to the governor in which he described himself as having been banished from his native country "through the unhappy circumstances of the Irish rebellion", and that he had been deprived of his original landholding in Liverpool by sale of execution: "Since which period your Excellency's petitioner has supported himself and his family at a considerable expense, by clearing and cultivating ground that he has rented." His application for a grant of land was endorsed by Michael Moore and Robert Cartwright but there is no record of the grant having been given, although there is a reference in 1826 to John Mernagh being among those whose land grants had been cancelled.[9]

In August 1826, Mernagh's elder daughter Elizabeth married Daniel Canvin who had come out from Bristol on the *Elizabeth* in 1820, and who worked as a blacksmith for Mrs Elizabeth Badgery, South Creek, Bringelly, where James Sheedy also lived, and the young couple settled in the area. The marriage ceremony was performed by Fr Therry while Mary Dwyer acted as one of the witnesses. By 1828, John Mernagh was working just a four-acre farm, half of which was under cultivation, and which also supported seven cattle.[10] His official listing as shoemaker in the 1828 census, however, must be taken on trust as it scarcely fits into the lifestyle of the Glenmalure man. It is possible that he was mending one of his boots when the census-taker called! Mary Johnson died about this time and probably before the marriage of their younger daughter Bridget in September 1828 to Patrick Farrelly (Farley). Bridget was 16 years old and working in Sydney where she lodged at Thomas Scarr's in Castlereagh St. It was there that she met Farrelly, a stonemason who had come out on the Cambridge, and the marriage also took place at St Mary's Church, with Fr Therry again officiating.

The name of Martin Burke appeared regularly in the early 1820's on the list of constables entitled to draw rations from government stores as did Phoebe Tunstall and her two children.[11] In 1823, however his marital status was officially queried in this regard, and Colonial Secretary Frederick Goulburn contacted the Magistrates at Windsor: "I have the honour to enquire the

7.   *Sydney Gazette*, February 1824.
8.   Fiche 3099 4/1838 a. No 614 (AONSW)
9.   Fiche 3099 4/1838a. pp.585-588 (AONSW)
10. Mayberry Mss.
11. Reel 6011. 4/3509.p.477 (AONSW)

place and date of marriage of Martin Burke, the Pittwater constable to the woman with whom he resides, together with the names and residences of their progeny." And as no official record of his marriage existed, Martin Burke had to explain the special circumstances in a letter to D'Arcy Wentworth:

> Sir, In compliance with notice received this is to acquaint you that I have been married at Sydney in 1807 by the Reverend W.[J.] Harold, Catholic clergyman. By this marriage I have no children – but my wife's two. I have always supported and was allowed their rations at Governments store. . . . . I beg leave to observe to you that I have some enemies (of the lower order) who would, if it lay in their power, do me any injury because of my executing Government duty in the district where I live.[12]

D'Arcy Wentworth forwarded his letter to the Colonial Secretary, with some additional relevant details: "Martin Burke has further stated that the marriage was celebrated in the presence of Joseph Barry and his wife who are now at the Derwent." This put an end to the uncertainty and Burke continued to concentrate the 700-acre holding which he had leased. He built a farmhouse close to the sea at Mona Vale, planted a large vegetable garden and increased his herd of cattle. And to pay for the improvements he sold his own Newport grant to John Farrell for the sum of £35 in November 1823.[13] In February, his step–daughter Sarah married David Foley, a wheelwright who had come out from Ireland in the *Guilford* in 1818. Fr Therry performed the ceremony in St Mary's Church, Sydney and the couple came to live in Pittwater to help with the running of his leasehold. In that year also, John Clarke, the soldier he had befriended during the *Tellicherry* voyage, was demobilised and became entitled to a grant of 100 acres in any surveyed part of the colony. He applied for a grant at Mackeral Beach which, by previous arrangement, Burke purchased from him in 1824 and Clarke also came to live at Mona Vale.

Robert McIntosh, whom Burke had known since his days as an innkeeper in Sydney, was granted 200 acres at Bayview by Macquarie, and was also appointed as a Pittwater constable in 1819. But in the following year he was given a three-year sentence in Newcastle for embezzling government property and the McIntosh family, who had remained in Sydney, leased the property also to Martin Burke. By 1822 he had 34 head of cattle on the farm, of which 30 acres were cleared, 3 acres were under maize, with 1 acre each of potatoes and fruit trees.[14] In 1825, he subleased the 700 acre Wentworth holding to David and Sarah Foley (the lease had 3½ years to run) and the deed included a covenant "reserving to the said Martin Burke the grazing of whatever cattle

---

12. *Ibid.*, p.538.
13. *Martin Burke – Father of Pittwater*, p.56.
14. *Ibid.*, p.70.

he then had, or may hereafter have, on the said farm, and also to retain for his, the said Martin Burke's own use, one room in the dwelling house on said farm, together with about half an acre of garden ground."[15]

D'Arcy Wentworth retired as Superintendent of Police in 1825 and was succeeded by Captain Rossi who had a military background. He immediately introduced an upper and lower age limit for constables and when a complaint was lodged against Burke by a local man William Miller in 1826 Rossi wrote to the new Colonial Secretary Alexander McLeay:

> In the course of the enquiry it appeared that Martin Burke was the proprietor of cattle and further that he took in cattle of others as a grazier, that he had no stockmen, nor had he any stockyard to lodge the cattle at night. The consequence had been that the neighbours have frequently suffered by the trespass committed by these cattle and it was added and proved that no redress could be obtained for the injury thus received from the circumstances of Martin Burke being pound keeper as well as constable for the district. Martin Burke admitted this fact also that he did not keep any account of the proceeds of the poundage which he said were but small and these he considered as his perquisite.
>
> It is evident that Martin Burke cannot be made to suffer for any trespass committed by his cattle since he is the person to whom the fees for poundage are paid. Therefore, in this instance, the man's interest is certainly at variance with his public duty. Under these circumstances I deem it my duty to suggest that the situation of constable and pound-keeper in the Pitt Water district may in future be held by a person holding no property there. And I feel the less reluctance in recommending the removal of Martin Burke from his situation that I am informed by the Chief Constable that during the period that Burke has been a constable, about six years, he had taken up but one or two bushrangers, though that part of the country is well known to be much resorted to by the bushrangers and other bad characters.[16]

The last sentence contrasted with Burke's own previous statement that he had enemies among "the lower orders" because of the carrying out of his duties, but he was now in his mid-fifties, and may have welcomed his removal in order to concentrate on the further development of his land holdings in Pittwater over the next decade.

Following the death of Michael Dwyer in 1825, his wife Mary applied for a grant of 35 acres which she claimed had been allotted to her late husband on the Liverpool road. And accompanying her memorial was a letter from surveyor James Meehan who stated that following Dwyer's dismissal as Chief

---

15. Land Titles Office. Book K.No.837.
16. Colonial Secretary Corr. (1826) (AONSW)

Constable of Liverpool, "Governor Macquarie directed me to put him in possession of it and mentioned the same to Mr. Oxley when accompanying the Commission of Enquiry [Bigge's]. I am sure, on a reference, Mr. Oxley will recollect the circumstances."[17] Mary Dwyer was subsequently granted 100 acres in November 1825,[18] but the allocation was not taken up and she moved instead to Sydney to become Fr Therry's housekeeper, a position she would hold for many years. Shortly before his death Michael Dwyer, in consequence of a recently-enacted government assisted passages scheme, petitioned to have his four children in Ireland sent out to the colony, namely Mary Ann, John, Peter and Esther. Regular correspondence had been kept up over a period of 20 years, and in January 1828, following the intervention of Fr Therry, John Dwyer (age 27) and Peter Dwyer (age 26) arrived in Sydney on board the Marquis of Huntley. They were reunited with their mother whom they could scarcely have remembered and also met James (age 21) Bridget (age 20) and Eliza (age 16) for the first time. It would have been a bittersweet occasion for Mary Dwyer who saw, no doubt, in her sons the image of her late husband as he had looked at the time of their marriage in Wicklow 30 years before. And there was further comfort for her in October when Mary Ann (age 29) and Esther (age 24) arrived on board the *Sir Joseph Banks*. Mary Ann, the eldest of the family, had recently been widowed and brought William Hughes, her infant son, with her.

Eliza Dwyer, the youngest of the family, married Peter Bodicene in 1827. He was a free settler who came on the *St Michael* in 1819 and operated a wool business in George's St, Sydney where he employed Peter Dwyer as a sorter while John Dwyer obtained work as a warehouseman with J.B. Bettington. Esther Dwyer became a governess at the Catholic School in Hyde Park while Bridget Dwyer, also with the help of Fr Therry, became a teacher, working at various times of the year in Sydney and Parramatta, teaching about 80 children for which she was paid two pence per week per pupil. She also visited her cousins, the Byrne family, in Airds in the months following her father's death and acted as godparent, with Michael Byrne, at the baptism of Rose Agatha Byrne, the last of Sarah Byrne's 14 children. And less than a month later, in February 1826, Bridget Dwyer and Michael Byrne acted as witnesses at the wedding of Anne (Nanno) Byrne to William Byrne (no relation).[19]

The 1828 census showed that Hugh Byrne owned 210 acres, of which 163 were cleared, and with 66 acres cultivated. His herd of horned cattle had increased to 236 and he also owned six horses. But these were years of recession in the colony, aggravated by three successive years of drought from

---

17. Fiche 3130 4/1841 B. p. 250 (AONSW)
18. *Ibid.*,
19. Tucker Mss.

1826 to 1828, while in a five-year period until 1830 the price of cattle fell from £12 each to 12 shillings. He managed to survive the worst effects of the recession and continued to ply between his holdings at Airds and Burragorang while the lives of his children became inextricably linked with the development of nearby Campbelltown. Originally mapped out by James Meehan on the instructions of Governor Macquarie in 1820, the town had slowly taken shape and just a few buildings had been completed by 1827.[20]

They included an Anglican church while the foundations of St. John's Catholic Church had been laid in the town's eastern boundary. In that year allotments were allocated, and the applicants included Charles Byrne who stated in his petition for Allotment No. 88 that he required "a residence for carrying on the trade of butcher."[21] His application was endorsed by local magistrates William Browne and William Howe who described him as "a native of the colony and a very good character" while the same form of words were used to describe Michael Byrne who applied for Allotment No 91, and who was described as a cabinet-maker by trade, and that he intended carrying on his business in the town.[22] But the two brothers were beginning to dabble in land speculation, particularly after the system of free land grants ended in 1831, the same year that the allotments in Campbelltown were officially granted. Michael Byrne petitioned for his holding of 60 acres at Ilawarra to be registered (it did not appear on the list of official grants) and he claimed to have expended "a handsome sum" on his development. An his application for an additional grant was endorsed by Rev. Thomas Reddall who stated that "a short time ago he married a very prudent and industrious young woman, the daughter of a farmer in the district and born in the colony."[23] She was Jane Warby, twin daughter of John Warby, a former constable of Cowpastures and the stockman who had charge of the colony's wild cattle.[24] He had originally explored the area of Burragorang and took possession of his holding at Airds in 1816.

Charles Byrne purchased two further allotments in the town of Berrima (nos. 10 and 11, section 2) at a price of £2 per acre in 1832 and also applied for 200 acres of land at Burragorang, bounded on the east by the Woolindilly River and on the south by his father's land.[25] And at the same time, the Byrne brothers "took up a rich stretch of swamp and saltbush from Old Man Creek

20. *Campbelltown – The Bicentennial History.* Chapter Two.
21. Reel 1105, No. 5993 (AONSW).
22. *Ibid.*
23. *Ibid.*
24. Full genealogical information on the Warby family in Michelle Vale's book "Warby – My Excellent Guide."
25. Reel 1105 (AONSW).

to Uroly Creek: over 40 kilometres of frontage."[26] By the end of 1833 the entire Narrendera frontage had been occupied by landholders with Irish-Airds connections, but severe drought forced Charles Byrne to sell the western part of Brimbla (Yanco) in 1835 to James Devlin, a son of Arthur Devlin who, at the age of 25, was already a wealthy man. In the following year Charles Byrne also relinquished his holding in Brewarrena, the local Narrungdera Aboriginal tribe, led by warriors who were given nicknames such as Boney, Big Peter and Brian Boru (he was over six feet tall) having killed a servant of Michael Byrne's in 1837 and continued to create such havoc that he also was forced to abandon the station before the end of the decade.[27]

But Hugh Byrne still had not received the deeds to his Burragorang property and an incident which occurred in 1832 caused him to address a petition addressed to the new Irish-born Governor, Richard Bourke. It transpired that his cattle had recently been impounded from the section of land for which Charles Byrne had recently applied by another local settler James Riely (Reilly). He put them into a yard and attempted to exact a fine of one shilling per head for their return which, apart from the illegality of his action, was double the regular charge of an authorised poundkeeper. The fact that he was the local constable did not deter Hugh Byrne who noted that Riely had rented two sections of property from the government, but had no visible means of paying the rent, apart from the impounding of other people's cattle: "Petitioner having a large family of fourteen children of which five are married, and nine now living under petitioner's roof, claiming his support, that support he has to derive from two small farms near Campbell Town one of which he, by his industry purchased, and also by his travelling to and from to Burragorang." He requested that "a letter of instructions be written to Riely not to molest or trouble petitioner's cattle any more". His petition was again endorsed by Rev. Thomas Reddall who described Byrne as "possessing a considerable and valuable stock of horned cattle etc., – of his habits of industry, honesty of principle and of moral rectitude we can speak in the highest praise, having known him many years." And Reddall's letter was also signed by local magistrates Richard Brooks, Thomas Wills, William Howe, William Browne and Captain Antill, the leading citizens in the area. It was further proof of the standing of the Byrne family in the area.

An official reply to his complaint was scribbled across the first page of the petition stating that Byrne should be informed that if his cattle had been illegally impounded by Reily he should sue for damages, and that it did not fall within "the customary exercise of the secretariat's authority to interfere in such a case where the law is open by which redress for the alleged injury may be readily obtained." He was also told that his application for an additional

---

26. *History of Narranderra Shire* by B. Gammage.
27. *Ibid.*

200 acres had not yet been received, but that it would probably be refused because it was less than the amount allowed. It was also confirmed that Reily had been granted 1280 acres on a yearly lease, but that if Byrne chose to purchase the whole section Reily would be bound to vacate it. In the event, Hugh Byrne was in no position to make such a purchase while Reilly relinquished it to take up a freehold on another 200-acre property. And, ironically, when he later moved to another part of the valley the land was periodically leased to the Byrne family.[28] In 1835 Hugh Byrne finally received the deeds to his 100 acre property in Burragorang (granted to him a decade before) and he named it Apple Grove "because of the extensive stands of the splendid Angophora costata, the smooth-barked apple (so called by the early settlers from a resemblance to the European apple)".[29]

Martin Burke continued to work the 200 acre holding he had leased from Robert McIntosh at Bayview until the property was sold after the latter's death in 1829. In conjunction with John Clarke, he then transferred his stock to the 100-acre holding at Mackeral Beach which was made up of 40 acres at Little Mackeral Beach (Currawong) and a further 60 acres at Great Mackeral Beach. In 1832 he successfully resisted an attempt by another settler to lay claim to the property and immediately wrote to Surveyor-General Mitchel for the deeds of the land while confirming that he had purchased it from John Clarke in February 1824. He was also interested in purchasing land at a nearby neck of flatland at Coaster's Retreat called "The Basin" and applied in 1833 for just 20 acres for the purpose of making a vegetable garden. But his application was refused, the official reason being that 50 acres would be the minimum amount to be considered. He then arranged for Robert McIntosh Junior to acquire that amount and the land became available to him until 1839.

Phoebe Tunstall died in these years,[30] and as he approached his mid-sixties Martin Burke began to prepare for retirement. In November 1834 he sold his sixty-acre farm at Mackeral Beach for £50 to speculator John Marks with the proviso "that the said Martin Burke and his assigns shall occupy the house and outhouses . . . and three acres of land of the said land and receive the rents and profits thereof during the term of the natural life of the said Martin Burke."[31] One of his closest friends was local fisherman Paddy Flynn, and in December 1836 he gave his remaining 40 acre holding at Little Mackeral Beach to Flynn's young daughter Eileen by means of a 99-year lease. It provided that her father would hold it in trust for her until she married or reached the age of twenty one "and in the meantime to apply all benefits etc.

28. *Life in the Burragorang*, p.22.
29. *Ibid.*
30. The exact date of her death is unknown, nor has a death ceetificate been found.
31. *Martin Burke, Father of Pittwater*, p. 85.

for her use."[32] Martin Burke passed his final years living quietly in a wooden
hut beside Mackeral Beach and close to the Flynn and Sheehan families. He
became ill in 1842 and moved to the Sydney Asylum, a home for old men,
where he died peacefully at the age of 72 on 29 July, attended by Fr P.A.
Hogan, the Catholic chaplain.

The upturn of the economy in the 1830's, added to the decision by the
Government in 1831 to end the free land grant system, and to set a minimum
price of five shillings per acre on land sold at auction, led to an increase in
land speculation which Michael Byrne, in particular, continued to exploit. He
made a number of land purchases, including a 100 acre holding in the county
of Westmoreland on the Woolombri Brook (Lot 48) for £37 in 1836; two
further lots of 150 acres (Lot 267) and 100 acres (Lot 268) at the Hanging
Rock for £62-10s. (1836); a town allotment for £2 in Woolombri village
(1838); a further 100 acres (Lot 23) belonging to William Pownall at Woolombri
Brook (1838) while in October 1837 he applied to purchase 300 acres in
Camden on the Noorenda range, and which was bounded by his own 60 acres
and by Rev. John Reddall's 60 acre holding.[33] He had also received a license
in 1830 to operate the Royal Oak Inn which was situated at the southern end
of Campbelltown, and which was rented to him by William Bradbury for £58
per year. He took over control in the following year when his sureties were
given by Thomas Byrne and Michael Brennan from Airds. And from 1833 he
also operated the Joiners Arms Inn in the town.

In 1837 Mary Byrne (the ninth in the family) married Limerick-born
John Hurley who had come to the colony on the *Prince Regent* in 1824 to
serve a seven-year sentence. He was assigned to his fellow-Limerick man
Captain Terence Murray at Lake George and on being granted his freedom
settled in Campbelltown where he initially went into partnership with Patrick
Fennell in a number of enterprises, including auctioneering and the running
of the King's Arms Inn. Hurley was also a prominent member of the
Campbelltown Race committee, acting as Judge at the annual meeting while
Charles Byrne was one of the stewards and Sylvester Byrne clerk of the
course. Hurley became a noted breeder of racehorses and Clydesdales while
Michael Byrne had a famous horse Young Theorem standing at stud.

The first annual Campbelltown Races had taken place in 1836, the year
in which Charles Byrne built a single storey house on his town allotment, and
which is now called Richmond Villa. But he encountered financial difficulties,
and in 1840 mortgaged his house to John Vardy, his future brother-in-law for
£1000. In 1839 Michael Byrne built a striking two-storey sandstone house on
his allotment in Campbelltown – later to be called Glenalvon – but he also
suffered a number of setbacks, beginning with an unfortunate incident which

---

32. *Ibid.*, p.84.
33. Reel 1105 (AONSW).

occurred in December 1840 when he became involved in a brawl with a servant who subsequently died from the injuries he received. Michael Byrne and his brother-in-law Joseph Byrne (second husband of Nanno Byrne) and the owner of the Royal Oak Inn, had returned from the Cowpasture Races when an argument took place with John Lomas, who worked at the Joiner's Arms "upon which Lomas struck Byrne in the face; a general fight then commenced, during which the deceased was knocked down and severely kicked, and struck in several places with a brass-headed hunting whip."[34] At the initial Police Magistrates hearing both men were found guilty of manslaughter by a local jury and sent to Sydney for trial. The Chief Justice, in summing up, left the question to the jury as to whether the initial provocation by Lomas was sufficient to justify the subsequent assault, and after a few minutes consideration they returned a verdict of not guilty and the prisoners were released.[35] Michael Byrne's legal costs in the case were paid for by his brother-in-law John Keighran.

The 1837 Convict Muster showed that Hugh Byrne had four convicts assigned to him on his Burragorang property, and in that year also he was granted a squatter's license for Murrumbridge district. To the end of his life he continued to look after his herd of horned cattle and in 1841 was called as a witness by Luke Gorman, a former servant, when the title to the latter's property at Burragorang was unsuccessfully challenged.[36] Hugh and Sarah Byrne adopted an Aboriginal boy in 1842 whom they named Charles, but the exact circumstances of the adoption are unknown. Hugh Byrne died on 18 April 1842 and he was buried three days later in the family vault at St. John's Catholic cemetery, Campbelltown. The following obituary was published in the *Australasian Chronicle* on the same day. "At his residence Airds, after a short illness, which he bore with exemplary piety and fortitude, Hugh Byrne Esq., in his 78th year of age. It was truly edifying to the Christian who contemplated the dying scene of this venerable man, surrounded by moral sons and virtuous daughters and their progeny, joining in prayers to the author of all good, for a peaceful reception of his immortal soul into the mansions of eternal bliss." And a few days later the same newspaper gave a detailed account of the funeral.

> The long and mournful procession preceded by the hearse, with its dark nodding plumes, ascended the hill of Calvary, on the summit of which is erected the beautiful church of St. John. Having arrived at the southern entrance the corpse was borne with solemn step and silent tread along the aisle of the church, preceded by the rector reading aloud the

---

34. The Australian, 5 January 1841.
35. *Ibid*, 11 February 1841.
36. *Life in the Burragorang* by Jim Barrett, p.35.

Introit; it was deposited near the foot of the altar, and the priest, turning to the people, read the sublime and beautiful anthem – "A hymn
becometh thee, O Lord in Sion, . . . all flesh shall come to Thee," The
Gospel was then read . . . and from the aisle the richly-furnished coffin
was carried on the shoulders of four neighbouring gentlemen, and headed
by the clergyman whose voice repeating the "De Profundis" was heard
in the distance. The procession then took a circular course and ulti-
mately the corpse was deposited in its last long resting place near the
northern end of the cemetery where stands conspicuous the family mau-
soleum.

Hugh Byrne died intestate and his son Michael inherited his estate. But
the recession of the 1840's also caused Michael Byrne severe financial difficulties, and in 1844 the Coach And Horses Inn, situated on the road to Camden,
which he operated in conjunction with Charles Morris, was advertised to be
let, the premises being described as comprising of "a bar and taproom, 8
bedrooms, 4 sitting rooms and a large ballroom – an excellent detached kitchen
and laundry, stabling for 16 horses, a coach house and a large loft over a
stable, 2 substantial stockyards and a good well of water, a good paddock of 2
acres in which there is a large water hole, never known to be dry."[37]
    But worse was to follow, and in October 1844 Michael Byrne sought
voluntary bankruptcy when his principal creditors were his mother Sarah to
whom he owed £1,140 from the sale of cattle three years earlier, and his
brother-in-law John Keighran who took possession of Glenalvon as part-
payment for a debt of £880. The Joiners Arms and other properties of his
insolvent estate were advertised for sale in January 1845[38] but he managed to
retain possession of the inn and continued to play a prominent role in the
affairs of Campbelltown for the remainder of his life.
    In these years, the fortunes of the Dwyer family became linked with the
southern part of New South Wales. Mary Ann Hughes (nee Dwyer) married
for a second time to Patrick Hughes, a Wicklow man who had come out on
the *Countess of Harcourt* in 1822, and they moved to Goulburn where their
four children would be born. In 1837, Bridget Dwyer married John O Sullivan,
a native of Millcove, Berehaven, Co. Cork who had become friendly with her
two brothers during their voyage out from Ireland, and who was employed as
a bank manager in Goulburn, in addition to taking on the frustrating task of
looking after Fr. Therry's tangled financial affairs. In the following year John
and Peter Dwyer, both of whom had married some years before, moved from
Sydney to the area of Bungendore, south of Goulburn where a new settlement had been established, 2,000 feet above sea level, in the highlands of the

37. *Sydney Morning Herald*, 9 January 1845.
38. *Sydney Morning Herald*, 9 January 1845.

Brindabella range close to the recently-discovered Lake George. And with them came their sister Esther Dwyer who had married Owen Byrne, the son of another Wicklow man, Andrew Byrne. For their first venture they operated the Harp Inn which was strategically positioned outside the main Bungendore settlement in an area which led to a mountain pass and was also near the local barracks. Unlike their father, they were sober in their habits and hard-nosed businessmen, and the inn became highly profitable. By 1841, out of the 41 listed inhabitants of Bungendore, 24 were credited as living at the Harp Inn, and John Dwyer was also appointed as local poundkeeper, in addition to running the post office with John O Neill. In later years, the Harp Inn transferred to a new premises in Bungendore, and eventually became the Lake George Hotel. For their part, Owen and Esther Byrne set up their own establishment, simply called Byrne's Inn, which was also financially successful.

Richard Brooks, one of the two magistrates who had presided over the Liverpool Court House inquiry in 1820 when Michael Dwyer was dismissed as Chief Constable of the area, had moved to Bungendore in 1825 and held 4,000 acres near the southern end of Lake George. His estate was later divided when his daughters married Nathaniel Powell and Captain Henry Zouch. The latters's part of the estate was called Ashby after Zouch's birthplace in England, and when it was offered for sale in 1855 the 1,000 acre holding was bought by John Dwyer whose original Harp Inn bordered the property. Of the remaining Dwyer children, James who, at the age of 15, helped to run the ill-fated Harrow Inn, married Jane Perry from Co. Cavan at the age of 41 and the couple moved to the area of Lachlan where they reared a family of five children. There remains something of a mystery concerning Eliza Dwyer, the youngest of the family who married Peter Bodicene at the age of 16 in 1827. A son and a daughter were born to them, but it appears that about a decade later Eliza fell in love with George Butler who worked for her husband, and that they eloped together to Hobart Town. Eliza Dwyer did not return to her husband and bore six further children.[39]

Mary Dwyer continued to act as housekeeper to Fr Therry until he transferred to Van Diemen's Land. For the remainder of her life she lived in a house at Castlereagh St, Sydney, the rent of which was supposedly paid by local members of the Irish community,[40] but she also spent some time with her daughter Bridget and son-in-law John O'Sullivan in Goulburn. In the course of a letter to Fr Therry in January 1841, John O Sullivan wrote: "Mrs. Dwyer is here. She is looking very old and rather feeble",[41] while in August

---

39. A comprehensive genealogical study of the Dwyer family has been carried out by Alan Leslie Brown, (a descendant of Eliza Dwyer), Sydney.
40. Sheedy diary.
41. Fr.Therry Papers, Vol. 56. (cy 798) 15 January 1841 (Mitchel Library).

of the same year she went back in Sydney and Fr Therry, who was on his way
back to Van Diemen's Land, received a note that she wished to see him: "She
is exceedingly ill, suffering very much, may linger for a long time, but is not
likely to recover. My dear friend Esther is with her. Miss de Lacy is also
there; indeed she appears to have experienced the kindest attention from both
the Fitzpatrick families and her medical attendant. . . Having heard of Mrs.
Dwyer's accident, I thought it very desirable to see her without delay."[42]
Mary John Baptist de Lacy was a nun who would become Mother Superior of
the Sister of Charity, and they helped to look after Mary Dwyer in her
declining years.

The nature of her accident was not revealed and, despite the gloomy
prognosis, Mary Dwyer recovered and would live for a further 20 years. In
1844, John O Sullivan noted "I have left Mrs. Dwyer at Goulburn. She is
well, although rather feeble in her walk"[43] and eight years later, in June 1852,
Bridget O'Sullivan informed Fr. Therry: "My poor mother is on her death
bed, confined to her bed for three weeks and very weak. . . When this letter
reaches its destination she will be dead."[44] But Mary Dwyer again recovered
and in a postscript to a letter written in July 1853, Bridget O'Sullivan casually
stated "My mother is quite strong."[45] Fr Therry was back in Sydney in 1854,
and he sent greetings to John O'Sullivan "with affectionate compliments to
Mrs Dwyer, Mrs O'Sullivan and all members of your dear family."[46] The
return of Fr Therry may have prompted her to return to No. 368 Castlereagh
St, Sydney where she remained in contact with him. In June 1859, she had a
letter sent asking him to call as she was "very ill" while in February 1860 she
wrote: "I have been very ill last night . . . I am very anxious to see you." And
she wrote a final letter to Fr Therry on 25 May 1860: "I have been suffering
from influenza this last fortnight and am sinking fast. I feel very anxious to
see you before I die. If you could come you would confer a great favour on
your very humble servant."[47] Mary Dwyer died 18 days later at her home in
Castlereagh St. at the age of (circa) 79 and was buried beside her husband.

Sarah Byrne continued to live in Airds following the death of her husband Hugh in 1842, and later in that year her son Sylvester married Mary
Vardy, the daughter of John Vardy who farmed at Maryfields near
Campbelltown. Sylvester Byrne was a licensee of the Royal Hotel which was
taken over by his brother-in-law John Hurley in 1844 while his brother Michael

---

42. *Ibid.*, 11 August 1841.
43. *Ibid.*, Vol. 56.
44. *Ibid.*, Vol. 58, 2 June 1852, p.229.
45. *Ibid.*, Vol. 58, 13 July 1853.
46. *Ibid.*, Vol. 58 p.267.
47. *Ibid.*, Vol. 59.
48. *Life in the Burragorang*, p.35.

sold him the Apple Grove family property in Burragorang in 1856 where Sill's Creek is named after him.[48] Winifred Byrne, the twelfth child of the family, married Dr Isidore Blake who practised in Campbelltown and Yass, but there was further tragedy for Sarah Byrne in 1850 when another daughter, Sarah Merritt, died in Sydney at the early age of 34, and her three children were also reared by their grandmother at Airds. The two youngest daughters of the family married in the early 1850's; Elizabeth Byrne to Henry J. Eccleston, the couple moving to the Monaro district where the Ecclestons held a squatting license, and in 1853 Rose Agatha Byrne married Joseph Tucker who had arrived in the colony from England to take up a position as secretary to Archbishop Polding. He resigned his post in 1857 to become a succesful wine and spirits merchant in Sydney.[49]

John Hurley (husband of Mary Byrne) became one of the most successful businessmen in Campbelltown and also held squatting licenses in the Lachlan pastoral district amounting to 90,000 acres. He also acted as unpaid farm agent to Fr Therry who had a similar license at Billabong, and in this capacity was frequently in contact with John O'Sullivan at Goulburn. And when an upgrading of the road southwards from Campbelltown was proposed, both of their names, in addition to John Dwyer, appeared in a public notice.[50] Mary Hurley (nee Byrne) died in January 1859 and in the same year John Hurley was elected as a member for the newly created constituency of Narellan in the New South Wales Assembly, following representations made to him by a large influential group of local people.[51] He continued to represent the area (with some breaks) until he retired in 1880.

In 1859, Sarah Byrne sold one acre of the original land grant she had received at Minto, and seven years later she sold the remaining portion for £375 and moved to a house in Allman St, Campbelltown. She died there at the age of 94 on 2 January 1872, seven of her children having predeceased her. Her death was reported in the local *Freeman's Journal* under the heading "Death Of A Very Old Colonist":

> On the 2nd inst. a very old and respected resident of Campbelltown departed this life . . . Mrs. Byrne, it will be manifest, was not being behind in obeying the Divine injunction, for she succeeded in rearing a large family consisting of five sons and nine daughters, the latter of whom were well and respectably married. The old lady had the satisfaction of seeing her grandchildren of the fourth generation before she exchanged a terrestial for a more perfect and spiritual existence. Her great, great, grandchildren are eight in number. The writer of this

49. Tucker Mss.
50. *Sydney Morning Herald*, 18 October 1842, p.3.
51. *Campbelltown – The Bicentennial History*, pp.78-79.

notice had been for many years a near neighbour of Mrs. Byrne, and, therefore, had numerous opportunities of conversing with her on various subjects, but more particularly on those eventful and exciting events that occurred during the period antecedent to her departure from her native land. Up to a short time previous to her death her faculties were in full vigour; her memory remarkably tenacious, relating remote events which came within her own experience while in Ireland with a freshness and accuracy as to names and dates wonderful in a person of her advanced period of life. The wrongs of Ireland were her chief and most absorbing theme. Though passionately and deeply sympathising with her country people, her mind was entirely free from, and ucontaminated by any unreasonable feeling of animosity towards Englishmen. She led a pious, useful life. Some time before her death she received the full rights of her church. Her mortal remains were interred in the family vault at St. John's Church, Campbelltown, and her funeral, which was a very large one, comprised persons of various demoninations.

Her son Charles (who had built Richmond Villa) died in the following year at Cadgee where he had settled in 1848 and acted for many years as a magistrate. Part of his property became the greater part of the Gulph gold-field and the township of Merrigundah, but he was content to lease land to the gold diggers: "In his dealings with the diggers, he was never oppressive; on the contrary he was always extremely liberal, and many a trick to chisel him out of a fee, he has good-naturedly winked at. His rule was to give the digger a chance before he demanded payment; and, of course, he enjoyed the utmost popularity amongst the digging community. As a landlord, neighbour and employer, he was much respected; and in regard to the private relations of life he bore the highest character."[52]

John Mernagh, the last surviving member of the Wicklow rebels, also lived to a great age. In the early 1840's he accompanied his daughter Elizabeth and son-in-law Daniel Canvin when they moved to the area of Ballalaba on lands acquired by the Badgery family in 1837. Canvin later worked as a blacksmith for T.J. Roberts, brother-in-law of Andrew Badgery, on his Exeter Stud Farm at Jembaicumbene, to the south west of Braidwood. The stud became famous for breeding racehorses, including Archer, the winner of the first two Melbourne Cups in 1861 and 1862. John Mernagh lived to see the marriage of his grandchild Sarah Canvin in 1852 and died at the age of 80 at Burlang, Ballabala-Major's Creek, near Braidwood, on 2 July 1857. His burial ceremony in the local cemetery was conducted by Fr. Thomas Farrell. The headstone of his daughter Elizabeth who died in 1872 is still standing in the

52. *Rural Gazette*, 1 March 1879.

Catholic section, but John Mernagh's ornate headstone, among others, was destroyed by an act of vandalism in the 1960's.[53]

Two years before his death in 1872, John Dwyer, the owner of the Ashby estate in Bungendore, divided the property into farms and allotments and sold out. His eldest son Michael Joseph had joined the Benedictine order and was one of the principal clergyman who received the remains of Fr. Therry in Sydney in 1864. In later years he became Dean of Sydney, a leading figure in the St. Joseph's Investment and Building Society, a member of the boards of Sydney Hospital, the Benevolent Society and Randwick Orphanage, and he also compiled the Catholic Directory. In 1868 there was a political sensation when Prince Alfred, Australia's first royal visitor, was shot by Henry James O'Farrell, a deranged Irishman. He quickly recovered from his wound but O'Farrell was sentenced to be hanged. Fr. Dwyer was chaplain to Darlinghurst Jail at the time and he attended O'Farrell at the time of his execution, in addition to thwarting the attempts of Colonial Secretary Henry Parkes to stir up sectarian feelings by claiming that the attack was part of a Fenian plot to murder the prince. Fr. Dwyer smuggled a duplicate copy of O'Farrell's confession out of the jail in which he denied any complicity with the Fenian movement, and he was subsequently dismissed as chaplain.

Mary Ann, the only daughter of John Dwyer, became a Benedictine nun in the Subiaco convent in Parramatta while his other son John Elicius seems to have lost contact with the family after his marriage to Isabel Carrington. The house at Ashby and the largest segment of the property was bought by Patrick Doyle, a grandnephew of his mother who had come out to New South Wales from Wicklow in 1858, and his sons subsequently became well-known farmers in the area. The Doyle family retained possession of Ashby until the 1930's and, for many years, a life-size portrait of Michael Dwyer hung in the house.[54]

The children of Arthur and Priscilla Devlin also played leading roles in the development of the colony. Their eldest son James trained originally as a wheelwright and master butcher, and became a businessman and government contractor. He acquired properties on the north coast of New South Wales on the Clarence river, and owned two stations, Glenugie and Corinda and, as already had been noted, dealt with Michael and Charles Byrne at Narrenderra. His first wife was Mary Ann Hartigan whom he married at St. Peter's Church, Campbelltown in 1831 (all of the Devlin children were reared as Protestants after the death of their father), and following her early death he married Susannah Hughes, the daughter of teacher Matthew Hughes. They had ten children and in 1842 James Devlin built a new home for his family at Ryde which is regarded as one of the finest examples of colonial architecture in

---

53. Mayberry Mss.
54. *Ripe from a Chord* by Fr Brian Maher.

Australia and was restored by the National Trust in 1980. Despite being declared bankrupt in the recession of the 1840's, James Devlin again prospered and acquired substantial properties in the Kissing Point area while he was one of the first squatters in the Murumbidgee station.

Arthur Devlin, the second son of the family, went to sea at the age of twelve, became an expert boatsman and was described as having "grown up to be a splendid specimen of the native Australian". At the age of twenty he imported a racing gig called the "Paddy" which for many years remained unbeaten and his crew, which consisted of himself, James Chapman, George Chapman, William Howard, Andrew Melville and George Mulhall, were described as "six young giants, all standing well over six feet tall and splendidly built". He prospered initially in the whaling industry, and in 1832 commissioned the building of the "Surprise", the first steamship in the colony. In the following decade he became master and part-owner of a number of ships and by the age of thirty was reputed to be worth £48,000. In later life he became a partner in a firm of gold buyers in Melbourne and was a founder member of the Athenaeum Club. He died in November 1893 as a result of injuries he received when falling down a flight of stairs at the Melbourne Opera House.[55]

Patrick Devlin, the third son of the family, is reputed to have spent most of his life in Queensland in the area of Rockhampton. He never married and worked as bushman, station superintendent and gold miner, which included a stint in the Californian gold fields. He was aged fifty when he died at his home in Prime St, Ryde in August 1865. Mary Devlin, the eldest of the family's three daughters, died in 1835 at the early age of twenty three, while the second daughter Ann was thirty seven when she died in 1854. Martha Devlin, the youngest member of the family, had been baptised by Fr. Connolly shortly after his arrival in the colony, and was just one year old when her father died in 1820. She married Thomas Beckford Simpson, a sea captain who worked at one time for her brother Arthur, and who was described as "an intelligent and humane man." The wedding took place at Kissing Point in June 1842 and was performed by Rev. G.E. Turner of St. Anne's Church of England. They raised a family of two sons and four daughters. Martha Devlin died in 1908 at the age of eighty nine.

55. Brigadier Stan Devlin, Canberra, Devlin Mss.

Postscript

As the nineteenth century progressed the fame of Michael Dwyer, both as a rebel leader and peasant folk hero, grew in direct proportion to the increase in Irish nationalism. Accounts of his exploits during his five-year guerilla campaign became part of the oral tradition, although a certain degree of re-evaluation concerning his political orthodoxy was engaged upon in the Wicklow mountains when news filtered back that he had become a constable in New South Wales. These reservations became almost a guarded secret, to be whispered around firesides at night, and were totally swallowed up in the tide of nationalistic deification which occurred, particularly following the publication of T.D. Sullivan's ballad which related in stirring fashion his escape from the cottage at Derrynamuck:

> Around the little cottage they formed into a ring,
> And called out: "Michael Dwyer! Surrender to your King!"
> Thus answered Michael Dwyer: "Into this house we came.
> Unasked by those who own it; they cannot be to blame.
> Then let those guiltless people, unquestioned, pass you through,
> And when they've passed in safety, I'll tell you what we'll do."
> 'Twas done." And now", said Dwyer, "your work you may begin;
> You are a hundred outside – we're only four within.
> We've heard your haughty summons, and this is our reply.
> We're true United Irishmen – we'll fight until we die.

This ballad was later complemented by a haunting song *The Three Flowers*, composed by Norman Reddin, in which the name of Michael Dwyer is linked with Robert Emmet and Wolfe Tone:

> She took and kissed the first flower once
> And sweetly said to me:
> "This flower came from the Wicklow hills,
> Dew wet and pure," said she.
> "Its name is Michael Dwyer
> The strongest flower of all.
> But I'll keep it fresh beside my breast
> Though all the world might fall."

The sentiments expressed in these verses were kept alive also in Australia by the thousands of Irish emigrants who had settled there, while plans to commemorate the centenary of the 1798 rebellion coincided with the announcement in Sydney in 1898 that the remains of those who had been buried in the Devonshire Street cemetery were to be reinterred as the Central railway was due to be built on the site. A committee he headed by Dr. Charles McCarthy appealed to Irish people all over Australasia "to commemorate the honour and memory of the Wicklow chieftain, Michael Dwyer and all other insurgents whose remains lie here." A large sum of many was donated and work on the imposing monument in Waverley Cemetery began. In 1878, Dean Michael Joseph Dwyer had the remains of his grandparents transferred to a vault in Devonshire Street cemetery, and on 22 May 1898, their remains were first taken to St. Mary's Cathedral where a service was held and an oration given by Cardinal Moran. After Mass the remains were carried around the aisles on the shoulders of ten men, and the subsequent funeral procession to Waverley Cemetery was of massive proportions.

The first carriages contained the grandchildren, great-grandchildren and great-greatgrand children of Michael and Mary Dwyer who had travelled from all parts of Australia while the hearse was drawn by six black horses wearing ribbons of blue and white on their headgear and green cloths embroidered with Irish emblems in gold at their sides. The glass sides of the hearse were taken out and the top converted into a canopy, toppped with a Celtic cross capped with a laurel wreath, and from its base ran garlands which capped the drapery of Irish flags, and blue and white silk representing the colours of both Ireland and Australia. Over 400 carriages and 4,000 people took part in the procession while an estimated number of 100,000 people lined the route. At Waverley cemetery Dr. Charles McCarthy gave the principal oration in a manner which fitted the charged emotional atmosphere of the occasion: "Of all that noble band of patriots who rose in dark and evil days to right their native land there is no-one whose relics we could be more honoured and blest in possessing and reverencing than those of the central figure among the exile here – the brave insurgent Chief of the Wicklow Mountains – Michael Dwyer."

It was an extraordinary day for the Irish for, in addition to honouring the memory of Michael and Mary Dwyer, they were paying homage to the land of their forefathers while at the same time adverting to their own growing power, prosperity and influence in Australia.

Monuments have been erected also in Ireland in honour of Michael Dwyer and his comrades in the towns of Wicklow and Baltinglass while at the roadside in the valley of Glenmalure a simple granite monument bears the names of Michael Dwyer and Fiach McHugh O'Byrne, the famous fourteenth century chieftain. In 1948, the cottage at Derrynamuck where Sam McAllister died, and from which Dwyer managed to escape, was restored and declared a national monument by Sean T. Ó Ceallaigh, President of Ireland while in the same year Taoiseach Eamonn de Valera, during a visit to Australia, visited the Waverley Monument as did President Patrick Hillery in 1985.

No folk hero of the stature of Michael Dwyer could ever live up to the heroic image and the sanitised reputation which an emerging nation bestowed posthumously on him. Dwyer himself had no unique political phlosophy; he won no major battles; his ambitions always remained modest, but were central to the aspirations of successive generations of peasant farmers throughout Ireland who continued to struggle, throughout the nineteenth century, to win for themselves the basic human right of owning their own property, of living in peace, and of being able to provide a decent standard of living for themselves and their families. Having failed, many were forced to emigrate, following eviction, to Australia where their life-long ambitions were to be fulfilled. The legacy of Michael Dwyer and his comrades are two-fold. By holding out in the Wicklow mountains for five years, following the savageries of the Rebellion, they gave a renewed sense of pride and self-respect to those whose own hopes had been cruelly denied. And in Australia their legacy has come in the shape of generations of their descendants who have helped to create an individualistic nation and to impress upon it the need for eternal vigilance regarding the fundamental right of human freedom.

John Hurley, 1859

APPENDIX ONE

List of Rebels Proclaimed by Military

The following ROBBERS, MURDERERS, and DESERTERS, are now wandering about, and are occasionally concealed by disaffected Persons in the Counties of Wicklow, Wexford, Carlow, Kildare, Dublin etc. and Rewards will be paid for securing such of them, as are first mentioned, agreeably to a Proclamation dated the 8th of July last (1800):

1st. DWYER MICHAEL, aged about thirty-one years, five feet nine or ten inches high, very straight in the back, short neck, square shoulders, a little in-kneed, rather long-legged, with a little rise on the shin-bones, very long feet, black hair and complexion, broad across the eyes, which are black, short cocked nose, wide mouth, thin lips, even teeth, but stand separate, very long from the nose to the end of the chin, full breasted, and rather full-faced, born in Imale. Five Hundred Guineas for taking him.

2nd. MERNAGH JOHN, about thirty years old, six feet high, full-bodied, but light limbed, dark complexion, marked with the small pox, black hair, heavy eye-brows, and thick lips, somewhat round-shouldered, born in or near Glen Malur. Two Hundred Guineas for taking him.

3d. HARMAN JOHN, twenty-two years old, five feet ten inches high, fair complexion, brown hair, well made, large grey eye, and speaks thick, born near Seven Churches. Two Hundred Guineas for taking him.

4th. PORTER JOHN, aged twenty five years, five feet five inches high, slender made, light-limbed, dark brown hair, small eyes, sallow flecked complexion, halts a little, right leg a little crooked, born near Seven Churches. Two Hundred Guineas for taking him.

5th. THOMAS ANDREW, aged twenty four years, abiyt five feet six inches, brown hair, swarthy fresh complexion, straight and well made, born near Anamoe. Two Hundred Guineas for taking him.

6th. BURKE WILLIAM, about five feet ten inches high, dark hair, lightly marked with the small pox, dark complexion, stout made, twenty one years old, broad shoulders, a little in-kneed, born in Knockrath, coarse voice. Two Hundred Guineas for taking him.

7th. BURKE MARTIN, five feet eleven inches high, dark hair, rather fair complexion, long nose, bending downwards at the point, uneven teeth, long face, straight in the back, but stoops in the shoukders down from his neck, strong legs and thighs, a little bowed at the knees, walks very upright, thirty years old, born at or near Imale. Two Hundred Guineas for taking him.

8th. GENOUD WILLIAM, five feet eleven and a half high, about thirty three years old fair complexion, dark brown hair, rounded shoulders, but well made, by trade a carpenter, born in the parish of Athy, county Kildare, has been living in the lands of Carigeen and Graney, in said county upwards of ten years. Two Hundred Guineas for taking him.

9th. BYRNE CHRISTOPHER, about five feet eleven inches high, light hair, grey eyes, fair complexion, a little marked with the small pox, round face, strong and lusty, stoops some, what in walking, about twenty one years old. Two Hundred Guineas for taking him.

10th. BYRNE JOHN, his brother, five feet seven inches high, round face, fresh coloured, light hair, blue eyes, strong made, about thirty years old.

11th. BYRNE PATRICK (son of Bartle), about five feet ten inches high, sandy hair, lightly freckled, halts in his walk, loosely made.

BYRNE BARTLE (brother to Pat), about five feet eight inches high, sandy hair, freckled complexion, light limbed, stoops in the shoulders, twenty-one years old.

CULLEN JAMES, about five feet eleven inches, slender made, black hair, shot through his hand at Hacket's-town, forty years old.

BYRNE HUGH, about five feet eight inches high, freckled, fair face, light or sandy hair, well made, shot through the thigh, twenty four years old.

HARMAN LAWRENCE, thirty four years old, five feet six inches high, light brown hair, grey eyes, heavy limbs, round faced, dark sandy complexion, (brother to John Harman).

HARMAN NICHOLAS, twenty-nine years old, five feet eight inches high, slender made, light brown hair, long visage, light limbed, long thin nose, brown eyes, a wild look, cannot speak plainly, (brother to John and Lawrence).

DOYLE JAMES, about twenty four years old, five feet eight inches high, soft face, rather well-looking, charged with the murder of John Leeson.

MANGAN JOHN, about twenty-five years old, five feet seven inches high, round made, good countenance, part of one finger of his left hand cut off by a reaping hook, born near Coolbeg, charged with the murder of John Leeson.

BYRNE JOHN (son of Owen Kittagh,) five feet seven or eight inches high, straight and light limbed,but broad, and a little stooped in the shoulders, pale and freckled, dark haired, about twenty three years old.

BYRNE TERENCE (brother to John), five feet eleven inches high, long thin face, frsh colour, dark hair, cross made, and stooped shoulders, about twenty five years old.

BRADY EDWARD, five feet six inches high, black hair, grey eyes, and black eye-lashes, round face, strong made, speaks a little thick, about twenty two years old.

DOYLE GEORGE, five feet eleven inches high, light made, pole face and hard features, speaks remarkably quick, twenty three years old.

KELLY, JAMES (son of Ned), twenty-one years old, well made, smooth face, fresh complexion, brown hair, five feet seven and a half high, born in Glen Malur.

KELLY, JAMES (son of Tom), twenty-five years old, five feet six inches high, light make, marked with the small pox, black hair.

TOOLE MILES, twenty-six years of age, six feet high, black hair, pale yellow complexion, well made, but light limbed, Antrim deserter and robber.

HANIGAN CHARLES, a deserter from the Antrim Militia, twenty five years old, five feet ten inches high, black hair, red face, in-kneed and sour countenance.

GRANT WILLIAM, late of Belleneclash, a deserter from the Antrim Militia, and captain of United Irishmen, aged about twenty seven years, five feet nine inches high, light brown hair, lightly freckled, well made, a little stooped.

GRANT THOMAS (brother of William), deserter from the Antrim militia, aged about twenty five years, five feet seven inches high, light brown hair, lightly freckled, well made, thin visage and down looking.

BUTLER RICHARD, about five feet ten inches high, aged twenty five years, dark brown hair, heavy eye-brows, dark complexion, lightly made, born near Whaley-Abbey.

ARNOLD JOHN, about twenty six years of age, six feet high, well made, high cheek bones, ruddy complexion, brown curled hair, with a cut upon his face.

FLYNN JAMES, about twenty-one years of age, five feet eight inches high, slender made, a handsome face, with very fair hair and complexion.

CLARY JOHN, twenty five years of age, five feet six inches high, strong made, a little bow-legged, stooped shoulders, dark brown hair, small black eyes, and sallow complexion.

REDMOND DENIS, forty years of age, six feet, stoops much, slender made, marked with the small pox, large eye-brows, hollow eyes, dark brown hair, and has a remarkable impediment in his speech.

CAVANAGH LAWRENCE, forty years of age, five feet ten inches high, well made, very corpulent, remarkably short neck, very thin hair, and marked with the small pox.

BYRNE MICHAEL, thirty four years of age, five feet eleven inches high, stooped shoulders,heavy limbed, brown hair and eyes, sallow complexion, high cheek bone, with a moon on one of his cheeks, a strong coarse voice, and has a moon on his neck.

BRYAN WILLIAM, thirty years of age, five feet ten inches high, dark hair, well-limbed, full-bodied, round face, a native of Kilnamana, near Glanely, by trade a bricklayer.

BYRNE NICHOLAS, about twenty-seven years old, five feet eleven inches high, strong, athletic, broad shoulders, smooth but large features, dark heavy countenance, grey eyes.

BYRNE JAMES (his brother), about five feet eight or nine inches high, sandy complexion and sandy whiskers, ruddy face, straight and well made, about thirty five years old, grey eyes, lightly marked with the small pox.

BYRNE JOHN, deserter from the Antrim Militia, very red hair, freckled face and hands, about twenty three years old, five feet eight inches high, broad and strong shoulders, strong limbed.The above three born near Rathdrum.

DOYLE JAMES, Rebel Captain, about five feet six inches high, freckled face, grey eyes, heavy eye-brows, well made, about twenty-eight years years.

BURKE DANIEL, deserter from the North Cork Militia.

BYRNE MARTIN, about thirty years old, born near Anamoe, black hair, hollow nose, stooped in the shoulders, well made, about five feet eleven inches high.

BYRNE ANDREW (brother to Martin), aged about twenty-years, five feet eleven inches high, big lips, full mouth, grey eyes, which are large, bowed legs, round shoulders, and fair hair.

BYRNE RICHARD, about five feet eleven inches high, round shouldered and stooped, twenty-five years old, round,pale smooth face, dark complexion and black hair.

BYRNE JAMES (his brother), about five feet eleven, about twenty one years old, smooth faced, light shouldered, heavy limbed, brown hair, grey eyes, a wild look and a swaggering walk.The last two born near Rathdrum.

MAHON ———. a tailor, five feet six inches, strong man, heavy limbed, about twenty-six years old, black hair, smooth face, and well looking, fresh complexion, lately resided in Imale.

BRYAN, PATRICK, a tailor, about five feet five and a half, a chubby fellow, strong made, about thirty five years old, black hair and beard, and pock-marked, speaks affectedly, a native of Imale.

George Stewart, Lieut. Col.
Assistant Adjutant General.

(47)

APPENDIX TWO

The Family of Michael and Mary Dwyer

1. Mary Ann. Born 1799 Wicklow. Died 1869. Married (1). Patrick Hughes, Dublin c.1826. 1 son. (2). Patrick Grace, 2 sons, 1 daughter.

2. John. Born 2 January 1801 Wicklow. Died 1882. Married Ann Kennedy 1832. 2 sons, 1 daughter.

3. Peter. Born 1801 Wicklow. Married Mary White c.1835. Died 1876. Married Mary White c.1835. Died 1876. 10 sons, 1 daughter.

4. Esther. Born 1804 Wicklow. Died 1874. Married Owen Byrne 1833. 1 son, 3 daughters.

5. James. Born 1807 New South Wales. Died 1874. Married Jane Perry 1847. 1 son, 4 daughters.

6. Bridget. Born 1808 Van Diemen's Land. Died 1878. Married John O'Sullivan 1837. 1 son, 3 daughters.

7. Eliza. Born 1812 New South Wales. Died 1888. Married Peter Bodicene 1827. 1 son, 1 daughter. Also 4 sons, 2 daughters to George Butler ???

Bridget Bowler, daughter of Sarah Byrne

The Family of Hugh and Sarah Byrne

1. Philip. Born *c*.1798 Dublin. Remained in Ireland and was reared by Sarah Byrne's parents, Philip and Mary Dwyer (nee McDonald)

2. Michael. Born 1800 Wicklow. Died 1879 Campbelltown. Married Jane Warby *c*.1829. 6 sons, 4 daughters.

3. Rosanna. Born 1803 Wicklow. Died 1825 Campbelltown. Married William Craft 1 son, 1 daughter.

4. Anne. Born 1805 on the *Tellicherry*. Died 1864 Ten Mile Creek, Yass. Married (1) William Byrne 183-. 2 sons, 4 daughters. (2) Joseph Byrne 18—. 2 sons. (3) Patrick Mc Keogh 1855.

5. Catherine Agnes. Born 1807 Liverpool. Died 1859 Campbelltown. Married John Keighran 1825. 5 sons, 10 daughters.

6. Charles. Born 1809 Liverpool. Died 1873 Nerringundah via Moruya. Married Elizabeth McCarthy 1833. 1 son.

7. Bridget. Born *c*.1811 Liverpool. Died 1875 Five Mile Creek, Albury. Married Samuel Bowler 1829. 3 sons.

8. Mary. Born *c*.1813 Liverpool. Died 1859 Campbelltown. Married John Hurley 1837. 3 sons, 3 daughters.

9. Sarah. Born *c*.1816 Liverpool. Died 1850 Sydney. Married Henry Merritt 1836. 2 sons, 2 daughters.

10. James. Born *c*.1818 Airds. Died 1853 Campbelltown. Unmarried.

11. Sylvester. Born 1820 Airds. Died 1880 Nymagee via Cobar. Married Mary Ann Vardy 1842. 2 sons, 5 daughters.

12. Winifred Mary. Born 1822 Airds. Died 1889 Darlinghurst, Sydney. Married Dr. Isadore Blake. 6 sons, 5 daughters.

13. Elizabeth Mary. Born 1824 Airds. Died 1893 Dalgety via Cooma. Married Henry J. Eccleston 1851. 3 sons, 3 daughters.

14. Rose Agatha. Born 1826 Airds. Died 1864, Newtown, Sydney. Married Joseph Edward Tucker 1853. 2 sons, 3 daughters.

The Family of Arthur and Priscilla Devlin

1. James. Born 1807 Sydney Cove. Died 1875 Wagga. Married (1) Mary Ann Hartigan 1831. 2 sons. (2) Susannah Hughes 1835. 6 sons, 4 daughters.

2. Arthur. Born 1810. Died 1893 Melbourne. Married (1) Ann Hudson 1832. 2 sons, 3 daughters. (2) Esther McLeland 1843, 3 sons, 1 daughter. (3) Winifred Corry. 2 daughters.

3. Mary. Born 1813. Died 1835. Unmarried.

4. Patrick. Born 1815. Died 1865 at Ryde. Unmarried.

5. Ann. Born 1817. Died 1854.

6. Martha. Born 1819. Died 1908. Married Thomas Beckford Simpson 1842. 2 sons, 4 daughters.

The Family of John Mernagh and Mary Johnson

1. Elizabeth. Born 1810 Hawkesbury River. Died 1884 Braidwood. Married Daniel Canvin 1826. 4 sons, 6 daughters.

2. Bridget. Born 1812. Died ? Married Patrick Farrelly (Farley) 1828. 1 son.

APPENDIX SIX

Ship's Indent – Tellicherry, August 1805

Sentence – 7 years (unless stated)

MALE PRISONERS

ANTRIM (1): Joseph Kelso (March 1803) Age 53.

ARMAGH (1): Joseph Carlahan (April 1805) Age 60.

CARLOW (7): Richard Doyle (1803) Age 29; Myles Dolan (1803) Age 32; John Ryan (1803) Age 40; Pat Mulhall (1803) Age 21; John Fitzpatrick (Life) Age 29; Hugh "Brander" Byrne (Life) Age 25; Laurence Fenlon (Life) Age 27.

CLARE (4): Maurice Flavahan (1803) Age 30; Jer Griffin (1803) Age 31; Pat O Mara (1803 – Life) Age 31; James Sheedy (1804 – Life) Age 32.

CORK CITY (1): Richard Dooley (Spring 1805) Age 21.

CO. CORK (1): Darby Donovan (Spring 1805 – Life) Age 62.

DOWN (1): Michael Maguire (October 1803 – Life) Age 27.

CO. DUBLIN (24): Thomas Price (June 1804) Age 25; William Lawler (August 1802 – Life) Age 40; Daniel Kelly (February 1803 – Life) Age 26; Darby Murray (February 1803 – Life) Age 33; John Kearney (February 1803 – Life) Age 36; John Nowlan (July 1803) Age 27; Thomas Shaughnessy (July 1803 – Life) Age 33; John Hughes (July 1803 – Life) Age 34; John Mc Cabe (July 1804 – Life) Age 30; Pat Mc Mahon (July 1804 – Life) Age 26; Henry Kelly (November 1804 – Life) Age 27; Laurence Townsend (June 1804): Arthur Doyle (July 1803) Age 26; James Griffin (October 1802 – Life) Age 34; Robert Fox (December 1803 – Life) Age 21; Pat Tiernan (July 1803) Age 34; Owen Clarke (November 1804 – Life) Age 30; Edward Doyle (July 1803) Age 23; Peter White (July 1803 – Life) Age 24; Roger Keogh (May 1803) Age 24; James Williams (December 1803) Age 30; Thomas Cuff (July 1805) Age 31; Tim Murphy (July 1805 – Life) Age 23; James Magrath (June 1805) Age 34.

DUBLIN CITY (22): Lawrence Bailey (September 1803 – Life) Age 34; Walter

Clare (September 1803 – Life) Age 22; Bartholomew Tiernan (January 1804 – Life) Age 28; John Connolly (February 1805) Age 28; Henry Austen (April 1805) Age 16; John Reynolds (June 1805) Age 30; Lawrence Magee (July 1802 – Life) Age 40; Bernard Brennan (July 1803 – Life) Age 45; John Reilly (May 1804) Age 30; William Ward (August 1804) Age 19; Michael Kenna (January 1805) Age 24; Daniel Leary (March 1803) Age 30; Daniel Sleavan (November 1804) Age 27; John O Neal (July 1804) Age 32; John Mooney Age 30; Thomas Holden Age 23; John Shannon Age 27; Hugh Woods Age 22; Francis Darby, Age 26; Daniel Rowson, Age 19; William Coughlan Age 60. (all June 1805).

KILDARE (14): John Cogan (Summer 1802 – Life) Age 29; Michaal Magrath, Age 34; Patrick Gore, Age 25; Pat Farrell, Age 29 (All Spring 1803) ; Stephen Hyland, (Spring 1803 -Life) Age 37; Martin Dogherty, (Summer 1803 – Life) Age 24; Philip Ennis (Spring 1804 – Life) Age 31 Pat Masterson,Age 44 and Denis Farrell, Age 24 (Spring 1804 – Life); Edward Francis, Age 26 (Spring 1805 – Life), Hugh Conlan, Age 28 (Spring 1805) Laurence Fox, Age 52 (Spring 1803); James Behan, Age 31 (Summer 1802); Christopher Gallagher, Age 50 (Lent 1803).

KILKENNY (7): John Flynn (1803) Age 22; Nicholas Lacey (1803); Denis Ryan (1803 – Life) Age 25; Pat Hawes (1803 – Life) Age 36; James Johnson (1804) Age 25; Pat Kinevan or Kirwan (1804) Age 60; Barnaby Butler (1803) Age 24.

KING'S COUNTY (LAOIS) (1): James Hutchinson (1805 – Life).

CITY OF LIMERICK (6): James Malone (1802) Age 30; James Henchy (1802) Age 23; Michael Fitzgerald (1803) Age 26; John Redmond (1803) Age 34; Pat Murnane (1804 – Life) Age 21.

MONAGHAN (2): Henry Murphy (Spring 1804) Age 35; Michael Begaan (Spring 1803) Age 24.

MAYO (6): Thomas Gibbons (1803 – Life) Age 65; Laughlin Monahan (1805 – Life);John Jones (1803); Pat Keenahan (1804) Age 37; John Dent (1804) Age 30; Thomas Tighe (1805) Age 16.

LONDONDERRY (1): Edward James (Spring 1803) Age 42.

LONGFORD (2): William Scott (1804) Age 25; John Murphy (1805) Age 25.

ROSCOMMON (1): Bryan Gannon (Spring 1803 – Life) Age 35.

TIPPERARY (13): Pierce Condon (1803 – Life) Age 44; Pat Dawson (1803 – Life) Age 30; Thomas Meagher (1803 – life) Age 30; Stephen Halpenny (1803 – Life) Age 30; Thomas Hyers (1804) Age 21; Denis Sullivan (1804) Age 27; John Quin (1804) Age 34; Pat Kenna (1804) Age 30;

Edmund White (1804 – Life) Age 27; William Halpenny (1804 – Life) Age 33; James Halpenny (1804 – Life) Age 30; Pat Meagher (1804 – Life) Age 28; Pat Cleary (1805) Age 25.

CITY OF WATERFORD (1): Charles Mc Mahon (1804) Age 23.

WESTMEATH (1): Pat Cox (Spring 1805) Age 21.

WEXFORD (1): Patrick Prendergast (1805) Age 22.

WICKLOW (2): John Bryan (Spring 1803) Age 50; John Reynolds (Spring 1803 – Life) (No age given).

FEMALE PRISONERS

ARMAGH (1): Bridget Mc Mahon (July 1804) Age 17.

CLARE (2): Margaret Hayes (1803); Eliza Kennedy (1803) No age given.

DUBLIN CITY (21): Mary Barry Age 24, Catherine Mc Laughlin Age 27, Mary Rice Age 28 (January 1803); Mary Bradshaw (September 1802) Age 40; Catherine Brady (June 1803) Age 30; Mary Mc Nulty (June 1805) Age 30; Sarah Cooksey (October 1803) Age 30; Anastasia Shanley (October 1803) Age 24; Mary Kennedy Age 33, Catherine Hill Age 22, Margaret O Brien Age 26, Mary Smith Age 40 (all January 1804); Mary Gough (May 1804) Age 23; Mary Byrne (March 1804) Age 23; Ann Mathews (May 1804) Age 23; Eleanor Burke (January 1804) Age 40; Eliza Cooper (August 1804) Age 27; Mary Lamb (September 1804) Age 28; Mary Shannon (December 1804) Age 28; Bridget Johnson (February 1805) Age 25; Margaret Kelly (October 1803) Age 40; Catherine Ennis (October 1803) Age 25.

KERRY (1): Mary Grady (1804) Age 19 – Life.

CITY OF LIMERICK (5): Catherine Hinchy (1802) Age 40; Ann Mollowney (Moloney) and Bridget Shea (1803) – no age given; Catherine Leeson (1804) Age 20; Eleanor Leonard (1804) no age given.

MEATH (2): Mary Johnson (Spring 1805) Age 29; Eleanor Tyrrell (Spring 1805) Age 29.

MONAGHAN (1): Mary Begley (Spring 1804) Age 25.

LONDONDERRY (1): Ann Forbes (Spring 1803) Age 30.

WESTMEATH (1): Mary Fagan or Nagle (Spring 1805) No age given.

Bibliography

Australian Dictionary of Biography, ed. Douglas Pike (1966)

Bateson, Charles, *The Convict Ships* (1787-1868)

Barrett, Jim, *Life In The Burragorang* (1995)

Birch A, and Macmillan D., *The Sydney Scene* (1788-1960)

Bowd, D.G., *Macquarie Country - a history of the Hawkesbury* (1969)

Byrne, Miles, *Memoirs*

Byrne, Paula, *Criminal Law and Colonial Subjects (1810-1830)*. 1993

Caley, George, *Reflections on The Colony of New South Wales*, Ed. J.E.B.Currey (1966)

Cargeeg, George, *The Rebel of Glenmalure* (1988)

Clarke, C.M.H., *History of Australia* (Vol. 1), 1962

Cloney, Thomas, *A Personal Narrative of those transactions in the county of Wexford in 1798* (Dublin 1832)

Clune, Frank, *The Norfolk Island Story* (1957)

Costello, Con, *Botany Bay* (1987)

Cullen, Luke, *The Anne Devlin Journal* (ed. J.J. Finnegan, 1968)

Cunningham, Peter, *Two years In New South Wales* (2 vols., 1827)

Dickson, Charles, *The life of Michael Dwyer* (1944)

Elliott, Marianne, *Partners In Revolution: The United Irishmen and France* (1982)

Ellis. M.M., *Lachlan Macquarie* (1947)

Fisher, J.R., *The End Of The Irish Parliament* (1911)

Gammage, B., *History of Narrandera Shire*

Gregg, Pauline, *A Social And Economic History of Britain (1760-1965)*

Hainsworth D.R., *The Sydney Traders* (1992)

Harris, Alexander, *Settlers And Convicts* (1847)

Henry, Brian, *Dublin Hanged* (1994)

Historical Records of Australia (1915)

Historical Records of New South Wales (1898)

Hughes, Robert, *The Fatal Shore* (1987)

Kiernan, Colm, *Ireland and Australia* (1984)

Kiernan T.J., *Ireland and Australia* (1984)

Landrett, Helen, *The Pursuit of Robert Emmet* (1949)

Lea-Scarlett, Errol, *Queanbeyan District and People* (1968)

Lewis, Milton, *A Rum State* (1992)

Liston, Carol, *Campbelltown: The Bicentennial History* (1988)

Mackaness, C.J., *Life of Vice-Admiral Bligh* (2 vols., 1931)

Macken, James J., *Martin Burke – The Father of Pittwater* (1994)

Macquarie, Lachlan, *Journal Of A Tour of New South Wales 1810* (eds. Shepherd and Newman)

McDonagh, Michael, *The Viceroy's Post Bag*

Madden, R.R., *The United Irishmen* (1860)

Maguire, Paul, *Inns of Australia* (1952)

Neal, David, *The Rule of Law in a Penal Colony* (1994)

O'Brien, Eris, *The Life And Letters of Archpriest J.J. Therry* (1922)

The Dawn of Catholicism in Australia, Vol. 1 (1928)

O'Brien Gerard, *Parliament,Politics and People* (ed.) (1989)

O'Farrell, Patrick, *The Irish In Australia* (1986)

O Shaughnessy, Peter (ed.), *A Rum Story* (1988)

Reece, Robert (ed.), *Irish Convict Lives*

Ritchie, John (ed.), *The Evidence to the Bigge Report* (1971)

Robinson, Portia, *Women of Botnay Bay* (1988)

Rowan, *Archibald Hamilton: Autobiography* (1840)

Shaw, A.G.L., *Convicts And Colonies* (1966)

Sheedy, Kieran, *Upon The Mercy Of Government* (1988); *Feakle – A History* (1990); *The Clare Elections* (1993)

Smith, Babette, *A Cargo of Women* (1992)

Smyth, Jim, *The Men of No Propoerty (Irish Radicals and Popular Politics in the Late 18th Century)*, (1992)

Sydney Gazette, Vols. IV and V (16 March 1806-30 August 1807), Facsilimile edition

Teeling, Charles Hamilton, *History of the Irish Rebellion 1798 and Sequel* (1876)

Vale, Michelle, *Warby: My Excellent Guide* (1995)

Wentworth, W.C., *A statistical, historical and political description of the colony of New South Wales* (1819)

Whitaker, Anne-Maree, *Unfinished Revolution* (1994)

Wickham,William, *Correspondence* (2 vols.), edited by his grandson. (1870)

PUBLICATIONS, PAMPHLETS AND ARTICLES

Blackstock, Alan, "A Forgotten Army" (*History Ireland*, Winter 1996)

Fitzpatrick, Jeremiah, "Thoughts On A Penitentiary" (1790)

Fowler, McGill, Richardson, "Campbellstown Street Suburbs" (1995)

Maher, Brian Fr., "Chords From a Harp"

Mason, John St. John, "Pedro Zendono – Inquisitor of Kilmainham" (1807)

Pedro Redivivus, "Prison Abuses in Ireland" (1810)

Munro, Jim, "Where Pioneers Lie.St John's Cemetery Campbelltown" (1991)

O'Donnell, Ruan, "Michael Dwyer, The Wicklow Chief" (ed., Reece), *Irish Convicts Lives*, pp. 13-50

O'Dwyer, Barry, "Michael Dwyer and the 1807 Plan of Insurrection", *JRAHS LXiX* pt. 2, September 1883, pp. 73-82

O'Tuathail, P., "Wicklow Traditions of 1798" (*Bealoideas, The Journal of the Folklore of Ireland Society*, v. 1935, pp. 153-88

Potts. W.H., "Early Struggles of Wheat Farmers of N.S.W.", *Royal Australian Historical Society Journal*, Vol. 8-9 (1923)

Tandy, James, "An Appeal To The Public" (1807). An Accurate and impartial report of the action brought against Brabazon Morris (1807)

Trevor, Edward, "Dr. Trevor's Statement – a vindication of himself" (1809)

Wood, G.D., "Convicts", *Royal Australian Historical Society Journal*, Vol. 8, Part IV (1921)

Young, Angela., "Ripe for the Harvest" (1980)

NEWSPAPERS

Freeman's Journal, Dublin Journal, Dublin Evening Post, Belfast Newsletter, London Times, Cork Merchantile Chronicle, Clare Journal, Waterford Mirror, New Cork Evening Post, Limerick Chronicle, Sydney Gazette, The Australian, Sydney Morning Herald.

DOCUMENTS

National Library of Ireland (Documents); National Archives of Ireland; Public Record Office, London; Hampshire Public Record Office; Mitchel Library, State Library of New South Wales; Archive Office of New South Wales; Land Titles Office, Sydney.

NATIONAL ARCHIVES OF IRELAND

Prisoners' Petitions and Cases, Rebellion Papers, State Prisoners Papers.

PUBLIC RECORD OFFICE (LONDON)

Home Office Papers – 100/34-179 Ireland, private, secret and confidential correspondence 1792-1814.Ireland entry books (1793-1805) 122/3,123/6.Privy Council – 1/3564, 2581-3. Secret Information – Irish insurrection 1803.Suspected persons, Ireland 1804 – 1/3586, 3596-9, 3602-6,3624, 3627-8.

HAMPSHIRE PUBLIC RECORD OFFICE

William Wickham, Correspondence and Papers (1786-1840), Ref: 38M49, 28M49/A.

MITCHEL LIBRARY, STATE LIBRARY OF NEW SOUTH WALES

Banks Papers. Bonwick Transcripts (Bigge Enquiry), Hassal Correspondence, Mackaness Papers, Macarthur Papers, Fr Therry Papers.

ARCHIVE OFFICE OF NEW SOUTH WALES

Colonial Secretary's papers, Court of Criminal Jurisdiction, Governor's Court Papers.

Index of Names

Also published by The Woodfield Press

The Wicklow World of Elizabeth Smith (1840-1850)
edited by Dermot James and Séamas Ó Maitiú

The Sligo-Leitrim World of Kate Cullen (1832-1913)
revealed by Hilary Pyle

Ballyknockan: A Wicklow Stonecutters' Village
Séamas Ó Maitiú and Barry O'Reilly